The Williamite Invasion of 1688

The Last Successful Invasion of England

Mark Shearwood

'This is the Century of the Soldier', Fulvio Testi, Poet, 1641

HELION & COMPANY

Helion & Company Limited
Unit 8 Amherst Business Centre
Budbrooke Road
Warwick
CV34 5WE
England
Tel. 01926 499 619
Email: info@helion.co.uk
Website: www.helion.co.uk
X (formerly Twitter): @Helionbooks
Facebook: @HelionBooks
Visit our blog https://helionbooks.wordpress.com/

Published by Helion & Company 2026
Designed and typeset by Mary Woolley, Battlefield Design (www.battlefield-design.co.uk)
Cover designed by Paul Hewitt, Battlefield Design (www.battlefield-design.co.uk)

ISBN 978-1-806722-74-7

British Library Cataloguing-in-Publication Data.
A catalogue record for this book is available from the British Library.

For details of other military history titles published by Helion & Company Limited contact the above address or visit our website: http://www.helion.co.uk.

We always welcome receiving book proposals from prospective authors.

Contents

Abbreviations

BL British Library: London
CUP Cambridge University Press
EA Exeter Archives
HL Parliamentary Archives (House of Lords), London
IOW Isle of Wight Archives
NA National Archives: Kew
NLA Dutch National Military Museum: Amsterdam, The Netherlands
NP Newport Records Office: Isle of Wight
NU Nottingham University Archives
OSK Austrian State Archives: Kriegsarchiv, Vienna
OUP Oxford University Press
RM Rijksmuseum: Amsterdam, The Netherlands
SA Staffordshire Archives

Conventions

Currency conversion: each Dutch florin contains 3.5 grams of gold and each English Guinea contains 8.38 grams of gold, therefore one Guinea is equal to 2.4 Dutch florins.

Dates: All dates are given in the English Old Style, which was ten days behind the Continental New Style (this changed to an 11-day difference in 1700). Where a source quotes both days, it will be represented as i.e. 5/15 January. To avoid any confusion, the new year will be taken to be 1 January and not 25 March.

Original source material does not always agree on the same dates for events; this can be due to a mix of Old Style and New Style dates being used, dates recorded for when information regarding an event was received rather than when it happened, when orders were first given and not when the actual commands were carried out, and just plain human error. Where there are differences between the original accounts in the dates, I have for clarity, and to reduce any confusion for the reader, stuck with a singular timeline of the events. Any exceptions, with their sources, can be found within the footnotes. All errors are mine.

During this period, there was not any standardised spelling. I have wherever possible standardised the spelling of the names of persons mentioned and used modern spellings for locations where those locations have been confirmed.

Timeline

1660

29 May Restoration of the monarchy under Charles II

1677

4 November Marriage of Prince William III and Mary Stuart, Princess Royal

1685

6 February Death of Charles II and accession of James II and VII
23 April Coronation of James II and VII
11 June Start of the Monmouth Rebellion – Duke of Monmouth lands at Lyme Regis (Dorset)
6 July Battle of Sedgemoor, Somerset
15 July Duke of Monmouth executed – end of the Monmouth Rebellion
8 October Revocation of the Edict of Nantes in France

1686

June Court case of Godden v. Hales confirms King's dispensing powers

1687

12 February Declaration of Indulgence issued in Scotland
4 April Declaration of Indulgence issued in England
August William III sends Willem Hendrik van Nassau-Zuylenstein to England
October Queen Mary of Modena becomes pregnant

1688

January Pamphlets printed in the Dutch Republic confirming Mary of Modena's pregnancy

17 January James II requests the return of the Anglo-Dutch and Scots-Dutch brigades from Holland
April Arthur Herbert and Edward Russell meet William III in Holland
May Hans Willem Bentinck visits Elector of Brandenburg
10 June Birth of James Francis Edward Stuart
6 July Arthur Herbert delivers the invitation to invade England to William III
7 July William III meets with close advisers to agree on invasion plans
9 July William III orders the Dutch invasion fleet to be fitted out
August Share price of the Dutch East India Company plummets due to the prospect of war

September
29th States General gives William the authority to invade England
30th William's *Declaration of the Reasons Inducing him to Appear in Arms in England* is published in The Hague.

October
19th Invasion fleet sets sail but is forced back due to a great storm
29th Invasion force due to sail but delayed

November
1st William's fleet departs from Hellevoetsluis (Helvetsluys)
2nd Fleet turns south past Norfolk and the English fleet's expected position of Gunfleet
3rd Fleet Clears the English Channel
4th Fleet passes Portsmouth, one of the expected landing sites
5th William arrives at Torbay
6th The Williamite army moves forward in two lines of advance
7th William arrives at Forde House, Newton Abbot
8th William arrives in Chudleigh
9th William arrives in Exeter and stays until the 21st
16th Lord Cornbury defects to William and arrives in Exeter with about 100 dragoons
21st William marches from Exeter to Honiton
22nd William marches from Honiton to Axminster
23rd Bentinck marches with 1,200 horse and dragoons to Sherborne
26th William marches to Crewkerne; Trelawney and all his officers defect to William
27th William marches to Sherborne
30th William marches to Wincanton

December
1st William marches to Hundon
3rd Dutch ambassador arrives (after King James II had issued a passport)
4th William marches to Salisbury
5th William stays in Salisbury; Lord Oxford arrives in William's camp
6th William marches to Collingbourne Kingston

7th William marches to Hungerford
9th Isle of Wight declares for William
10th William's headquarters moves to Newbury
11th James II departs London; Feversham orders the English army to disband
13th William's headquarters moves to Abingdon; the Irish Fright
14th William moves to Oxford
15th Carlisle declares for William
16th James II arrives back in London
17th William arrives in Windsor, the Williamite army surrounds London
18th James II's second departure from London
19th James II arrives in Rochester under Dutch guard
23rd James II departs Rochester
24th James II flees the country and seeks refuge with Louis XIV of France
25th William is offered the authority to rule the country by the Lords until the Convention in January 1689 can confirm his right to rule
28th William accepts the Lords' request to rule England.

1689

January
22nd Convention sits at Westminster and formally offers the crown to William, pending negotiations

April
11th William and Mary are crowned King and Queen of England in Westminster Abbey

May
11th William and Mary accept the crowns of Scotland.

1

Introduction

The works of military historians have been dominated by studies of conflicts, along with the study of operational histories and regimental histories. The military historians of the late seventeenth century have continued this practice, with works focusing on the army of James II, William III and the war in Flanders, Ireland, and Scotland.[1] While these are important works, they emphasise the issue within this trend by only studying the military when it is active within a conflict with pre-defined criteria, such as in the histories of battles and campaigns, or through ongoing skirmishes or guerrilla warfare. The Glorious Revolution fails to meet these criteria, with limited actions between the forces of William of Orange and the English army, and therefore has not been fully investigated by military historians as a military campaign. This is in part due to the propaganda produced by William and his supporters, both prior to and during the invasion, which was designed to de-escalate the military aspect of the campaign and to place the events as support for the English people and definitely not an invasion by a foreign power. Decades of Whig historiography and propaganda have added to this belief that the events of November 1688 were anything other than a military invasion resulting in the forceful overthrowing of James II, the rightful monarch of England, Scotland, and Ireland. This false narrative has been repeated by numerous historians and politicians, including the English Prime Minister (PM) Margaret Thatcher in her speech to Parliament on 7 July 1988 during the tercentenary celebration of the Glorious Revolution.[2] While the speech does concede that the events of 1688 were not entirely bloodless, and the PM

1 J. Childs, *The Army, James II, and the Glorious Revolution* (Manchester: Manchester University Press, 1980); J. Childs, *The British Army of William III, 1689-1702* (Manchester: Manchester University Press, 1987); J. Childs, *The Williamite Wars in Ireland 1688-1691* (London: Continuum Books, 2007); M. McNally, *The Battle of Aughrim 1691* (Stroud: The History Press, 2008); J. Fortescue, *British Campaigns in Flanders, 1690-1794* (London: Macmillan & Co., 1918); M. McNally, *St Ruth's Fatal Gamble: The Battle of Aughrim 1691 and the Fall of Jacobite Ireland* (Warwick: Helion & Co., 2018); S. Reid, *Battle of Killiecrankie: The Last Act of the Killing Times* (Barnsley: Pen & Sword, 2018); S. Stansfield, *Early Modern Systems of Command: Queen Anne's Generals, Staff Officers and the Direction of Allied Warfare in the Low Countries and Germany, 1702-1711* (Solihull: Helion & Co, 2016).

2 *Hansard*, HC Deb., vol.136, cols.1233–63, 7 July 1988, <https://api.parliament.uk/historic-hansard/commons/1988/jul/07/revolutions-of-1688-89-tercentenary>.

refers to the conflict in Ireland and Scotland, the speech continues the Whig narrative. There are a number of errors and misunderstandings within the speech and the common understanding of the events of November 1688 that this book seeks to rectify. Firstly, the PM states that 'this was a revolution carried through by the actions of Parliament itself', referring to the fact that both the English and Scottish parliaments had resolved the invasion, with the Bill of Rights (England) and the Claim of Rights (Scotland).[3] Second, it states that 'these events saved us [England] from the violent revolutions' of our Continental neighbours, paving the way for 'universal suffrage and full parliamentary democracy'. Both these points made for good political soundbites, in 1988 as well as in the preceding 300 years. However, these events were not, and could not have been, foreseen prior to William's landing or the disbandment of the English army, or after James II's eventual flight to France. Lastly, the speech stated that the revolution ensured that the will of the people would be exercised through Parliament rather than by intimidation. As this book will prove, the will of the 'people' was not taken into account, and the bulk of the English soldiers refused to side with William during the invasion. In addition, there can be nothing more intimidating than a foreign army on English soil while negotiations were under way for validation of William's (and Mary's) claim to the throne.

The events covered within this book are commonly known as the Glorious Revolution and involved the change of monarchy from King James II to King William III and Queen Mary II. This 'revolution' is typically stated as happening over a period from William's landing in England on 5 November 1688 to the flight of James II to France on 22 December 1688. A second, later date of 13 February 1689 is occasionally used, which is when William and Mary accepted the joint crowns of England at the Banqueting House, in London, after Parliament declared that James II had abdicated the throne.[4] William and Mary would eventually be offered the crown of Scotland on 11 April 1689 and were subsequently crowned on 11 May 1689.[5] The first time the events were recorded publicly as a revolution was on 3 January 1689, when the London paper *The Orange Gazette* reported on 'the Revolution that had occurred'.[6] William later referred to the events as 'this late Revolution' in a speech before the House of Lords during 1689.[7] The events have been referred to at various times as the Bloodless Revolution, the English Revolution, the Extraordinary Revolution, a Famous Revolution, the Great Revolution, the Peaceful Revolution, the Sensible Revolution, a Stupendous Revolution and

---

3 'Bill of Rights [1688]', Legislation.gov.uk, <https://www.legislation.gov.uk/aep/WillandMarSess2/1/2/introduction>; 'Claim of Right Act 1689', Legislation.gov.uk, <https://www.legislation.gov.uk/aosp/1689/28/contents>.

4 The start date of the 'revolution' has also been recorded as June 1688, when the letter of invitation was sent out to William by the 'Immortal Seven'.

5 J. Hertzler, 'Who Dubbed it "The Glorious Revolution"', *Albion: A Quarterly Journal Concerned with British Studies*, Winter 1987 (19.4), p.580.

6 *The Orange Gazette*, no. 2, 31 December 1688 – 3 January 1689.

7 Hertzler, 'Who Dubbed It "The Glorious Revolution"', p.579.

even as the Bourgeois Revolution.[8] Some modern historians have started to use the term the 'Unglorious' or 'Inglorious Revolution' in order to separate themselves from the overwhelming Whig propaganda. The term 'Glorious Revolution' was first used by John Hampden (Member of Parliament for Wendover, 1689–90) in his testimony before the House of Lords in late 1689.[9] Bishop Gilbert Burnet had used the term 'the Glorious Instrument of our Deliverance' in a speech before the House of Commons in January 1689, when he was praising William and the events of November 1688.[10] It was next used by Bishop Gilbert Burnet in his sermons during 1706, when he referred to the events as 'the Glorious Revolution'.[11] Historians have also described the events of 1688 as a coup, and occasionally the events of 1688 have been described as an invasion. That said, the majority of studies of British history throughout the period since William's arrival have followed the Whig premise of calling the events the 'Glorious Revolution'. This is for several reasons, primarily to justify the overthrowing of the rightful King of England and to legitimise the actions of the Convention Parliament in electing William of Orange and Princess Mary to the throne of England, along with the subsequent succession of Queen Anne. The term 'Glorious' was subsequently used to differentiate these events from the later revolutions in America and France and to prove England's 'moral superiority' over countries involved with violent revolutions. Later Whig propaganda has instilled the idea of a 'Glorious Revolution' within the collective memory of the country.[12] Colley Cibber, who took up arms for William by enlisting in the regiment raised by the Duke of Devonshire, described the events in his memoirs: 'I question if in all the histories of empire there is one instance of so bloodless a revolution as that in England in 1688.'[13] William's actions both prior to and after invading England strengthened this approach and helped to standardise this definition of these events. His use of propaganda before, during, and after the invasion highlighted his actions as being in the best interest of Protestant England and that he had only arrived on the shore to support the (Protestant) English. His original stated intentions and aim were to help a wayward King James back onto the correct Protestant path, to protect the Protestant faith and the Church of England, and to guide James II and England away from the 'evil' clutches of 'Papism' and Louis XIV's France. Celebrations on the centenary of the invasion praised 'that glorious and immortal hero KING WILLIAM THE THIRD, who rescued this country from tyranny and oppression, and

8 W.A. Speck, *Reluctant Revolutionaries: Englishmen and the Revolution of 1688* (Oxford: OUP, 1988), p.3; Hertzler, 'Who Dubbed It "The Glorious Revolution"', p.580.

9 L.G. Schwoerer (ed.), *The Revolution of 1688-1689: Changing Perspectives* (Cambridge: CUP, 1992), p.3.

10 Hertzler, 'Who Dubbed It "The Glorious Revolution"', p.582.

11 Schwoerer, *The Revolution of 1688-1689*, p.3.

12 These ideas of a glorious past resulting from the revolution and successive Whig governments were detailed in Thomas Babington Macaulay, *The History of England: From the Accession of James II*, 5 vols (London: Folio Society, 1985).

13 Colley Cibber, *An apology for the Life of Mr. Colley Cibber, Comedian, and Late Patentee of the Theatre-Royal*, 2nd ed. (London: John Watts, 1740), pp.60–3.

secured to us a free and happy constitution'.[14] Commentaries memorialising the events of 1688 were recorded in papers across the country.[15]

The main premise of this book is that these events were not a revolution, glorious or of any description, nor were they a coup, although in the humble opinion of this author, a coup would be a more accurate definition than a revolution. Instead, they were a planned invasion of England by a foreign power. While the results of the invasion caused a revolution in the way we viewed the monarchy, and in the relationship between the monarchy and the state through the Bill of Rights (1689), thus revolutionising England, and then British politics, these were not the intended results of William's expedition as he departed Hellevoetsluis on 1 November 1688. The invasion did have the backing of what would later be described as a 'fifth column' within society, generally a small minority of the upper classes of England, Wales, and Scotland, including members of what would become known as the Treason Club.[16] The Treason club held meetings at the Rose Tavern in Covent Garden, London, and was run by Richard Savage, Lord Colchester, commander of the Fourth Troop of Horse Guards.[17] Even though there were not any pitched battles on English soil (but there were in Scotland and Ireland), and although William wanted to avoid bloodshed on English soil, he had planned this as a military operation with the expectation of having to engage the English army. William's planning and actions, along with the counter-invasion planning by James II, are detailed in the first half of the book. William's unopposed landing and his steady march through the South West towards London, along with the skirmishes between William's forces and the English army along William's line of advance, including possible engagement points where hostilities were averted, are detailed within the second half of the book.

It is important to understand that although this was an invasion by the Dutch head of state, William of Orange, utilising Dutch forces, this was not an invasion by The Netherlands and there was no formal declaration of war between the two states. This was due to the complex nature of the relationship between the individual Dutch states and William of Orange as Stadholder, and as Captain-General and Admiral-General of the Dutch land forces and navy. The invasion of England and securing the English succession for William's wife, Mary, was deemed a private matter by the Dutch state, although beneficial to the States General. The provocation behind the events of 1688 originated in the heir to Charles II's throne and the joint crowns

---

14 K. Wilson, 'Inventing Revolution: 1688 and Eighteenth-Century Popular Politics', *The Journal of British Studies*, 28.4 (1989), pp.353–54.

15 For example, see the *Leeds Mercury*, 11 November 1788; *Bristol Gazette and Public Advertiser*, 13 November 1788; *Manchester Mercury*, 11 and 18 November 1788; *Cumberland Pacquet*, 10 November 1788; *Norfolk Chronicle*, 8 November 1788; and *Morning Chronicle*, 4 November 1788.

16 William Pull, *William III: From Prince of Orange to King of England, A History 1650-1689* (London: Unicorn, 2021), pp.125–6; J. Childs, *General Percy Kirke and the Later Stuart Army* (London: Bloomsbury Publishing, 2014), p.123.

17 H. Smith, *Armies & Political Changes in Britain 1660-1750* (Oxford: OUP, 2021), p.108; NA: SP 44/164, f.324.

of England and Scotland apostatising from his Anglican faith and openly declaring his Catholic faith and therefore, in the eyes of his dissenters, his loyalty to the Pope, to Rome and also, by default, to Louis XIV of France. While James did not have any legitimate heirs, the prospect of a 'limited' Catholic sovereign seemed to be acceptable to the majority of the population as the next in the succession were his staunchly Protestant daughters Mary and Anne, but with the birth of his son in June 1688, the prospect of a Catholic dynasty was used as the spark to launch an invasion and change of monarchy. While there was a concatenation of events that started with William's plans to invade England and finished with the revolution of both parliamentary democracy and a constitutional monarchy under William III and Mary following the Declaration of Rights, these were neither planned for, foreseen, envisaged, nor even hoped for by those individuals who instigated the events of 1688, either in the Dutch Republic or in England. On the 250th anniversary of the Glorious Revolution, G.M. Trevelyan wrote that: 'In the affair of the Revolution, the element of chance, of sheer good luck, was dominant,' conceding that the events of the revolution were 'neither willed nor inevitable'.[18] In 1789 the Nonconformist cleric and political radical Richard Price stated that had society not gained 'the right to choose our own governors' in the events of 1688, along with 'the right to resist power when abused' and liberty of conscience in religious matter', it would have been an 'invasion of rights' and 'a rebellion'.[19] Therefore, any reference to these events as a revolution is at best hindsight and at worst a continuation of Whig propaganda originated by the likes of Thomas Babington Macaulay.[20]

England in the late Seventeenth Century

Life in England during the 1670s and 80s under Charles II could best be described as living in a powder keg. The country was rife with political dissent and religious plots and fears surrounding the Catholic faith and fears of absolute monarchy and slavery, as seen under Louis XIV of France. The persistence of anti-Catholicism amongst all levels of English society resulted in it playing an increasingly important part within politics, including an increase in the belief of 'Popish' plots against the country. The vilification of the Catholic population was based on both the previous persecution of Catholics in England and Ireland and Catholic reprisals including the St Bartholomew's Day massacre in 1572 and the common practice of referring to Queen Mary as 'Bloody Mary' for ordering over 280 religious dissenters to be burned at the stake. Fears of new reprisals against the majority Protestant population were constantly repeated in handbills and reports of events on

18 G.M. Trevelyan, *The English Revolution, 1688-1689* (Oxford: OUP, 1938), p.240; John Morrill, 'The Sensible Revolution', in Jonathan Israel (ed.), *The Anglo-Dutch Moment: Essays on the Glorious Revolution and its World Impact* (Cambridge: CUP, 2003), p.74.

19 Steven Pincus, *England's Glorious Revolution 1688-1689: A Brief History with Documents* (Boston: Yale University Press, 2006), pp.53–4.

20 Macaulay, *The History of England*.

the Continent, including Louis XIV's revocation of the Edict of Nantes in 1685. The Edict of Fontainebleau in October 1685 revoked all the rights and religious freedoms of the Huguenot population in France, denying them work, education, freedom of worship, and the right to leave the country. An increase in Huguenot refugees in England in 1685 and 1686 amplified the religious tensions as their stories of persecution were repeated throughout the country. There was a widespread belief that the Great Fire of London of 1666 was a Jesuit plot to destabilise the country. When the monument to those lost in the fire was built (between 1671 and 1677), the inscriptions on two of the sides included anti-Catholic propaganda.[21] The north side stated: '*Sed Furor Papisticus Qui Tamdiu Patravit Nondum Restingvitur*,' which translates to: 'But the Papist Fury That Has Lasted So Long Has Not Yet Abated.' On the east side the inscription originally read: 'burning of this protestant city, begun and carried on by the treachery and malice of the popish faction'. Anonymous pamphlets were distributed throughout London and the country warning that this was only the start of events, along with rumours that there were thousands of armed Frenchmen and 'Papists' about London and the kingdom.[22] The Rye House Plot of March 1683 confirmed the public fears regarding 'Papists' during this period. This was an assassination attempt on both Charles II and the Duke of York as they returned from Newmarket races, and although James was known to be Catholic at this time, this was still put down to the Popish plot originally put forward by Titus Oates between 1678 and 1681.[23] The multiple 'Popish plots' put forward by Titus Oates resulted in one of the most monumental proposed changes to the monarchy, which was the attempt by Parliament to exclude James, Duke of York from being the rightful and lawful heir to the throne. While the original attempts failed, Parliament would eventually succeed in excluding James II and his successors from the throne in 1689. Parliament introduced the first bill to exclude James from the line of succession in March 1679, with another two attempts in the following two years. On each occasion the Commons held a majority for exclusion and on each occasion Charles II prorogued Parliament as he did not want to abrogate his brother's God-given right to the throne.[24] James was known for his toughness and authority within government, with an urge to reform which was linked to a king who had absolutist tendencies, believing in the monarch's divine right to rule, likened to the absolute rule of Louis XIV of France and his direct control of a large standing army.[25]

The English army under Charles II was limited to a core strength of about 6,000 men, which included a small number of standing regiments and garrison troops made up of individual companies posted throughout the country.[26] Since the Civil War, Parliament and the country had been

---

21 John Miller, *Popery & Politics in England 1660-1688* (Cambridge: CUP, 1973), p.90.

22 Miller, *Popery & Politics*, p.103

23 Phillip Milton, 'John Locke and the Rye House Plot', *The History Journal*, 43.3 (2000), pp.647–68; Miller, *Popery & Politics*, pp.154–56.

24 Tony Claydon, *Europe and the Making of England 1660-1760* (Cambridge: CUP, 2007), p.223.

25 Claydon, *Europe and the Making of England*, pp.224–25; Miller, *Popery & Politics*, p.153.

26 Childs, *The Army, James II*, p.xviii.

concerned with the monarch having control of a large standing army and preferred for the defence of the realm to be placed in the control of the lord lieutenants of each county and the county militia under their command.[27] The call for the militia to be put under the control of Parliament was first put to the Commons in December 1641 with the introduction of the Militia Bill, which had the support of Oliver Cromwell, John Pym, and Sir Arthur Haselrig and passed as an ordinance in the spring of 1642.[28] This view against a professional standing army was used as the central argument against Cromwell's insistence on keeping the New Model Army during the Interregnum, and later against the plans of both Charles II and James II for a standing English army.[29] Even though these provisions would be written into article VI of the Bill of Rights as part of Parliament's negotiation with William of Orange and Princess Mary prior to the offer of the joint crown, William would continue to argue against this throughout the period of his reign.[30]

Power within England during the late seventeenth-century was held by a number of official positions appointed by the king. These included members of the Privy Council along with the secretaries of state for the northern and southern departments and the lord lieutenants of each county.[31] The secretaries of state shared the responsibility for all domestic affairs but had different responsibilities for international relations and England's overseas territories. The departments were divided by geographical responsibilities, with the Northern Department being responsible for diplomatic relations with the Scandinavian countries, the States General of Holland, Poland and Lithuania, Russia, and the Holy Roman Empire. The Southern Department was responsible for the affairs of the American colonies, Ireland, and the Channel Islands, as well as diplomatic relations with France, the Italian states, the Ottoman Empire, Portugal, Spain, and Switzerland. There was a separate Secretary of State for Scotland. Charles, the 2nd Earl of Middleton held the position of Privy Councillor and Secretary of State of the Northern Department under Charles II and continued in the role under James II; he also briefly held the position of the Secretary of State for the Southern Department from 28 October to 2 December 1688. The position of the Secretary of State for the Southern Department was held by Robert Spencer, 2nd Earl of Sunderland under Charles II from 14 April 1684 and under James II until 28 October 1688. Middleton and Sunderland were responsible for communicating the king's orders and instructions and interpreting his wishes.

27 Lois Schwoerer, *No Standing Armies: The Antiarmy Ideology in Seventeenth-Century England* (Baltimore: Johns Hopkins University Press, 1974), pp.56–57.

28 Schwoerer, *No Standing Armies*, pp.33–34.

29 Schwoerer, *No Standing Armies*, p.34.

30 B. Coward, *The Stuart Age: England 1603-1714*, 3rd ed. (Harlow: Pearson Education, 2003), pp.356–9; Schwoerer, *No Standing Armies*, pp.155–9.

31 For a full list of the Privy Councilors during the reign of James II, see Appendix III.

King James II of England, in a print by Cornelis van Dalen, Amsterdam, 1685–89. (Rijksmuseum, Amsterdam: 01 RP-P-BI-6765, Public Domain)

James II

James II was born on 14 October 1633 and was the second son of Charles I. He became King of England after his older brother Charles II died on 6 February 1685 as Charles did not have any legitimate children. While James Scott, 1st Duke of Monmouth claimed to be Charles II's legitimate son and heir, there is no evidence that Charles married his mother, Lucy Walters.[32] James converted to the Catholic faith around 1672; although his conversion was not openly admitted until 1676, it had already become an open secret to a large part of the population.[33] The open declaration of the heir's Catholic faith and his name being linked to 'Popish plots' in the spring of 1679 plunged the country into a political crisis unseen since the Civil War.[34] The country was transfixed by the question of succession and if it was either possible or right for a Catholic to succeed to the throne of England. The situation was partly due to James's inability to comply with the Test Acts of 1673 and 1678, which state that all holders of official offices had to take the oaths of allegiance and supremacy within three months of taking up any official position. This included James's appointment as Admiral of the Navy. James had been an exceptional admiral, reforming the English navy, including regarding the use and conduct of fireships, and had been involved in action against the Dutch during the Four Days' Battle of 1666.[35] The oaths state that the person making the declaration denied the process of transubstantiation, confirmed the sacraments used by the Anglican Church, attended Anglican church services on a regular basis, and that they recognised no person or power

32 Anne Keay, *The Last Royal Rebel: The Life and Death of James, Duke of Monmouth* (London: Bloomsbury, 2018).

33 John Miller, *James II* (New Haven: Yale University Press, 2000), p.59, Coward, *The Stuart Age*, pp.314–32.

34 Titus Oates manipulated the mood of the country by making a large number of unsubstantiated claims regarding 'Popish' plots to kill the kings and turn England into a Catholic vassal of Rome and France.

35 Frank Fox, *The Four Days' Battle of 1666: The Greatest Sea Fight of the Age of Sail* (Barnsley: Seaforth Publishing, 1996), pp.58–59, 207, 214.

above the king.[36] While these acts were aimed at all dissenting religions, the focus was against the Catholic faith and although they forced James to resign from any appointed position, including Admiral, they did not exclude him from becoming king. This resulted in the Exclusion Crisis, which lasted from May 1679 until March 1681, during which there were a number of legal attempts to exclude James from the lawful succession of the crown, all of which failed to pass both houses. Although the crisis was finally ended with the dissolution of Parliament in March 1681, the stain on James's reputation was never removed.[37] Following the death of Charles II, King James II tried to placate the fears of the Protestant majority by stating that he would defend the rights of the Church of England, with the transfer of power not only being peaceful but met with acclamation.[38] James II almost immediately declared his support for and defence of the Church of England, declaring this the following day in front of the Archbishop of Canterbury and the Bishop of Ely, which alleviated any lingering doubts regarding the Catholic king's intentions.[39] His enemies always insinuated that his intention was to create a Catholic country and these declarations did not persuade them otherwise. James's reign started with his nephew James, Duke of Monmouth trying to overthrow him in the failed Monmouth Rebellion.[40] Monmouth did not have any substantial support throughout the country, which resulted in his rebellion being quickly resolved, though it did shake James's faith in the ability of the army and militia to protect the country and his reign.[41] Following the rebellion, James II instigated a number of army reforms, including the instigation of yearly training camps lasting effectively all summer for the army on Hounslow Heath.[42] During James II's three-year reign, he increased the size of the army and implemented a modernisation of their equipment, including the widespread introduction of bayonets and battalion guns (light artillery pieces attached to infantry regiments and manned by soldiers) and a standardised regimental structure. During his reign, a total of 4,062 commissions were issued on behalf of James II. These include officers receiving their first commission, promotions, transfers to new regiments (a possible promotion depending on the status of the new

36 R. Beddard, *A Kingdom without A King: The Journal of the Provisional Government in the Revolution of 1688* (Oxford: Phaidon Press, 1988), p.16.

37 Coward, *The Stuart Age*, p.332.

38 Mark Goldie, *Roger Morrice and the Puritan Whig* (Woodbridge: Boydell Press, 2016), p.9.

39 Miller, *James II*, pp.58–9, and Jacqueline Rose, *Godly Kingship in Restoration England: The Politics of the Royal Supremacy, 1660-1688* (Cambridge: CUP, 2013), p.184.

40 Keay, *The Last Royal Rebel*. See also L. Brennan, *The Duke of Monmouth: Life and Rebellion* (Barnsley: Pen and Sword, 2018); D. Chandler, *Sedgemoor 1685: From Monmouth's Invasion to the Bloody Assizes* (Staplehurst: Spellmount, 1995); C. Chenevix Trench, *The Western Rising: An Account of Monmouth's Rebellion* (London: Longmans, Green, 1969); J. Tincey, *Sedgemoor 1685: Marlborough's First* Victory (Barnsley: Pen and Sword, 2005); and S. Carter, *Fighting For Liberty: Argyll & Monmouth's Military Campaign Against the Government of King James, 1685* (Warwick: Helion, 2020).

41 For further information on the militia and their involvement in the suppression of the rebellion, see: C. Scott, *The Maligned Militia: The West Country Militia of the Monmouth Rebellion* (Farnham: Ashgate, 2015).

42 M. Shearwood, 'A Summer on Hounslow Heath: Combined Army Operations in late Seventeenth-Century England', *War in History*, 29.3 (July 2022).

regiment), and a small number of demotions.[43] Of these commissions, only 404 (or just under 10 percent) can be associated with Catholic or dissenting officers, which is equal to the general population of dissenters within the country. In the 1676 census of London only 1 percent of the population of the city identified as Catholic, with the numbers of Catholics rising in London in 1689 by between 112 percent and 148 percent, based on the 1689 'Catholic' census of London.[44] While James's aim was for uniform acceptance of all religious beliefs, some of his actions were seen as being purely pro-Catholic and authoritarian. These included the engineered trial of Godden v. Hales (1686), where the courts ruled that the king's royal prerogative entitled him to dispense people from taking the Test Act, charging seven bishops with seditious libel for petitioning the king and refusing his command (1688), and interfering with the election of the President of Magdalen College, Oxford, by trying to get a Catholic elected.[45] These actions were used by James II's enemies and opponents to claim that England under James II would be transformed into an absolute monarchy similar to France under Louis XIV. In addition, they claimed that the king intended to turn England into a Catholic country, with all non-Catholics being subjugated and persecuted. James II had two daughters, Mary (b. 30 April 1662) and Anne (b. 6 February 1665), with his first wife, Anne Hyde, who died in 1671. Both of James's daughters were devoutly Protestant and Mary was seen as his legitimate heir until 1688 when James had a son with his second wife, Mary of Modena. Mary was implicated in the supposed Catholic plots, including the 'Warming Pan Scandal' of 1688, which alleged that Mary had not given birth to James II's legitimate son. James Francis Edward Stuart's birth on 10 June 1688 was seen as the start of a Stuart Catholic dynasty. In addition to his legitimate children, James had a number of illegitimate children, including James FitzJames, 1st Duke of Berwick (b. 21 August 1670), who was the king's eldest illegitimate son, a Catholic, and held a number of commands in the English army.

43 The commissioning information has been taken from the author's PhD thesis, 'The Catholic "Other" in the Army of James II and William III, 1685-90', unpublished, University of Leeds, 2022, and from Charles Dalton, *English Army Lists and Commission Registers, 1661-1714,* vol. 2 (London: Eyre & Spottiswoode, 1894), as well as numerous archival materials, including State Papers and Ordnance Papers.

44 E. Wrigley, *The Early English Census* (Oxford: Oxford University Press, 2011), p.104; A. Whiteman, *The Compton Census of 1676* (Oxford: OUP, 1986), pp.lxxxiv, 38–9, and 57. The London diocese census records 263,285 conformists, 20,893 Nonconformists, and 2,069 Papists (HL/PO/JO/10/1/402, ff. 19–20, 22–8, 41–2, 74–84). When looking at census figures, we must remember that minority groups are always under-represented in any census; the US Congress stated the 1940 census underreported persons of colour by at least 10.3 percent.

45 W. Gibson, *James II and the Trial of the Seven Bishops* (Basingstoke: Palgrave, 2009), pp.98–100; Rose, *Godly Kingship in Restoration England,* p.92; Coward, *The Stuart Age,* pp.339–40.

William III

William III, Stadholder and King of England, in a print by Gerard Valck, Amsterdam, 1689–1726. (Rijksmuseum: RP-P-OB-17.492, Public Domain)

William III, Prince of Orange, Stadholder of the Netherlands, later William III of England and William II of Scotland, was born Willem Hendrik on Monday, 14 November 1650, eight days after his father died, and inherited the title of William III, Prince of Orange of the House of Orange-Nassau. William's mother, Mary Stuart (Princess Royal), was the eldest daughter of King Charles I of England and Henrietta-Maria of France. At the behest of Charles II, William married Mary Stuart, the eldest daughter of James, Duke of York on 4 November 1677. The negotiations for the marriage started in 1674 after the signing of the Peace of Westminster (February 1674), with the marriage intended to strengthen the ties between England and the Dutch Republic following the disastrous series of Anglo-Dutch Wars (1652–54, 1665–67, and 1672–74).[46] William was therefore linked to the English succession both by birth through his mother and through his wife. These links would be subsequently used to support the legitimacy of offering him the crown of England and subsequently Ireland and Scotland. William's Calvinist faith, along with his marriage to the Protestant daughter of James II, made him the obvious choice for the conspirators (including the Immortal Seven) to overthrow the Catholic king. William became stadholder of each of the Dutch provinces during 1672 (each province had the authority to elect their own stadholder) and on 20 April 1675 he was appointed by the States General as hereditary Captain-General and Admiral-General of all the Dutch forces.[47] William's main aims were always the promotion of the Dutch Republic and its protection against the expansionist policies of Louis XIV. William developed a large coalition of Catholic and Protestant countries against Catholic France and formed various anti-French alliances – the Union of Wetterau in 1679, the Laxenburg Alliance in 1682, and the League of Augsburg in July 1686.[48]

William sent his cousin William Nassau de Zuylenstein to England in 1687 with the intended purpose of informing the queen-consort of the death of her mother, the Dowager Duchess of Modena, and again in June 1688 to

46 Pull, *William III*, pp.307–8; Coward, *The Stuart Age*, p.312
47 Pull, *William III*, p.319.
48 Coward, *The Stuart Age*, pp.343, 366.

congratulate the queen-consort on the birth of her son. Both trips, while diplomatic in their stated purpose, were also used to both gauge the support for William's invasion and converse with the conspirators. Zuylenstein would return to The Hague in early August 1688 accompanied by the author of the invitation letter, Henry Sydney, 1st Earl of Romney. William rewarded Zuylenstein on his return with a promotion to the rank of major-general of the Dutch army.

William's intent to invade England, Ireland, and Scotland was published in October 1688 in his declaration of *The Reasons Inducing Him to Appear in Arms in the Kingdom of England, for Preserving of the Protestant Religion, and for Restoring the Laws and Liberties of England, Scotland, and Ireland*.[49] The declaration lays the blame with king's 'evil councillors' for 'overturning [of] the religion, laws, and liberties of the realm' rather than with the king himself. It also states that Princess Mary had been interested in the succession to the crown since England invaded the States General of the United Provinces in 1672 in a 'most unjust war'. The inclusion of Mary's 'interest' in the succession is used to legitimise William's actions and intent in overthrowing James, as it links the Dutch actions back to Charles II. William states that all those employed in civil or military positions should not be a 'Papist' and were required to take both the Oath of Allegiance and Supremacy and the oaths laid out in the Test Acts. When William was in control of the army, he initially only required the army and navy to take the Oath of Allegiance and Supremacy and they did not have to take the oaths in the Test Acts. One of the main stipulations of the declaration was for a free and lawful parliament under the protection of (Dutch) force of arms along with a good agreement between the Church of England and Protestant dissenters. The last paragraph gives an insight into William's later actions in Ireland in 1690–91 as it states that he intends to 'bring the Kingdom of Ireland to such a state… that Protestant and British interests there may be secured'. This section gives the clearest indication that William did not just want to restore the Church of England's supremacy in England, but that he also wanted to extend it into Ireland and reduce its independence. A later manifesto published by William and Mary in English, Dutch, and Latin openly stated their objections to James II's Declaration of Indulgence and the perceived threat to Protestant England. It confirmed the Dutch view of personal religion, that no Christian should be persecuted for their faith, and that as in the United Provinces, each person should be free to worship with full liberty of conscience.[50] The manifesto stated that the penal laws should be rescinded to allow freedom of worship although it did clearly state that the Test Acts should remain in force in relation to the Catholic faith, stating that 'the Protestant Religion and the safety of the nation, would be exposed to most certain dangers'.[51]

---

49 William, Prince of Orange, *The Reasons Inducing Him to Appear in Arms in the Kingdom of England, for Preserving of the Protestant Religion, and for Restoring the Laws and Liberties of England, Scotland, and Ireland* (Hague: N.P., 1688).

50 Gaspar Fagel, *A letter Writ by Mijn Heer Fagel, Pensioner to the Great and Mighty Lords, the States of Holland and Westfriesland* (Holland and Westfriesland: J. Schelsus, 1687), pp.1–4.

51 Fagel, *A letter Writ by Mijn Heer Fagel*, pp.1–4.

Revolution House, Chesterfield, formerly the Cock and Pynot inn, where two of the 'Immortal Seven' met in the summer of 1688 to discuss the invitation of William III, Prince of Orange. (Author's Collection)

Immortal Seven

When historians consider the events of 1688 as a revolution, they are looking at the outcome: changes to the governance of England; issuing the Declaration of Rights (1689); and the change from an absolute monarchy to a constitutional monarchy. However, none of these events could have been foreseen prior to 1689 and they certainly were not planned for by the group who wrote and signed the letter inviting William of Orange to England.

The letter was written by Henry Sydney, 1st Earl of Romney and signed by Edward Russell, Charles Talbot, 12th Earl of Shrewsbury, William Cavendish, 4th Earl of Devonshire, Thomas Osborne, 1st Earl of Danby, Richard Lumley, 2nd Viscount Lumley, and Henry Compton, Bishop of London. While most of these men were entitled to sit within the House of Lords, they were not speaking for any part of the government at the time they instigated the request, and while Sydney and Talbot raised troops for James II during the Monmouth Rebellion, both had resigned their commissions prior to 1688. Edward Russell had been a naval captain prior to falling into disfavour with King Charles following the revelations of his connection to the Rye House Plot of 1683 and moved to the Netherlands to serve William after signing the letter. The seven signatories later became known as the 'Immortal Seven' and were all rewarded by William after the invasion, including with grants of positions and titles, including dukedoms. The letter was signed on 30 June 1688 and stated that:[52]

52 NA: SP8/1/224.

> We have great satisfaction to find by 35, and since by M. Zulestein, that your Highness is so ready and willing to give us such assistances as they have related to us. We have great reason to believe that we shall be every day in a worse condition than we are and less able to defend ourselves, and therefore we do earnestly wish we might be so happy as to find a remedy before it be too late for us to contribute to our own deliverance; but although these be our wishes yet we will by no means put your Highness into any expectations which may misguide your own counsels in this matter, so that the best advice we can give is to inform your Highness truly both of the state of things here at this time and of the difficulties which appear to us. As to the first, the people are so generally dissatisfied with the present conduct of the Government in relation to their religion, liberties, and properties (all which have been greatly invaded), and they are in such expectation of their prospects being daily worse that your Highness may be assured there are nineteen parts of twenty of the people throughout the Kingdom who are desirous of a change.[53]

Lieutenant-General Godard van Reede, in a print by Jacob Hounraken, Amsterdam. Van Reede was a senior commander in William's invasion force and later commander of his forces in Ireland. (Rijksmuseum: RP-P-1903-A-22966, Public Domain)

As stated in the letter, this was just part of a long correspondence with William of Orange, with a number of the signatories going over to Holland and joining William prior to the invasion. This letter was not an invitation by seven concerned lords based on their fears regarding a 'Popish' dynasty following the birth of a legitimate son to James II, but rather the carefully orchestrated conclusion to a yearlong conspiracy to overthrow the legitimate sovereign. The letter incorrectly stated that there would be the 'greatest numbers of deserters' from the army and navy when he arrived, and that 'not one in ten who would do them any service in such a war'. These statements are based on the seven's knowledge of the members of the Treason Club and their efforts to undermine the morale of the army and their assertions that they would be able to get each of their regiments to defect with them to William. While planning for the Dutch invasion, members of this group still used subterfuge to cover their tracks in case their plans did not come to fruition. Danby was one of many members of the gentry and nobility to offer support to James during the October of 1688 and also offered to raise troops to defend the country, when in reality he had no intention of doing such a thing.[54] All of the signatories would later receive substantial rewards from William: Henry Compton, Bishop of London conducted William and Mary's coronation and Cavendish, Danby,

53 The number 35 is code for Edward Russell, who had held the position of Admiral of the English fleet.

54 *London Gazette*, Monday, 8 October to Thursday, 11 October 1688, no. 2389, p.2.

and Talbot all received dukedoms. There were other conspirators involved in organising the invitation, including the MP for Richmond, the Honourable John D'Arcy, who met with the Earl of Devonshire and the Earl of Danby at the Cock and Pynot inn, Whittington, Chesterfield, in 1688 to discuss inviting William to take the throne.[55]

55 The inn is currently known as The Revolution House and is operated as a museum by Chesterfield Council (closed at the time of writing this book). Items including a chair used by the conspirators are currently held at Hardwick House, near Chesterfield, which is a National Trust property.

2

Invasion Planning

There is no doubt that William of Orange had started to plan for the invasion of England long before the birth of James's son and the invitation written by the 'Immortal Seven'. William had dispatched personal envoys to friendly states during the second half of 1687, including sending Simon van Petticum, who was the head of his Domain Council, to the court of Brunswick-Lüneburg.[1] While this and other diplomatic meetings did not result in signed treaties and confirmed agreements regarding the supply of troops and financing for William's intervention in England in 1688, they did set the scene and enabled William to be confident about support for his proposed operation to gain control of the English crown and therefore the English army and navy, and to a lesser extent the Scottish army. The prospect of a close relationship between James II and Louis XIV based on a united religious belief revised fears and memories of the Third Anglo-Dutch War, when France and England brought the Dutch Republic to near collapse and ruin.[2] It is unknown if William had any plans for the mainly Catholic Irish army, as while the Irish army was almost as large as the English army, it was categorically inferior to the English army in the quality of both its soldiers and equipment.[3] The Irish army was supposedly entirely Catholic following Richard Talbot, Earl of Tyrconnell's purge of Protestant officers and soldiers during 1686–87.

William's plans for the invasion of England were known to a very close circle of advisers as far back as late 1687; these included William Bentinck, Gaspar Fagel, Pensionary of Holland, and Everard van Weede van Dijkvelt.[4] Bentinck acted as one of William's closest advisers and as his ambassador and was sent to meet with the Elector of Brandenburg in April 1688 in order to 'confide to him the designs of the Prince of Orange'. Other alliances and treaties were signed with Saxony and Hesse-Cassel, Celle, and Hanover. These treaties included mutual defence treaties, including for the Middle and

1 Pull, *William III*, p.543.

2 K.H.D. Haley, 'The Dutch, the Invasion of England, and the Alliance of 1689', in L. Schwoerer (ed.), *The Revolution of 1688-1689: Changing Perspectives* (Cambridge: CUP, 2003), p.26.

3 Childs, *The Army, James II*, pp.56–7.

4 Marion Grew, *William Bentinck and William III (Prince of Orange); The Life of Bentinck Earl of Portland from the Welbeck Correspondence* (London: J. Murray, 1924), p.104.

Lower Rhine areas, as well as for the replacement of Dutch troops with troops from various German states. These alliances allowed for the Dutch troops to be withdrawn to Holland and used for the proposed invasion of England without weakening William's efforts against Louis XIV and risking territories becoming vulnerable to French invasion.[5] The diplomatic interventions during 1687 and early 1688 confirm that the 'invitation letter' sent by the 'Immortal Seven' in July 1688 was not the instigator, as Whig history would have us believe, but just one piece in a long-held plan by William to ensure the dominance of Holland and its allies over Catholic France. Despite William's appearance as the leader of what seemed to be an anti-Catholic coalition, he was certainly not anti-Catholic in any traditional sense; rather, he was anti-French and opposed to French expansion within Europe. The Dutch army had large numbers of Catholic troops within its ranks and there were more Catholic soldiers within William's invasion army than at any time within the army of James II.[6]

William's Catholic allies included Emperor Leopold I of the Habsburg Empire and Pope Innocent XI, who were both involved in their own conflicts with France and Louis XIV. The Pontiff's agreement to William's plans was based on his declaration that he had no intention of subjugating the Catholic population of England, or the Catholic religion, and that his only aim was securing the true inheritance of his Protestant wife Mary to the throne of England, Scotland, and Ireland. Following the birth of James Francis Edward Stuart on 10 June 1688 (he would be named Prince of Wales in July 1688) and the arrival of the invitation, Bentinck departed for his second diplomatic mission to the courts of Brandenburg, Hesse-Cassel, Hanover, Celle, and Wolfenbüttel on 24 July 1688.[7] Frederick III of Brandenburg advised that he would be able to send troops to help William in his endeavour, with the negotiations between Bentinck and the Prime Minister of Brandenburg, Paul Fuchs, concentrating on whether William would contribute to the costs of the recruitment and mobilisation of these soldiers.[8] Fuchs and Bentinck agreed on a total of 5,000 foot and 1,000 horse, a mixture of cavalry and dragoons, to be made available to Holland. These troops for the most part would be used to allow Dutch troops to withdraw and return to Holland for the proposed invasion, with a 'good number of troops' to be dispatched to Cleves in Germany as soon as possible.[9] The rate to be paid would be between 8 and 10 Reichsthaler for each foot soldier and 25 Reichsthaler for each mounted trooper (cavalry or dragoons).[10] William required and received the approval

5 Miller, *James II*, p.191.

6 Marc Van Alphen, 'Soldiers and Sailors', in Marc Van Alphen et al. (eds), *Military Power and the Dutch Republic: War, Trade, and the Balance of Power in Europe 1648-1813* (Leiden: Leiden University Press, 2021), p.355; J. Israel, 'The Dutch Role in the Glorious Revolution', in J. Israel (ed.), *The Anglo-Dutch Moment: Essays on the Glorious Revolution and its World Impact* (Cambridge: Cambridge University Press, 1991), p.144.

7 Grew, *William Bentinck*, p.112.

8 Grew, *William Bentinck*, p.113; J. Carswell, *The Descent on England: A Study of the English Revolution of 1688 & its European Background* (London: Barrie and Rockliff, 1969), p.119.

9 Grew, *William Bentinck*, p.118.

10 Grew, *William Bentinck*, p.119.

of the States General for his use of German troops to take over the duties of the Dutch troops involved in the invasion, and also received their permission for William to invade England.[11]

William arranged a similar contract with King Christian V of Denmark in 1689 for the transfer of 6,000 foot and 1,000 horse to England for William's campaign in Ireland. This contract paid a lump sum to Denmark, and William was responsible for the payment of the Danish troops. In addition, William was allowed to recruit replacements for troops killed or wounded, but had to pay an agreed sum for each soldier killed while in William's service.[12] This agreement for recruiting foreign troops for service was not new and was an easy way for nations to increase their fighting forces quickly and to a level not achievable by their own population.[13] By the end of August 1688, Bentinck had obtained an additional 12,000 troops for service in William's army and coalition from Brandenburg, Celle, Hesse-Cassel, and Württemberg. In a dispatch to Louis XIV on 14 September 1688, the numbers were stated as 12,000 from Brandenburg, 6,000 from the Elector of Saxony, 4,000 from the Dukes of Celle and Wolfenbüttel, and 3,000 from Hesse-Cassel.[14] The German troop numbers have also been reported to have been around 14,000, made up of 6,000 Brandenburgers, 4,000 from Brunswick-Lüneburg-Zeller, 2,400 from Hesse-Cassel, and 1,000 from Württemberg.[15] In addition to the German troops, the States General hired an addition 6,000 Swedish veterans, the majority from the Swedish enclaves in Germany and the rest directly from Sweden.[16] Louis XIV was so concerned that James II would not be able to prevent the Williamite invasion that he instructed his most trusted diplomat, Jean-Antoine de Mesmes, known as d'Avaux, to inform the States General that he would come to James's aid if the Dutch invaded.[17] In late August 1688 news reached England that the Dutch had started to recruit 9,000 additional seamen and had announced that they were willing to pay higher wages to English seamen.[18] William was also arranging for the purchase of large quantities of military saddles and horse furniture and arms.

William was so concerned with the possibility of conflict between the Dutch and English fleets that on 26 September 1688 he informed his secretary, Bentinck, to repeat to Admiral Herbert, commander of the invasion fleet, that 'he must avoid fighting as much as he can, for, since the result is uncertain, though we are stronger, this is no time to show his

11 K. Haley, 'The Dutch, The Invasion of England, and the Alliance of 1689', in L. Schwoerer (ed.), *The Revolution of 1688-1689: Changing Perspectives* (Cambridge: CUP, 2003), p.21.

12 K.H. Galster, *Danish troops in the Williamite Army in Ireland, 1689-91* (Dublin: Four Courts Press, 2012).

13 P. Wilson, '"Mercenary" Contracts as Fiscal-Military Instruments', in S. Norrhem and E. Thomson (eds), *Subsidies, Diplomacy, and State Formation in Europe, 1494-1789: Economies of Allegiance* (Lund: Lund University Press, 2020), pp.78–9.

14 Grew, *William Bentinck*, p.125.

15 M. Glozier, *The Huguenot Soldiers of William of Orange and the Glorious Revolution of 1688: The Lions of Judah* (Brighton: Sussex Academic Press, 2002), p.105.

16 Israel, 'The Dutch Role', pp.108–9.

17 Miller, *James II*, p.192.

18 Narcissus Luttrell, *A Brief Historical Relation of State Affairs, from September 1678 to April 1714*, vol. I (Oxford: OUP, 1857), p.456.

[Herbert's] bravery'.[19] On 29 September the Grand Pensionary of Holland granted William the authority to launch his invasion of England, citing the secret alliance between Louis XIV and James II, and instructed the prince to use all measures to obtain the consent of the rest of the provinces.[20] William arranged for broadsheets to be printed and distributed throughout the English fleet through his network of supporters and conspirators. Similar broadsheets were also sent for distribution to the army. The broadsheet stated that it was James and not William that had brought the nation under foreign control (that of Louis XIV of France), and that they were under the command of French and Irish papists and that any support for James against the Williamite forces was 'inconsistent with their duty to God, and the Laws of England'.[21] The broadsheet finished with a direct appeal to English seamen: 'The same considerations are likewise humbly offered to all English Sea-men, who have been the Bulwark of this Nation against Popery and Slavery ever since Eighty Eight.'[22] The reference to 'Eighty-Eight' refers to the defeat of the Spanish Armada in 1588 and William is clearly playing on the cultural memory of the English people to link his endeavour with Elizabeth I's reputation as the saviour of the country. The use of 'this Nation against Popery and Slavery' rather than 'England against Popery and Slavery' is an obvious attempt by William to place himself at the centre of the nation, and James as the enemy of the English people. A further broadsheet directed towards the English fleet stated that William had fully empowered and trusted Admiral Herbert, who most of the English navy would have known at least by name and who many would have served under. The broadsheet concluded with a prayer designed to rouse the feelings of English sailors and linking them to the Dutch sailors in their aim to protect the Protestant faith.[23] The Grand Pensionary of Holland issued a declaration on 19 September 1688 stating that:[24]

> His Highness, The Prince of Orange desires to go over to England with a sufficient force, not to obtain possession of that country, nor to dethrone the king, but in the interest of the Protestant religion, and to prevent a coalition of the kings of England and France for invading this country.

William published his *Declaration of William, Prince of Orange, the Reasons inducing him to Appear in Arms in England* in The Hague on 30 September

19 William III to William Bentinck, 16 September 1688 (OS), in N. Japikse (ed.), *Correspondentie van Willem III en van Hans Willem Bentinck, eersten Graaf van Portland* (s'-Gravenhage: M. Nijhoff, 1927), p.97.

20 Carswell, *The Descent on England*, pp.172–3.

21 Anon., *A Letter of Advice to all Protestant Soldiers, and Sea-men Showing how Inconsistent it is with their Duty to God, and the Law of England, to Fight for a Popish Interest* (London: N.P., 1688).

22 Anon., *A Letter of Advice to all Protestant Soldiers.*

23 Anon., *Prince of Orange Letter to the English-Fleet and the Form of Prayer used in the Dutch* Fleet (N.L.: N.P., 1688).

24 J. Ferguson, *Papers Illustrating the History of the Scots Brigade in the Service of the United Netherlands, 1572-1782: Extracted by Permission from the Government Archives at the Hague* (Edinburgh: SHS, 1899), p.566.

1688 (10 October 1688 in Holland). The declaration opens stating that William Henry, Prince of Orange is invading England 'for preserving the Protestant religion, and for restoring the laws and liberties of England, Scotland, and Ireland'.[25] The declaration is an account of the (illegal) acts that have 'overturned the religion, laws, and liberties of these Realms [England, and Scotland]' and rather than blaming James II, the declaration puts the blame on the king's councillors.[26] The supposed crimes committed by the king's councillors include abolishing the laws regarding the Oaths of Allegiance and Supremacy and allowing Papists and Nonconformists to hold ecclesiastical, civil, and military employment. In addition, it claims that the setting up of the Court of Ecclesiastical Commission, the replacement of the President of Magdalen College, Oxford, the King's Declaration for Liberty of Conscience and the subsequent trial of the seven bishops were all reasons for his intervention in England.[27] The bishops were accused of seditious libel for issuing and printing a petition to the king stating their reasons for refusing the king's order. James's insistence that both military officers and civil authorities answered positively to the 'three questions' further isolated the king and provided William with propaganda for his invasion. The three questions were: 'first, if they were appointed to office or elected to Parliament would they favour the "taking off" of penal laws including the Test Act? Second, would they use their influence to elect candidates committed to this policy? Third, would they support James's declaration for Liberty of Conscience by living amicably with Catholics?'[28] There would have been a great expectation for officers within the army to answer positively to these three questions and to comply with the wishes of the king. This pressure resulted in a number of officers either losing or giving up their commissions as a result of their political or religious beliefs. Between James II's accession to the throne in 1685 and the summer of 1688 there were, according to Childs, some 40 or 50 officers who lost their commissions due to their beliefs.[29] These numbers are inconsequential when looking at the numbers of officers, both Protestant and Catholic, commissioned by James II during his reign. It does show how William's *Declaration… of the reasons inducing him to appear in arms* enabled the Williamite cause to win 'the propaganda war hands down'.[30] While there has been a large focus on the fact that William brought over a printing press with the invasion fleet, most of the Williamite propaganda was printed on English presses by English publishers and booksellers. Williamite agents provided publishers and booksellers with a large number of copies of all William's declarations (without any charge) in order for them to produce

25 William, Prince of Orange, *The Declaration of William, Prince of Orange, of the Reasons Inducing Him to Appear in Arms in England* (Hague: Arnout Leers, 1688).

26 T. Harris, *Revolution: The Great Crisis of the British Monarchy, 1686-1720* (London: Penguin Books, 2007), p.279.

27 See Gibson, *Trial of the Seven Bishops*.

28 Gibson, *Trial of the Seven Bishops*, p.69.

29 Childs, *General Percy Kirke*, p.120.

30 T. Claydon, 'William III's Declaration of Reasons and the Glorious Revolution', *The History Journal*, 39.1 (1996), p.88.

more and sell them to their customers.[31] This was in addition to 60,000 copies of William's declaration being printed in Holland and secretly transported to England.[32]

Futile Concessions of James II, September 1688, in an anonymous print from the Northern Netherlands. William was intent on invading England to secure the crown for himself and his wife, with the situation out of the control of James II. (Rijksmuseum: RP-P-OB-77.619, Public Domain)

Invasion Fleet

Plans for the naval and military invasion force were well underway by June 1688, with agreements from both Amsterdam and Rotterdam for the use of their ships both as part of the invasion force and as naval escorts. Amsterdam and Rotterdam provided the majority of the warships for the invasion, with the transports being private and East India Company (VOC) merchant ships being all hired by the end of September 1688.[33] Before the troops were first embarked for the invasion, some of the small ships were in danger of being overwhelmed by an oncoming storm; the men of war and larger transport ships weighed their anchors and headed for an area between two and three leagues from the shore, between Holland and Zealand.[34] The fleet initially set sail on 19 October from its loading port of Texel, but on the first attempt were met by serious storms on the North Sea and while the fleet did not lose any ships, the men, horses and supplies did not fare so well with approximately

31 Claydon, 'William III's Declaration of Reasons', pp.89–90.
32 Israel, 'The Dutch Role', p.121.
33 Pull, *William III*, p.560.
34 Luttrell, *A Brief Historical Relation of State Affairs* vol. I, p.13.

500 horses lost due to suffocation.[35] The soldiers on the ships were in a terrible condition following the storm, with reports stating that they had been:

> Tumbl'd about the ship, many wax'd exceeding sick, and vomited continually after a dreadful rate; you could hear the men groan after a pitiful manner; other were fighting, and not a few praying, and committing their souls unto God, for they thought their bodies must be meat for the fish of the sea.[36]

Reports of casualties amongst the troops are vague and varied, with some reports suggesting that William had not lost any soldiers during the storm, while others state that a ship was lost containing four companies (120 men) from a Holstein regiment of foot along with sixty Huguenot officers and soldiers.[37] The Governor of the Isle of Wight, Sir Robert Holmes, reported on 20 October that the Dutch fleet had lost a fireship with all her men.[38] The fireship was replaced by the time that the invasion fleet eventually set sail on 1 November 1688. A number of ships were damaged and had their sails torn, with several ships being 'driven near the coast of England'.[39] It was several days before the fleet managed to return, this time to Hellevoetsluis, and waited for the storm to subside and for the 'Protestant wind' to return. While the ships were undergoing repair, the horses were disembarked from the ships to allow them to recover, with William having to replace the dead and injured horses. The delay resulted in thousands of troops being held in and around Dutch ports, resulting in the price of supplies and lodgings increasing in those areas. To counter this, William issued orders dictating the maximum price for a night's lodging, along with the maximum price for eggs and for each pound of bacon, beef, butter, cheese, mutton, and veal.[40] By 30 October all the ships within the fleet had been re-provisioned and troops and horses re-embarked by working through the night in order for the fleet to be ready to sail on 1 November and take advantage of the prevailing winds.[41]

We have detailed information regarding the disposition of William of Orange's transport fleet from a number of sources, including from the hand-drawn plan by William Bentinck, the future 1st Earl of Portland. This drawing does not include the Dutch warships that were drawn up in a protective screen around the fleet. We not only know the number of ships involved but also their cargos and their position with the convoy, which was divided into nine divisions, excluding the lead ships which contained William of Orange and his immediate circle.[42] The fleet was divided into three squadrons or

35 Grew, *William Bentinck*, p.130, Anon., *An Exact diary of the Late Expedition of His Illustrious Highness the Prince of Orange (now King of Great Britain) from His palace at the Hague, to His Landing at Torbay and from thence to His Arrival at White-Hall* (London: Richard Baldwin, 1689), p.23.

36 Anon., *An Exact diary of the Late Expedition*, p.19

37 S. Smiles, *The Huguenots: Their Settlements, Churches and Industries in England and Ireland* (London: John Murray, 1905), pp.216–7.

38 NA: SP 31/4, f.151–3.

39 Anon., *An Exact diary of the Late Expedition*, p.21.

40 Anon., *An Exact diary of the Late Expedition*, p.24.

41 Anon., *An Exact diary of the Late Expedition*, p.28.

42 NU: PwA 2197/2, Plan of the order of sailing of the Dutch fleet; n.d. [c.1688].

divisions, with each ship carrying a mark or token to identify their division, a red flag for the English and Scottish, a white flag for Prince's guard and the Brandenburgers, and a blue flag for the Dutch and French.[43]

The convoy was headed by two picket ships, followed by the *Brill*, the ship carrying the Prince of Orange, this was followed by a further ten ships, seven containing Wayman Lord Macclesfield, English gentlemen, Marshal Schomberg, Nassau, Voorst, Scottish lords and an additional three ships carrying provisions and baggage belonging to His Highness.[44]

Following behind these ships was the first three divisions as follows:

> Graaf van Solms with Colonel Bohum, leading a division of 24 ships containing: 15 ships of Guards on foot with their horses, six ships with dragoons, one ship carrying artillery, two ships carrying the equipment for Willem Meesters.
>
> General Major Mackay leading a division of 22 ships containing: 19 ships of English troops, one ship with their horses, two ships carrying artillery. The Scots Brigade embarked on ten ships, with Mackay on board the *De Boom*, while his regiment was on the *Gortmolen*, *'s Gravebhage*, and *Young Ruyter*. Balfour's regiment embarked on the *d'Eendragt*, *Juffrouw Hester*, and *'tWapen van Amsterdam*, with Wacop's regiment onboard *de Blaeuwe Pot*, *De Koog in de Saen*, and *De Trouw*.[45]
>
> Palsgrave leading a division of 22 ships: 19 ships with infantry, one ship with their horses, two ships with artillery.

The second line of three divisions contained:

> Colonel l'Estang leading a division of 30 ships: four ships of bodyguards, 22 ships with dragoons' horses, four ships with his highness and the Gentlemen of Owverkerck's horses,
>
> Count Van Lipp leading a division of 13 ships: 12 ships with cavalry horses, and one ship with men (presumably the cavalry).
>
> Colonel J. Hersum leading a division of 11 ships: 10 ships with horses, and one ship with men.

The final line consisted of:

> Colonel Holtsappel leading a division of 21 ships: 15 ships of horse guards, two ships with His Highness's carriages, and one ship with French and their horses.
>
> Major Doccum leading a division of 25 ships: 12 ships with cavalry horses, one ship with men, nine ships with volunteer artillery and artillery ships, and three ships with Lord Leven's and Lord Picton's men.

---

43 Anon., *An Exact diary of the Late Expedition*, p.28.

44 NU: PwA 2197/2.

45 Ferguson, *History of the Scots Brigade*, pp.566–7.

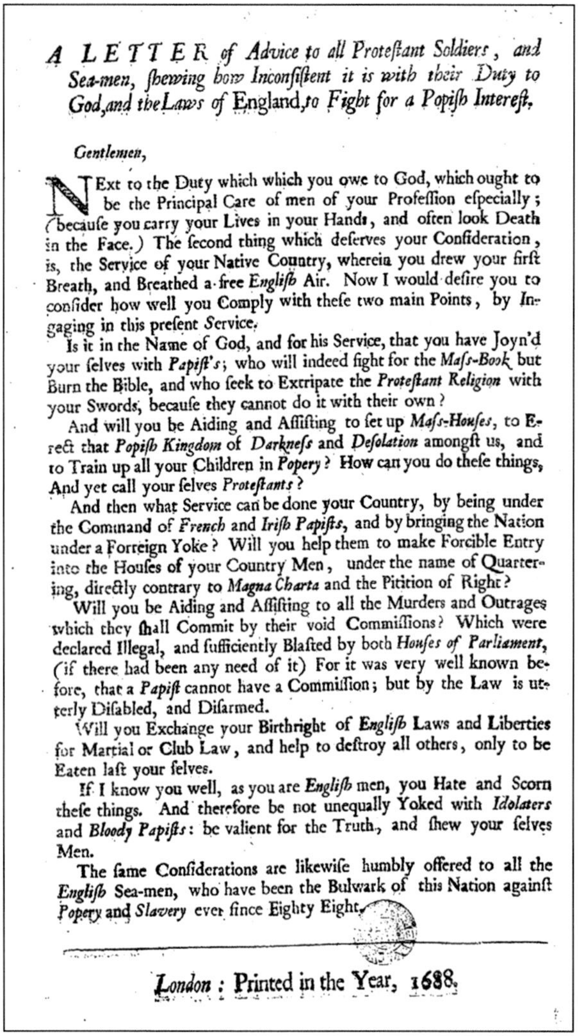

A LETTER *of Advice to all Proteſtant Soldiers, and Sea-men, ſhewing how Inconſiſtent it is with their Duty to God, and the Laws of* England, *to Fight for a Popiſh Intereſt.*

Gentlemen,

NExt to the Duty which which you owe to God, which ought to be the Principal Care of men of your Profeſſion eſpecially; (becauſe you carry your Lives in your Hands, and often look Death in the Face.) The ſecond thing which deſerves your Conſideration, is, the Service of your Native Country, wherein you drew your firſt Breath, and Breathed a free *Engliſh* Air. Now I would deſire you to conſider how well you Comply with theſe two main Points, by Ingaging in this preſent *Service.*

Is it in the Name of God, and for his Service, that you have Joyn'd your ſelves with *Papiſt's*; who will indeed fight for the *Maſs-Book* but Burn the Bible, and who ſeek to Extripate the *Proteſtant Religion* with your Swords, becauſe they cannot do it with their own?

And will you be Aiding and Aſſiſting to ſet up *Maſs-Houſes*, to Erect that *Popiſh Kingdom* of *Darkneſs* and *Deſolation* amongſt us, and to Train up all your Children in *Popery*? How can you do theſe things, And yet call your ſelves *Proteſtants*?

And then what Service can be done your Country, by being under the Command of *French* and *Iriſh Papiſts*, and by bringing the Nation under a Forreign Yoke? Will you help them to make Forcible Entry into the Houſes of your Country Men, under the name of Quartering, directly contrary to *Magna Charta* and the Pitition of Right?

Will you be Aiding and Aſſiſting to all the Murders and Outrages which they ſhall Commit by their void Commiſſions? Which were declared Illegal, and ſufficiently Blaſted by both *Houſes of Parliament*, (if there had been any need of it) For it was very well known before, that a *Papiſt* cannot have a Commiſſion; but by the Law is utterly Diſabled, and Diſarmed.

Will you Exchange your Birthright of *Engliſh* Laws and Liberties for Martial or Club Law, and help to deſtroy all others, only to be Eaten laſt your ſelves.

If I know you well, as you are *Engliſh* men, you Hate and Scorn theſe things. And therefore be not unequally Yoked with *Idolaters* and *Bloody Papiſts*: be valient for the Truth, and ſhew your ſelves Men.

The ſame Conſiderations are likewiſe humbly offered to all the *Engliſh* Sea-men, who have been the Bulwark of this Nation againſt *Popery* and *Slavery* ever ſince Eighty Eight.

London: Printed in the Year, 1688.

A Letter of Advice to All Protestant Soldiers, London, 1688. These handbills were distributed throughout England in an attempt to dissuade the English army from fighting for James II. Similar propaganda was dispersed throughout the fleet by Williamite sympathisers. (Author's Collection)

Colonel Schaeck leading a division of 23 ships: 21 ships with cavalry horses, and two ships with men.

Each division was accompanied by an additional five small ships (pinnaces). The fleet was protected by between forty and fifty-three men-of-war with either five frigates and five fireships, or ten fireships.[46]

While at sea, two ships were lost from the invasion fleet: the *Akerboon*, which was rated as a 60-gun third-rate ship when launched in 1664, but by 1688 its armament had been reduced to 42 guns, and the *Bommell,* a 24-gun fifth-rate ship launched in 1668.[47] After the invasion William, on behalf of the Dutch state, charged the English government a total of 2,478,080 florins for the hire of the fleet, the sailors' wages, and supplies, with an additional charge of 59,500 florins for the loss of the two ships.[48]

Invasion Force

William's ultimate hope might have been for a peaceful transition of power, confirming his publicly stated aim of being England's and the Church of England's saviour, but he was prepared for a full military campaign. He had, however, made preparations for his hoped-for peaceful outcome. He had recruited senior English army and navy officers to his cause through a network of officers in the army and navy, and also through the Anglo-Scots brigades in service with the Dutch army. Many of these officers formed the 'Treason Club'; the club's network was extended through regimental and friendship networks. The president of the club, Lieutenant-Colonel Richard Savage, along with other senior army officers including Churchill, Kirke, and Trelawney, aimed to destabilise the English army and ultimately to persuade their regiments to desert to William's forces upon

46 William Pull puts the figure of 400 transports, 53 warships, and 10 fireships, while John Carswell puts the strength of the military escort at 52 ships, Grew puts the numbers of warships at 40, and W. Troost puts the figures at 260 transports and 48 warships. John Childs quotes a contemporary report by a William Leck from Holland from 16 October 1688, stating that William's invasion fleet consisted of 450 transport ships which were guarded by 80 warships. Pull, *William III*, p.559; Grew, *William Bentinck*, p.115; Carswell, *The Descent on England*, pp.167–70; W. Troost, *Stadhoulder-koning Willem III, Een Politieke Biografie* (Hilversum, 2001), p.71; Childs, *The Army, James II*, p.169.

47 J. Bender, *Dutch Warships in the Age of Sail 1600-1714* (Seaforth Publishing, 2014).

48 *House of Commons Journal*, Volume 10: 7 February 1689, pp.20–22.

their arrival.[49] The view of William's advisers was that the bulk of the English army's resolve would waiver in its support for a Catholic king upon his arrival and he would not have to face the English army in battle. However, he could not take the chance that the English army would instead stand united behind its king in defence of the nation, so he needed to mobilise a force superior to that available to James II.[50] William had started to plan for the invasion during 1687, with the inspection of his Dutch troops in Munster and Nijmegen, 'not very far from the Brandenburghers camp'.[51] Troops were reported being dispatched down the River Rhine and River Moselle on flat-bottom boats.[52] Letters were reaching England as early as January and February 1688 reporting increased activity within Dutch ports and shipyards. The letters reported that 'there were great preparations making there, as if an actual war', with ships being immediately fitted out, new forces being raised, and an increased urgency in recruiting seamen.[53] The fleet had been originally loaded with enough provisions to last the force for one month's operations within England. Unfortunately, not all the storm-damaged supplies were replaced prior to the actual invasion, with extra supplies having to be obtained by the troops while in England. The invasion force was planned to encompass 10,800 infantry in 18 battalions of foot, of approximately 600 men each, 3,280 cavalry, horse, and dragoons, and between 4,000 and 5,000 horses.[54] The eventual force consisted of 15 regiments of foot consisting of 16 battalions with a paper strength of 11,322 men. The report in the *London Gazette* puts the figures at 16 regiments consisting of 164 companies and 10,692 men.[55] The extra regiment in the reports is due to entering the Regiment Birkenfeld twice, one under Birkenfeld and one under Prince Birkenfeld.

The force consisted of elements of some of the best and most experienced regiments of the Dutch army. While this was not a state-sanctioned invasion by the States General, it had all the appearance of a full Dutch invasion. William brought over all six regiments from the Anglo-Dutch and Scots-Dutch brigades, which had proven their loyalty to William and to the Dutch states. In addition to these experienced troops, William's force also consisted of the majority of the elite Dutch Guard regiments, including two battalions of the Gardes te Voet (foot guards), six companies of the Gardes te Paard, William's personal bodyguard of the Gardes du Corps, and the Dutch Guard regiment of dragoons, the Gardes Dragonders, or Eppinger's dragoons.

The cavalry consisted of 16 regiments of horse, although two of these 'regiments' consisted of only one company: the Gardes du Corps with one expanded company of 197 men, and one company from the s'Gravemoer Regiment of Horse. The Gardes te Paard consisted of all six companies

---

49 J. Childs, *The Army, James II*; Childs, *General Percy*, p.123; S. Pincus, *1688: The First Modern Revolution* (Devon, PA: Yale, 2009).

50 Grew, *William Bentinck*, pp.114–5.

51 Anon., *An Exact diary of the Late Expedition*, p.9.

52 Anon., *An Exact diary of the Late Expedition,* pp.12–3.

53 Luttrell, *A Brief Historical Relation of State Affairs*, vol. I, p.433.

54 Carswell, *The Descent into England,* pp.168–9; Pull, *William III*, p.560. Carswell quotes 4,000 horses while Pull states the figure as 5,000.

55 *London Gazette*, Monday, 5 November to Thursday, 8 November 1688, p.2.

and 480 men. The 1685 regulations stated that a standard line regiment of Dutch horse consisted of three companies, each of 52 men. Of the remaining 13 regiments, nine arrived with those three companies; three regiments belonging to Quadt-Soppenbroek, Nassau-Zuylenstein, and Oyen sent over two companies; Waldeck's regiment was reported to consist of four companies. The two dragoon regiments consisted of 18 companies in total, with Eppinger's Dragoons having 10 companies of 88 men, while Marwitz's regiment had eight companies of 55 men. The difference in the size of these two regiments of dragoons is due to Eppinger's being a Guard regiment. A report published in the *London Gazette* on 8 November states that the mounted contingent of the Dutch force consisted of 2,360 horse and 1,300 dragoons.[56] The entry shows the following regiments having arrived with the Prince of Orange: The Life Guards, Waldeck's, Nassau's, Montpouillan's, Ginkel's, Lippe's, s'Gravemoer's, Nassau-Saarbrücken's, Flodroff's, Hayden's, Oyen's, and Quadt-Soppenbroek's regiments of horse, and Eppinger's and Marwitz's regiments of dragoons.[57]

Dutch cavalry regiments were armed with a sword, flintlock carbine, and two pistols, while the dragoons were equipped with a flintlock carbine, sword, pistol, and hatchet. The Dutch cavalry was not generally equipped with cuirasses until at least 1707. Each company included a captain, lieutenant, cornet, quartermaster, trumpeter, smith/farrier, and a clerk, while the Garde du Corps had an additional fourteen company officers, four trumpeters, a kettle drummer, and surgeon major.[58]

The infantry consisted of the 25 companies of the Gardes te Voet with a strength of 2,522 organised into two or sometimes three battalions, along with 14 line regiments. Each of these regiments had between 10 and 12 companies, with each company consisting of 55 men. For clarity, all regimental strengths are the paper strength of the regiment; actual strengths are unknown unless specified within the text. A full breakdown of the details for each regiment can be found in Appendix I.

Each company of Dutch foot consisted of a captain, lieutenant, ensign, two sergeants, two drummers, three servants, and a clerk, in addition to between 50 and 60 private soldiers. Dutch infantry were armed with a flintlock or matchlock musket and bayonet, while the regulations stated that one soldier in five was to be armed with a pike of at least 15 feet in length. Grenadier companies were armed with a flintlock musket equipped with a sling, bayonet, grenades, and a hatchet.[59]

56 *London Gazette*, Monday, 5 November to Thursday, 8 November 1688, p.2.

57 Spellings of the names have been changed to the correct Dutch spelling.

58 R. Hall, I. Stanford, and Y Roumegoux, *Flags and Uniforms of the Dutch Army 1685-1715: Volume 1: Cavalry, Dragoons, Artillery, & Subsidy Regiments* (Romford: Pike and Shot society, 2014), pp.37–43.

59 R. Hall, I. Stanford, and Y Roumegoux, *Flags and Uniforms of the Dutch Army 1685-1715: Volume 2: Infantry and the Forces of the Archbishopric of Liege* (Romford: Pike and Shot society, 2014), pp.16–19.

William's artillery train consisted of 21 field guns, each drawn by 16 horses.[60] The Dutch artillery regulations stated that each 12-pounder should be drawn by 13 horses, so it is likely that the entire field train consisted of these guns, with the additional horses being added due to the winter conditions and the expected state of the English road network during November and December.[61] In addition to the artillery, William also brought over a field smithy and bellows that would have been mounted on two wagons, allowing repairs to be carried out on the wagons and gun carriages of the invasion force. It would have been unlikely that the forge would have been big enough to repair any cannon barrels. Although the army needed to acquire most of its baggage wagons locally when in England, they brought over some wagons to carry the initial supplies of ball and powder for each gun, which was set at 100 cannonballs and 20 cartridges.[62] To crew the artillery, 16 artillery officers and 66 cannoneers accompanied the train. The numbers of non-military staff, including drivers for the horses, are not included within any figures found, as they were normally recruited locally. Any additional manpower for the artillery was usually seconded from the infantry.

Supply

The availability of supplies for an invading army had always been of prime concern to those planning for the offensive, with William being very aware of the consequences of sending a large army across the North Sea and the possibilities of failure if they were not fully supplied. There was no possibility of the army being able to forage for supplies while keeping up the premise that they were there to support the English people and William was keenly aware that James would have learned the lessons following Monmouth's failed attempt in 1685. William's campaigns against Louis XIV were only possible due to contracts with specialist merchants, pre-positioned supply bases, and an advanced supply network, none of which would be available when his forces landed in England. The invasion force would have to take all its supplies over with it, along with enough money to purchase both supplies and draught animals on arrival in England. John Carswell puts the list of supplies at 300 tons of hay, enough for 10 days' worth of rations for the horses required for the invasion force, given a daily ration of 16lbs of hay for each horse, four tons of tobacco, 1,600 hogsheads of beer, 50 hogsheads of brandy, and 10,000 pairs of spare boots.[63] William later brought a bill before the English Parliament for a sum of 186,000 florins for the provisions purchased in Amsterdam prior to the fleet's departure from Texel.[64] In addition to these consumables, the invasion force carried a portable bridge, moulds for striking

60 Olaf van Nimwegen, *De Subsistentie Van Het Leger* (Rotterdam: Museum Boijmans van Beuningen, 1998).

61 Van Nimwegen, *De Subsistentie Van Het Leger.*

62 Van Nimwegen, *De Subsistentie Van Het Leger.*

63 Carswell, *The Descent into England*, pp.168–69.

64 *House of Commons Journal* Volume 10: 7 February 1689, pp.20–22.

money, and bullion. William was well aware of the logistical challenges for any army, and especially for an invading army cut off from arsenals and supply bases and having to make a dangerous sea crossing. In addition, there was the prospect of any army conducting a winter campaign, which could have a catastrophic impact on the health and mobility of troops, especially on artillery and the supply train. Military doctrine dictated the numbers of supply wagons for each size of force, and this had not changed from the time of the Thirty Years' War to the Seven Years' War and later. During the War of the Spanish Succession Marlborough's forces that advanced from Bedburg to Schellenberg consisted of 25,000 infantry and cavalry, and required a train of about 1,700 supply carts drawn by 5,000 horses, which required an additional 2,000 men. Prince Eugene of Savoy is recorded as marching with an army of 26,000 men with 8,000 wagons and over 15,000 horses. The daily bread requirements for a force of 25,000 men would be 56,000lbs of bread or some 38,000 loaves; just to bake this amount would need 25 field ovens, with each oven needing four bakers/bricklayers, one cart to carry the bricks, one for the firewood, one for the flour, and one to carry grinding wheels in case milled flour was not available. While William's force was not as large as these two, it still would have required a significant number of wagons and produced a huge drain on local supplies. The slow advance of the Williamite forces can to some extent be explained by the lack of logistical elements attached to the army and the need for horses to forage while on the march.

While William of Orange had conducted detailed invasion planning, he did not have the time to obtain the number of ships required to transport the number of draught animals or wagons needed to transport all his artillery, baggage, and supplies for his army after the troops had landed in England. William resolved this shortage by requisitioning oxen and wagons from the general farming community of the South West. One such requisition was raised on 16 November in Exeter, where he set the daily rate for each draught of four oxen at 4 shillings, and for each draught of six oxen at 6 shillings. The order states that the oxen, along with carriages (wagons), yokes, and spare lanes (reins), were to attend Exeter at ten in the morning on 20 November 1688. It states that his commissioner for providing the oxen and carriages will go from house to house escorted by two soldiers, and will 'examine the quality of the oxen'. William was experienced enough to realise that he needed to keep the general population on 'his side' and therefore needed to pay for the supplies and animals that he required, as he was still advertising (at this point, at least) that he had arrived to defend the rights of the Protestant population of England. The presence of soldiers alongside William's commissioner does, however, show an implied threat of force and the ability to use military force to ensure that the population acquiesced to the commissioners' request to supply their oxen and carriages, and in some cases agreed to becoming paid labour and driving their wagons as part of William's ever growing transportation network.

3

England's Defences

The standard defences of England involved the billeting of either regimental or independent companies within town and forts around the country. In some cases, smaller forts and castles were garrisoned only by a few gunners and gunners' mates. The change from large regimental garrisons to a general policy of small detachments or company garrisons had its origins in the policy of the interregnum government following the Civil War, when there was a general lack of trust in regiments switching allegiance.[1] In addition to the garrisons, the country's defences were supplemented by the county militias, although the militias' role had been significantly reduced by James II. This was following their limited involvement during the Monmouth Rebellion, with James stating that 'the militia is a broken reed and should be discarded'.[2] Outside of London, only three towns' garrisons comprised the equivalent of a full regiment, these being Berwick, Plymouth, and Portsmouth. In 1686 the Berwick and Plymouth garrisons comprised 10 companies, while Portsmouth had 12 companies.[3] The port and arsenal town of Hull had a garrison of six companies, with the important towns of Carlisle and Chester, as well as the forts at Gravesend and Tilbury, along with the island of Jersey, had a garrison of three companies. Sheerness and Guernsey both had a garrison of two companies, while Chepstow, Landguard Fort, Sileby, Scarborough Castle, Tinmouth (Tynemouth) Castle, Upnor, Isle of Wight, and York garrisons all had one company.

In August 1688 the Board of Ordnance submitted inventories of the stores, arms, and supplies from the garrisons and ordnance stores throughout the country, which were sent to the king. In addition to stores held within the kingdom, lists were obtained from overseas stores, including from New York, which included the amount of gunpowder within the stores as well as the numbers and types of weapons within the stores.[4] The arsenal at Hull had a full issue of 1,000 matchlock muskets, but none of the 1,000 snaphance

1 H. Reece, *The Army in Cromwellian England 1649-1660* (Oxford: OUP, 2013), p.80.
2 Scott, *The Maligned Militia*, p.2.
3 BL: Add MS 15897, 'Pensions and Army Establishment of the Army', f.84.
4 Stafford: D(W) 1778/V/71, Part 1, f.124.

(flintlock) muskets it was meant to have been allocated.[5] Receipts showed that prior to the invasion, there were approximately 19,700 matchlock muskets, 17,850 various flintlock muskets, 3,662 bayonets, and 22,204 pikes in His Majesty's magazines, garrisons, forts, and castles within the Kingdom of England, Dominion of Wales and town of Berwick on Tweed.[6] In addition to these figures, there were another 6,500 muskets that required repair. In addition to the state of military stores held within the country's arsenals, all regiments were required to supply a list of equipment held within the regiment and a list of all missing or defective equipment.

James II ordered the strengthening of the defences of the River Medway in late April 1688 with the construction of a new gun platform at Sheerness. The platform needed to be large enough to accommodate 50 pieces of artillery and was to be linked to the far side of the Medway with a strong chain to block the movement of all vessels.[7] The work on the defences on the Medway had still not been completed by 19 October 1688, with the master of works informing Sunderland that he would need another 450 men in order to complete the works due to the lateness of the year and the bad weather.[8] Heavy frost was reported in England on 18 November, with snow reported in Oxford on 19 November, along with heavy drifts of snow on the same day near Coggeshall in Essex.[9] Sheerness had been previously sacked during the Anglo-Dutch Wars and any new gun platform here could also cover the south side of the Thames estuary. Lord Dartmouth, Master General of the Ordnance, was ordered to construct a new magazine in the fort at Sheerness on 20 May 1688. The old square tower of the castle was to be converted into the magazine and operated by two labourers, each to be paid £26 per year.[10] While Sheerness was getting a new gun platform and magazine, Captain Henry Villiers was writing to the Earl of Sunderland, complaining that the fortifications and garrison of Clifton fort and castle at Tynemouth were in a bad state of repair and without arms and cannon. He informed the earl that he had to borrow four 'small' guns from Clifton Fort and that he did not have enough muskets to equip the additional 10 men that had been added to his company.[11] In July 1688 Colonel Sackville Tufton was commissioned Governor of the fort of West Tilbury and ordered to re-entrench the fortifications and blockhouses as well as the towns of Tilbury and Gravesend.[12] The defences of the River Thames and River Medway were ordered to be strengthened on 19 August, with extra gunners at six location on or near the rivers.[13] The strengthened defences of the River Medway included Oakham Ness (near Kingsnorth Power Station), the Long Battery near Gillingham, Bishop's Fort, and Pinup Ness, while the Thames defences

5 Stafford: D(W) 1778/V/71, Part 1, f.186.
6 Stafford: D(W) 1778/V/1377, f.19.
7 Luttrell, *A Brief Historical Relation of State Affairs*, p.438.
8 NA: WO 55/335, f. 108r.
9 Childs, *The Army, James II*, p.168.
10 *Calendar of State Papers Domestic: James II, 1687-89*, ed. E.K. Timings (London, 1972), p.200.
11 *CSPD: James II, 1687-89*, p.297.
12 *CSPD: James II, 1687-89*, p.238.
13 NA: WO 24/8, Part 5, f.43.

were strengthened at Woolwich. The six batteries received a total of five extra master gunners and 22 gunners at an extra yearly cost of £584 to the state. The defences of Pendennis Castle in Falmouth were reported to have been 'long neglected and indifferently repaired' on 14 October when the Earl of Bath requested extra troops to defend the port.[14] Scarborough Castle and the fort at Bridlington were deemed to be in such a bad state of repair that all their 'guns, ammunition, and other habiliments of war' were ordered to be removed and returned to the ordnance stores in Kingston upon Hull.[15] While some of the forts and castles were deemed to be in a condition to be able to resist the enemy, most of the locations were critically short of the necessary supplies needed to mount a defence.[16]

The planned invasion of England by William of Orange was not a surprise to James II, his advisers, or even the English population. As with the invasion of Europe by the Allies in June 1944, when Germany was aware of the planned invasion, but not the exact date or the proposed landing site, the same could be said regarding the invasion of 1688. James had both spies and allies on the Continent that were keeping the king informed of the preparations being undertaken by William and his allies. James would have been well aware of troop movements within the Dutch states and its allies, as would the general population as these were regularly reported in papers available within coffee houses throughout the country.[17] On 27 and 28 August the navy sent press gangs and press boats along the River Thames, recruiting sailors for the English fleet and to ensure that men were not tempted to join the Dutch fleet, which was offering higher wages to sail with their vessels.[18] The Puritan minister, journalist, and diarist Roger Morrice reported in September 1688 that William of Orange 'would mount an expedition to England'.[19] News of William's plans to invade England were certainly known in early September 1688, when 19-year-old London law student William Croker wrote to his father in south Devon quoting reports of '100 Dutch sail at sea', plus the equipping of their army, '43,000 soldiers, well-armed and stout men'. In a later letter dated 27 September he informed his father that:

> Tis certainly thought here that the Dutch design to land in some part of England having a great many English and Scotch men with them, their fleet is composed of 80 sails their land forces on board 16,000 and have with them 40 flat bottomed boats some thousands of saddles, much horse furniture.[20]

Reports arrived in London on 30 September of a merchant ship out of Rotterdam that had been forced out of its berth in order for 'several great vessels' to be loaded with horses and hay and oats. The master of the vessel

14 NA: SP 31/4, f.112.
15 NA: SP 44/165, f.116.
16 NA: WO 55/335, f.99.
17 *The London Gazette*, Monday, September 17 to Thursday, September 20 1688, no. 2383, p.2.
18 Luttrell, *A Brief Historical Relation of State Affairs*, p.457.
19 Mark Goldie, *Roger Morrice and the Puritan Whigs* (Woodbridge: Boydell Press, 2016) p.2.
20 Exeter: 312M/8/F/2, *Hole of Parke*.

also stated seeing 23 hoys loaded with soldiers.[21] George Etherege, English ambassador to the Imperial German Court at Ratisbon, wrote to Lord Middleton on 11 October that the Duke of Schomberg was to join the Prince of Orange in his venture into England.[22] Sunderland informed the Earl of Bath on 23 October that James II had received information that the Prince of Orange was planning to land small parties of men at various points along the coast with the intention of creating panic amongst the population by 'giving false alarm'.[23] The letter stated that all the lord lieutenants should be made aware of this intelligence and that they should inform their deputies with the aim both of deterring any landings and to prevent any 'evil disposed persons' from joining up with any Dutch landing in their counties.

If the general population were unaware of the impending invasion, they were informed of it at the start of October 1688 by *The London Gazette*. The paper published a proclamation from King James II in its issue of 1 October 1688. The proclamation was dated 28 September and announced that:

> We have received undoubtable advise, that a great and sudden invasion from Holland, with an armed force of foreigners and strangers, will speedily be made in a hostile manner upon this Our Kingdom: And although some false pretences relating to Liberty, property, and Religion, contrived or worded with Art and Subtilty, may be given out (as shall be thought useful upon such an attempt) it is manifest however, (considering the great preparations that are making) that no less Matter by this Invasion, is proposed and purposed, than an absolute Conquest of these Our Kingdoms.[24]

The *Gazette* reported on 10 October that word had been received from the Marquis d'Albeville, Envoy Extraordinary from His Majesty of Great Britain to the court at The Hague, that the States General had not 'given an answer to the memorial presented to them on the 5th instant'.[25] The report also stated that troops continued to be loaded in Rotterdam, including the regiments of Guards (Garde te Voet).

The declaration put the country in effect onto a war footing, and in doing so the king recalled his previous writ of September 1688 to call Parliament to a session that should have happened at the beginning of November. The proroguing of Parliament has been cited by both Whig commentators and historians as justification for the descent against James II. This act has been used as conformation of his absolutism and, by default, his attempt to turn the country to Catholicism and into the control of Louis XIV of France and Rome. It can also be seen as a normal reaction to a declaration of war. In 1939, despite England having a well-established parliamentary democracy, Parliament was prorogued on 23 November 1939; in addition the election of 1940, which would have been in accordance with the Parliament Act of

21 CSPD, *James II, 1687-1689*, pp.289–90.
22 BL: Add MS 41837, ff.258–69.
23 NA: SP 44/97, f.2.
24 *The London Gazette*, no. 2386, Thursday, September 27 to Monday, October 1 1688, p.1.
25 *The London Gazette*, no. 2389, Monday, October 8 to Thursday, October 11 1688, p.2.

1911, was cancelled.[26] James had felt constrained by Parliament during the Monmouth Rebellion of 1685. He felt that certain members of both the Commons and the Lords had hindered him when trying to raise an army to face the Duke of Monmouth's forces in the South West. James objected to the Test Acts which, while not preventing him from commissioning loyal officers answering his call to defend the country, did prevent loyal Catholics from serving for more than three months.[27] The king's speech of 14 November 1685 makes clear his feeling on the Test Act's impact on his ability to commission loyal officers:[28]

> Let no man take exception that there are some officers in the army not qualified according to the late Test for their employment, the gentlemen I must tell you are most of them well known to me, and having formerly served with me in several occasions and shewed the loyalty of their principles by their practices, I think them fit now to be employed under me.

As a result of this apparent unfairness to and discrimination against officers who had loyally volunteered to serve the king and to protect the country while being ineligible to hold commissions within the army outside of the three-month grace period allowed by the Test Act, James II issued them with pardons. James issued a total of 70 pardons within the first tranche.[29] These pardons have repeatedly been stated as pardoning 'Catholic' officers;

Mary of Modena Leaving England for France, a print by Pieter Pickaert, Amsterdam, 1689. James II, concerned about the safety of his queen and son, ordered that they both leave England for the safety of France. (Rijksmuseum: NG-1087-8, Public Domain)

26 *Hansard*, HL Deb., vol.114, cols.1894–6, 23 November 1939; HL/PO/PU/1/1911/1&2G5c13.

27 Childs, *The Army, James II*, p.21.

28 Tom Harris (ed.), *The Entring Book of Roger Morrice: Volume III, The Reign of James II 1685-1687.* (Woodbridge: The Boydell Press, 2007), p.55.

29 NA: SP44/336, George, Earl of Dumbarton and other officers not having taken the Test, Pardon, 23 November 1685, ff.280–84.

Mary of Modena Arriving in France, a print by Pieter Pickaert, Amsterdam, 1689. (Rijksmuseum: NG-1087-12, Public Domain)

however, there is no reference to the religion of the officers involved within any of the documentation. The pardons only state that the king is exempting 70 officers from taking the test. The exemption would be needed for all Nonconformist officers, as well as for Catholic officers.

By the time of this announcement to the public, the king's plan for the defence of the realm was already well under way by increasing the size of the English army. There were four well-established ways to increase the size of any army: increase the size of the current regiments, troops, and companies of the existing army; increase the number of standing regiments as well as the numbers of independent troops and companies; recall troops from other duties; and arrange to hire troops from friendly nations. This last option was not realistic, as although James had been offered assistance from Louis XIV, he could not accept this offer as it would have had the possibility of turning the army and the country against him. Each of the remaining three options came with their own issues, with the easiest normally being recalling troops from other duties and increasing the size of established regiments, troops, and companies, as this option required very little time, expense, and bureaucracy. The size of the army had always been adjusted dependant on the needs of the monarch and the nation and the fears and consideration of Parliament, who were generally afraid of a large standing army and the possibility of the monarch using the army to control Parliament and the country. This was an issue for Charles II as well as for James II. In 1667 Samuel Pepys recorded that:

> Discontented Parliament-men are fearful that the next sitting the King will put for a general Excise, by which to raise him money, and then to fling off the Parliament, and raise a land-army and keep then [parliament and the people] like slaves.[30]

30 S. Pepys, *The Diary of Samuel Pepys Vol. 8, 1667* (London: Harper Collins, 2010), p.324

Charles II had issued commissions for an additional 12 regiments of foot following the Dutch attack on Chatham in June 1667 with the consent of Parliament, resulting in the Commons voting that the new regiments should be disbanded in the July of 1667, before most of them had actually been formed.

John Churchill, Duke of Marlborough, deputy commander of the English army, in a print by John Smith, London, 1702–42. (Rijksmuseum: SK-A-3935, Public Domain)

The English Army

When the English army assembled on Hounslow Heath for its summer exercises in June 1686, its size and composition has been stabilised following the Monmouth Rebellion the previous year. The standard size of a troop of horse or dragoons was 40 men, and for a company of foot it was 50 men, although these numbers varied in the senior regiments of horse, dragoons, and foot. The standing army consisted of the following regiments:[31]

Four troops of horse guards, each of 200 men, each with a troop of horse grenadiers of 64 men

One regiment of horse consisting of nine troops of 50 men (Earl of Oxford's Regiment)

One regiment of horse consisting of nine troops of 40 men (Queen Consort's Regiment)

Eight regiments of horse consisting of six troops of 50 men

One regiment of dragoons consisting of eight troops of 40 men

Two regiments of dragoons consisting of six troops of 40 men

One independent troop of dragoons consisting of 60 men

His Majesty's Regiment of Foot Guards consisting of 26 companies of 80 men*

Coldstream Regiment of Foot Guards consisting of 13 companies of 80 men**

Scottish Regiment of Foot Guards consisting of 21 companies of 50 men**

31 Strengths of regiments and companies was counted in enlisted men, and did not include officers, NCOs, or musicians. Officers' servants were never included within the lists.

Two regiments of foot consisting of 13 companies of 50 men**

Ten regiments of foot consisting of 11 companies of 50 men**

One regiment of fusiliers consisting of 11 companies of 50 men and one company of 40 men (miners).[32]

When he gained the throne, James II had inherited fifteen independent companies of grenadiers, which had been used as garrisons for the various forts and castles around the country. By the time the summer camp of 1686 had disbanded and the regiments retired into their winter quarters, 14 of the companies had been absorbed into regiments.[33]

Organisation of a Regiment and Company

Under Charles II, the English army could still be described as a traditional pike and shot-equipped army, with the exception of the few grenadier companies. Each 50-man company of foot was equipped with both pikes and muskets, with 18 pikes, 26 matchlock muskets, and nine snaphance or flintlock muskets.[34] The grenadier company were issued 53 snaphances fitted with slings and grenado pouches along with 50 bayonets and hatchets. Foot guard regiments with a strength of 80 men were equipped with 28 pikes, 40 matchlock and 15 snaphance muskets. Charles II was in the process of issuing bayonets to all the musketeers, with the regiments of foot guards receiving the bayonets first.[35] By late 1688 the English regiments of foot were generally divided into twelve companies of foot and one grenadier company, with each type of company having different equipment. Standard companies of foot were equipped with 12 pikes, 12 flintlock muskets, and 26 matchlock muskets, with bayonets for each musketeer. Although each company would have been issued with flintlock and matchlock muskets, operationally each company would have operated with just one type of musket. There are two main reasons why it would have been common for regiments to standardise the type of muskets within each company. The first reason was that generally the distance between infantry files was greater for matchlock-armed troops than for flintlock-armed troops and the second was due to the method and orders for loading sequences of each type of musket. Drill manuals for the time show 33 separate orders for matchlock musket drills and 27 for flintlock or snaphance muskets.[36] The pikemen could either be consolidated into one central block, into three groups (in the centre and on each flank), or kept

32 Stephen Ede-Borrett, *The Army of James II 1685-1688: The Birth of the British Army* (Solihull: Helion & Co., 2017), pp.164–6; Mark Shearwood, *The Perfection of Military Discipline: The Plug bayonet and the English Army 1660-1705* (Warwick: Helion & Co., 2020), pp.108–09. ** Including two companies of grenadiers; * Including one company of grenadiers.

33 Ede-Borrett, *The Army of James II*, pp.135–36.

34 NA: WO 55/397, ff.5–7. The extra three weapons were for the three corporals; the sergeants were issued halberds.

35 NA: WO55/397, f.8.

36 Shearwood, *The Perfection of Military Discipline*, pp.77–78.

within each company. Pikes were classified generally as either 'long' or 'short', with 'long' pikes being between 16 and 18 feet in length, while the 'short' pikes were between 10 and 14 feet in length.[37] The Grenadier company was solely armed with flintlock muskets with slings, hatchets, bayonets, and grenadoes (grenades). The standard for each man (foot or horse) was to be issued with 100 rounds, and for each grenadier within the company to be issued with six grenades.[38] Bandoliers were still in use within the English army, with a new supply being ordered for the Regiment of Foot Guards in October 1688; grenadiers were issued with cartridge boxes rather than bandoliers.[39] Each regiment of foot consisted of a colonel, lieutenant-colonel, major, chaplain, adjutant, chirurgeon (doctor), and quartermaster, while each company also consisted of a captain, lieutenant, ensign, three sergeants, three corporals, and two drummers. The colonel, lieutenant-colonel, major, and adjutant also held positions as company captains. The officers' allowance also included funds for servants and the chirurgeon was generally accompanied by two chirurgeon's mates.

The equipment and structure of each regiment of cavalry or dragoons did not realistically change from Charles II to James II, with the exception of an increase in the numbers of men within each troop. Each regiment of horse also consisted of a colonel, lieutenant-colonel, major, chaplain, adjutant, chirurgeon, and a kettle drummer, while each troop also consisted of a captain, lieutenant, cornet, quartermaster, three corporals, and two trumpeters. The regimental staff of each dragoon regiment consisted of a chirurgeon, adjutant, quartermaster and provost, and chaplain. Troops of dragoons had a similar structure to cavalry troops, with a captain, lieutenant, cornet, quartermaster, two sergeants, three corporals, two drummers, and two hautboys. In most regiments the colonel and lieutenant-colonel also held positions of captain of a troop. The officers' allowance also included funds for servants and additional horses, while the chirurgeon was generally accompanied by two chirurgeon's mates. In addition, each regiment would have a regimental agent, who was a civilian and who was responsible for ensuring that the crown paid its dues; they could also be involved in recruitment and acted as a permanent location for post going to the regiment. As with infantry regiments, it was a common practice for company officers to have additional duties by taking on the role and associated pay for regimental posts such as adjutant and quartermaster. Troopers within each cavalry regiment would have been equipped with a flintlock carbine, a brace of pistols, and a sword, while the troopers of each regiment of dragoons were issued with a carbine, a bayonet, and a sword.[40]

37 Shearwood, *The Perfection of Military Discipline,* p.59.
38 SA: D(W)1778/V/1380, Earl of Dartmouth, Board of Ordnance Papers, ff.1–20.
39 NA: WO 55/335, f.78.
40 Stafford: D(W) 1778/V/71, Part 1, f.136.

Modernisation of the English Army

The modernisation of the English (and Scottish and Irish) army started almost as soon as the Monmouth Rebellion was over. James II, unhappy with the performance of the various county militias, realised that the country needed a full-time, professionally trained army not only for foreign interventions but also for defence. Under Charles II, the army was a disparate organisation, with regiments billeted over vast areas, in some cases across different islands, and unable to train together, let alone train with other regiments. This resulted in regimental officers not being able to handle the simplest of drills and companies unable to act as a cohesive unit. The training of officers, NCOs (non-commissioned officers, including corporals and sergeants), and soldiers was carried out at company level using privately printed drill manuals that often featured out-of-date military drill and tactics. While officers would still rely on these drill manuals, James put a system in place for regular training camps for the majority of the army each summer. While the summer camps included elements of medieval tournaments, with processions, performances, and the public spectacle of mock battles, these were the late seventeenth-century equivalent of modern combined-arms exercises.[41] In a period where there was no centralised accommodation, these camps offered the chance for regiments to train as one unit. In addition, multiple regiments of foot, horse, and dragoons could train together alongside artillery, which was under the control of the Board of Ordnance. Depending on the weather, camps lasted from late May to late August, with the 1686 camp officially lasting for 61 days.[42] Records show that almost 13,000 soldiers and officers attended these training camps each year and that most regiments were in attendance, although not always with all their companies and troops.[43] In 1686, all nine of the English regiments of horse and three regiments of dragoons were present with all their troops, and of the infantry regiments present, ten were at full regimental strength, with a further two at half strength.[44] Three single companies were present in 1686, these being Sir Thomas Haggerston's company; Captain Richard Carter's Independent Company of Foot, based at Southsea Castle; and the senior or colonel's company from the Earl of Plymouth's Regiment of Foot.[45] While the camps did increase the competence of the army, they were not always popular with army officers. This unpopularity was due both to the extra time officers had to spend away from home and with their regiments and to increased costs while living within the vast camps, resulting in several officers

41 Shearwood, 'A Summer on Hounslow Heath', p.2.

42 NA: WO55/339, f.31, Lord Dartmouth from William Blathwayt, 24 August 1685; BL: Earl of Aylesbury Papers, Add MS 15897, Account of the English Army, f.88.

43 Shearwood, 'A Summer on Hounslow Heath'.

44 BL: Add MS 15897, f.86.

45 BL: Add MS 15897, f.86; SP44/69, f.145; SP44/336, f.317. Sir Thomas Haggerston was a captain in Sir William Clifton's Regiment of Foot. It was common that when part of a regiment was present, it would be referred to by the senior officer present, in this case the company captain.

resigning their commissions.[46] While these camps were only concerned with raising the standards of the English army, they were seen by James's enemies as the king intimidating the population of London. This was due to the proximity of Hounslow Heath and therefore the army to London, this despite the large numbers of the capital's citizens coming on day trips to view the mock battles. Charles II had used Blackheath to view the English army and as a staging point for the army; it was never used for the same long-term training, or combined-arms training. The summer camps allowed regiments to train as one unified unit and allowed officers to conduct manoeuvres using the whole regiment or several regiments at once. New officers were able to gain experience from senior, more experienced officers, and from the introduction of standardised drills and the ability to practice large-scale battles and siege tactics. James introduced new tactics and equipment during the summer training, including the introduction of two battalion guns into each infantry regiment. Apart from the introduction of bayonets to all troops, this was the most important change to the structure of the English army until the withdrawal of the pike from all regiments. These battalion guns were between 1lb and 3lb guns, operated by soldiers within the regiment, and were kept within the regiment when they returned to their winter quarters at the end of the training season.[47] Colonel Kirke's and Colonel Trelawney's regiments of foot received new 2–3lb guns, while Colonel Cornwall's, Sir Edward Hales's, Colonel Tufton's, and Colonel Buchan's regiments of foot received old drakes and falconetts, again with a 2lb to 3lb calibre.[48] In addition to the battalion guns, all regiments of foot received plug bayonets and the grenadier companies were trained in using their grenades in normal infantry combat as well as when assaulting fixed positions. During his reign, James II sent military observers to Europe to gain an understanding of the latest military tactics and weapons, and to see European armies in combat. He sent a number of officers to view the Habsburg army: Jacob Richards in October 1685, Edward Clark in March 1687, and his son James FitzJames, Duke of Berwick, who participated in the Siege of Buda, which was recreated on Hounslow Heath in 1687.[49] While James II did modernise the English army during his reign, in the months prior to the invasion he also relied on tried and tested equipment. On 25 September 1688 James II ordered a full suit of armour made for Charles II to be delivered to the commander of the English army, Lewis, Earl of Feversham, and a second full suit of armour made for him to be delivered to the deputy commander of the army, John, Lord Churchill.[50] While these were gifts for the commanders of the army,

46 Harris, *The Entring Book of Roger Morrice, Vol. III*, p.105.

47 NA: WO55/400, Lord Dartmouth from Lord Sunderland, 8 August 1686, ff.88, 101–03, 137.

48 Three-pounder drakes and falconetts were English Civil War-era artillery pieces which were both heavier in weight than the new 3-pounders; the falconetts also had a much longer barrel.

49 NA: SP44/70, State Papers, Earl of Middleton, 1686, f.191; Charles Petrie, *The Marshal Duke of Berwick: The Picture of an Age* (London: Eyre & Spottiswoode, 1953), pp.27–30; G. Carleton, *Memoirs of Captain George Carleton, An English Officer: Including Anecdotes of the war in Spain under the Earl of Peterborough; and many Interesting Particulars Relating to the Manners of the Spaniards in the beginning of the Last Century* (London: J. Davis, 1811), p.18.

50 NA: SP44/165, f.68.

and status symbols rather than practical equipment, James II also ordered 800 suits of harquebuss armour proofed against musket shot to be delivered from the Ordnance stores in the Tower of London to the four troops of Life Guards.[51] Prior to this order, the only English regiment of horse issued with armour was Oxford's Regiment of Horse; this regiment was issued with breast and back plates as well as with cavalry helmets. The officers of Lord Brandon's Regiment of Horse were issued 'suits of armour' on 18 October 1688, out of the stores at the Tower of London.[52] Previous orders had been given on 24 September 1688 for 'thirty suits of our newest and best proofed armour' to be sent to the 'officers of each of our regiments of horse'.[53] James II ordered that the 'several regiments of horse' that received armour were to 'leave the said equipment at their current location and for the Principal Officers of the Ordnance [Board of] to arrange for its return' to the Tower of London on 6 November.[54]

The lack of arms was still an issue in late October, with Lieutenant-Colonel Molyneux of Colonel Gage's Regiment of Foot complaining that although his regiment was complete in terms of soldiers, it still needed arms, and that the arms that had been assigned to him had been sent to Ireland.[55] The letter also shows that by late October 1688 there was a lack of new officers available to receive commissions into the new regiments. This could have been for a number of reasons: lack of experience, lack of money to pay for the commission, or a reluctance to join the army just before an invasion as part of an inexperienced regiment. While elements of the army were still short of arms and men, the artillery was being prepared for operation within the kingdom. Lord Dartmouth, Master-General of the Ordnance, was instructed on 15 October to ready a great train of artillery after the king had received 'undoubtable advice that a great and sudden invasion' was about to happen.[56] The train was to consist of twenty artillery pieces, along with six field mortars as well as all the necessary ammunition, stores, and equipment. The train required a total of 177 men, including 13 bombardiers, five petardiers, and 33 gunners. It was also accompanied by a company of 60 pioneers.[57]

Unfortunately for the king, the summer camps of 1687 and 1688 also acted as a cultivation ground for James II's enemies within the army to recruit new members for the Treason Club. The Treason Club was a loose collective of army officers, navy officers, and politicians, which met during 1688 at the Rose tavern on Russell Street in Covent Garden to organise a fifth column against James II when William invaded.[58] Prominent members included Lieutenant-General Percy Kirke, Lieutenant-General John Churchill, Lieutenant Colonel Savage, Viscount Colchester, and Major-General Charles Trelawney. All these men commanded English regiments and could extend

51 NA: SP44/165, f.68.
52 NA: SP44/165, f.117.
53 NA: WO55/400, f.223; WO55/335, ff.74–75.
54 NA: WO4/1, f.108.
55 NA: SP31/4, ff.149–50.
56 NA: SP44/165, ff.113–14.
57 NA: WO 55/335, ff.89r–90.
58 Childs, *General Percy Kirke*, p.123.

considerable influence on their subordinates, whose actions seriously impacted the ability of the army to counter William's advance following his landing in November 1688. The English army finished its summer training in early August 1688, with all the regiments leaving Hounslow Heath on 8 August 1688, departing for their various quarters throughout the country.[59]

Increasing the Size of the Army

With the imminent threat of invasion in the late summer of 1688, James II had utilised three of the known ways to increase the size of the English establishment. First, he had transferred existing regiments from other establishments onto the English establishment or army list. Regiments could be transferred from the Scottish or Irish armies, which were separate legal entities, although still under the command and rule of James II, or from the regiments of the Anglo-Dutch and Scots-Dutch brigades in service with the Dutch States under William of Orange, as had been the case during the failed Monmouth Rebellion. The option to raise new regiments for the crown, or to raise new independent companies of infantry or troops of cavalry and dragoons, was the most logistically challenging, as it required these new colonels or captains to be able to pay for the new regiments or companies, be able to provide suitable officers, and recruit enough soldiers for these new units. The new regiments, companies, or troops would then have to be trained and equipped within a short period of time in order for them to be operational before the expected invasion by William of Orange.

As previously stated, the easiest way to increase the number of soldiers within the existing army was to increase the size of existing regiments by the addition of extra soldiers to each company and troop, and to also increase the size of the remaining independent companies and troops. This was one of the normal options in time of conflict and had also been used following the Monmouth Rebellion. James II issued a warrant on 24 September 1688 for the raising of additional troops for each company and troop within the English army.[60] The warrant stated that an additional ten men were to be raised for each troop of horse and dragoons, resulting in an extra 510 cavalry troopers, 40 extra horse grenadiers, and 200 dragoons. The infantry regiments received orders to recruit an extra 2,150 men, which equated to an extra 10 men for the combined 215 companies. In addition to the increase in the numbers of private soldiers, the warrant ordered the recruitment of an additional 346 sergeants and drummers to be added to the existing regiments. In addition to extra men for each company, James II ordered the creation of 15 additional companies of foot, to be divided between His Majesty's regiments of foot, giving each regiment 13 companies. Prince George of Denmark's Regiment of Foot received one extra company, while the following regiments of foot received two additional companies: Colonel Cornwall's, Earl of Bath's, Lord Montgomery's, Earl of Lichfield's, Earl of Huntingdon's, Sir John Hales's, and

59 Luttrell, *A Brief Historical Relation of State Affairs*, p.454.
60 NA: WO55/400, Ordnance Warrants, ff.213–14.

Colonel Tufton's. Lord Dumbarton's Regiment of Foot received an additional five companies of foot. Each of the new companies comprised 50 men, three sergeants, three corporals, and two drummers. Colonel John Hales received orders to allow some of his officers to 'beat the drum' in any parts of the country that he saw fit to recruit the additional men needed for the extra company.[61] These changes theoretically increased the size of the English army by an additional 4,606 enlisted men, with each new company having a captain, lieutenant, and ensign.[62]

In addition to increasing the size of existing regiments, James II issued new commissions for colonels to raise new regiments on his behalf. Commissions were issued for two new additional regiments of horse, and for three additional regiments of foot. Each regiment of horse was to comprise of six troops, with each regiment of foot to have the now standardised 13 companies, including a company of grenadiers.[63] James II also ordered the creation of 12 independent troops of horse and 32 independent companies of foot.[64] James II was issuing orders for new independent companies and troops to be raised as late as 20 October.[65] The probability is that the majority of the new troops of horse would have been incorporated into the two new regiments of horse, while some were never actually raised, with two commissions for new troops only being issued on 21 November and 27 November, only days before the English army was disbanded.[66] Only one of the troops was confirmed to have been raised and equipped: the troop raised by Sir Thomas Burton, which was officially disbanded on 4 January 1689.[67] Four of the captains commissioned to raise new troops of horse followed James II over to Ireland following the disbandment of the army and were subsequently commissioned into the Irish army.[68] Commissions were issued to officers of the 32 independent companies of foot between 29 September 1688 and 8 October 1688, with all but five companies having named captains, lieutenants, and ensigns. Although these companies were raised as independent companies, most were incorporated into the newly raised regiments of foot. Two companies were formed from pensioners from the Royal Hospital of Chelsea; both of these companies were fully formed and equipped and received marching orders on 4 November 1688.[69] As for the other companies, the two companies commanded by Captain William Low and Captain Matthew Smyth were merged into the Duke of Norfolk's Regiment of Foot, which was raised on 3 March 1689 in the service of

61 NA: WO4/1, f.102

62 Figures quoted in warrants for the size of regiments, companies, and troops generally only included enlisted men and not the numbers of officers; these were generally accounted for separately.

63 NA: WO55/400, f.223.

64 S. Ede-Borrett, *The Army of James II*, pp.161–62.

65 NA: SP44/165, ff.119–21, 132; SP44/69, f.237.

66 Commissions issued to Sir Louis Palmer, 21 November 1688, and Captain Stephen Tempest, 27 November 1688.

67 BL: Add MS 10123, Montagu Army Accounts, f.315. The company was formally raised on 3 November 1688.

68 Dalton, *English Army Lists*, p.179.

69 NA: WO5/3, f.321

William III. There are records showing eight independent companies being disbanded in late December, with the commanding officers receiving pay from William for the time they were musted between October and December 1688. These companies were under the command of Captain John Sibble, Captain William Gibbons, Captain Elias Beak, Captain Francis Ingoldsby, Captain Maurice Flynn, Captain Matthew Smith, Captain Anthony Powers, and Captain Henry Davies.[70]

When a new regiment was raised by royal warrant, a commission would be issued to the colonel of the regiment or company. The commission would state if the unit was to be raised as a regiment or company of horse, foot, or dragoons, how many troops and companies it would comprise, and how many officers of each rank were to be commissioned. It was general practice for only the colonel to be named; occasionally the lieutenant colonel and possibly the major, if present, would be chosen, otherwise all other officers were commissioned at the pleasure of the colonel. When Colonel Gage's Regiment of foot was raised in September 1688, named commissions were only issued for Mr Molyneux as the lieutenant-colonel, and to Mr Cunningham for the rank of major; all other commissions were blank.[71] Blank commissions were issued on behalf of the king and sent to the colonel to be filled, with copies of the completed commissions being returned to update the official records. The practice of blank, pre-signed commissions being issued on behalf of the king was not a new phenomenon – it was used by both Charles II, as well as by James II at the start of his reign, and later by William III.[72] The chaos caused by the invasion, the collapse of the army, and the following change of government has resulted in the records of numerous regimental commissions being left incomplete and the name of officers being commissioned within the last two months of James II's reign going unrecorded.[73] The same process was used for raising new independent companies or troops, with the commissions being sent to the captain of that company or troop. Commissions were issued to Lord Brandon and the Marquis de Miremont to raise new regiments of horse, and to the Duke of Newcastle and Colonel Solomon Richards to raise new regiments of foot.[74] Colonel Solomon Richard's Regiment of Foot would later swear loyalty to William III and would be one of the first regiments to be ordered to sail for Ireland for the relief of Londonderry. In addition to the gentry and nobility being granted commissions, other members of the aristocracy offered their

70 NA: WO 25/3138, ff.4, 6.

71 NA: SP44/56, f.443.

72 NA: SP44/163, f.249. Other blank commissions were sent to the Duke of Albemarle for a captain of horse and dragoons (BL: SP44/163, f.232); two blank commissions for adjutants were sent to Lord Feversham (SP44/164, f.228, 20 June 1685); two blank commissions for captains for volunteer troops of horse 'to be forthwith raised for our service' were sent to the Earl of Abingdon (SP44/163, f.209). See also *Calendar of State Papers Domestic: William and Mary, 1689-90*, ed. William John Hardy (London: HMSO, 1895), pp.221, 241, for instances by William III, and Dalton, *English Army Lists*, vol. I, pp.136, 220 for instances under Charles II.

73 Blank or unfilled commissions are recorded throughout the later entries of Dalton's *English Army Lists*, vol. 2. See pp.175, 179, 188, and 189.

74 *The London Gazette*, No. 2387, Monday, October 1 to Thursday, October 4 1688, p.2; NA: SP44/165, f.123.

support to the king, including the earls of Pembroke, Westmorland, and Danby (whose offer was just to cover his actual intent of serving William of Orange) and Lord Huntingtower.[75]

Colonel Gage's Regiment of Foot is a good example of the delays and shortages new regiments faced. Although the original commissions for the regiment were raised in mid-September, they had not been received by the proposed lieutenant-colonel, William Molyneux, by the end of the month. Molyneux writes to Lord Sunderland on 30 September to complain of a lack of commissions and equipment, stating that they had 'neither the arms or equipment in the county to furnish one company'. The letter also stated that without the commissions it would be impossible to levy any men for the regiment.[76] The shortage of available manpower to fill the extra companies and regiments commissioned within the army resulted in a number of regimental colonels resorting to pressing men for 'land service' during October and November 1688. This resulted in the Company of Watermen petitioning the king on 2 November to free the members and apprentices of the society from the press, quoting legislation from February 1627.[77]

William understood that in order to ensure the loyalty of English army officers following his overthrow of the king, he would need to guarantee the payments owed to officers who had raised independent companies and new regiments raised by James II. These payments to officers to cover regimental pay and costs help us to confirm which regiments were actually raised by James and which, if any, were just raised on paper. William ordered payments for all colonels and captains that could provide muster rolls during late January and early February 1689. These payments included colonels that had had their regiments disbanded and officers that had followed James II to France. Payments went to the Marquis de Miremont, Lord Brandon, Colonel Caines, Lord Montgomery, Colonel Hales, the Earl of Huntingdon, Sir James Lesley, Sir Edward Hales, the Duke of Newcastle, Colonel Henry Gage, Colonel Tufton, and Colonel Solomon Richards.[78]

Militia

The English militia were under the direct control of the lord lieutenant of each county and their use was restricted under the Militia Acts of 1661, 1662, and 1663. They were responsible for 'securing the peace of the nation'.[79] The requirements regarding the numbers of militia horse and foot each county was obligated to raise was based on the size and population of each parish, hundred, and county.[80] While James II diverted funds from the militia to the standing army after the failed rebellion, the obligations of each lord lieutenant

75 *The London Gazette*, No. 2389, Monday, October 8 to Thursday, October 11 1688, p.2.
76 *CSPD: James II, 1687–89*, p.289.
77 NA: PC2/72, ff.86–87.
78 NA: WO25/3138, ff.1, 7, 17.
79 Scott, *The Maligned Militia*, pp.55–56, 59.
80 Scott, *The Maligned Militia*, pp.59–100.

regarding the numbers of militia required to be raised were not changed between 1685 and 1689. In 1689 the English militia had a theoretical strength of 6,245 horse and 79,286 foot.[81] London had a specific structure, with both a militia and auxiliary units, with the returns not stating the number of companies of each, just the total muster figures. This consisted of eight regiments of horse, 67 independent troops of horse, 73 regiments of foot, and 29 independent companies of foot. Raising the militia was not always straightforward. The Dorset militia could not be legally raised and paid until the advance of their pay for the Monmouth Rebellion three years prior had been reimbursed.[82] James's feelings for the militia were well known. He believed that they had not done their duty during the Monmouth Rebellion and that they were not able to defend the country in time of invasion, which was their primary function besides keeping the peace. On 9 November 1685 James II gave a speech to both houses of Parliament where he stated:

> What an inconsiderable number of Men begun it [the Monmouth Rebellion] and how long they carried it on without any opposition, I hope everybody will be convinced that the Militia, which have hitherto been so much depended on, is not sufficient upon such Occasions.[83]

James II's general level of distrust of the militia, as well as the wide-ranging levels of uncertainty regarding the population's loyalty throughout the country, is clearly evident within the king's orders during the build-up to the invasion. Instructions were sent to the Duke of Norfolk on 2 October 1688 to call up the Norfolk militia. The king thanks the duke for his service and instructs him to 'call together such part of the horse militia as you can confide in, who, in case of invasion, may hinder evil-disposed persons from joining the enemy'.[84] Norfolk replied to Sunderland on 15 October that he had raised part of the militia, 'always on foot', to stop anyone from joining with the enemy and could raise the full militia within one day.[85] Further instructions were sent to the Duke of Newcastle on 4 October instructing the militia horse under his command to be raised 'under such officers as you can trust' with the same instruction to prevent evil persons going over to the enemy.[86] Similar instructions were sent out to the lord lieutenants regarding the militia within their respective counties, confirming that the issue of suspected divided loyalties was not just localised to one militia or county.[87] Militia along the coast, from Durham in the north to Cornwall in the south-

---

81 NA: SP8/8, The Numbers of the Militia in the Several Counties in England and Wales, f.81. The figures quoted are for England only as Wales had a different militia structure, split into Monmouthshire, North Wales, and South Wales, which had a theoretical strength of an additional 555 horse and 6,400 foot. For a full account of the militia by county, see Appendix V.

82 NA: SP31/4, f.158.

83 Anon., *The History and Proceedings of the House of Commons: With the Speeches, Debates, and Conferences Between the Two Houses*, Vol. 2: *1680-1695* (London: NP, 1742), p.180.

84 NA: SP44/56, f.447.

85 NA: SP31/4, f.135.

86 NA: SP44/56, f.448.

87 NA: SP44/56, f.450.

west, were instructed to seize and secure horses and to provide information regarding their owners and if any persons had 'brought-up [horses] to these parts'.[88] Lord Teynham, on being appointed Lord Lieutenant of Kent, informed Sunderland on 8 October that no part of the militia, horse or foot, had been mustered and that they were in 'the same ill condition' as most of the county militias. He also states that he had issued 14 commissions for the county militia, including four for his deputy lieutenants that had all been refused and returned to him.[89] There was a concern that as his five troops of militia horse had not been raised, it would allow discontent to grow against the king within the county. The Dorset militia should have consisted of two regiments of foot and two troops of horse, but even as late as 20 October, two weeks before the eventual invasion, the regiments were still lacking in officers and men, in addition to arms and uniforms.[90]

The Earl of Bath raised concerns to Sunderland on 9 October regarding discontent within the South West caused by James II's changes to the corporations of the towns within the counties and his inability to raise the militia.[91] While there is evidence of definite discontent within the English counties, and within the nobility and minor aristocracy who were the mainstay of the militia system, this was not universal and the majority of the country was still loyal to the king. Walter Partridge of Scarborough wrote to Sunderland on 8 October that all the gentlemen in the area and within the corporation are 'steadfast for the king' and that he was willing to serve the king in 'any station he may see fit'.[92] The letter goes on to state that he was a member of the Church of England. As well as the general policing duties, the militia were also raised to garrison forts and defences around the country, with the Cornish militia used to garrison Pendennis Castle.[93] New commissions were issued for officers within the trained bands of the first regiment of the Cinque Ports on 17 October 1688 – this was the militia in charge of the defence of the five ports on the south-east coast.[94] James II ordered the Duke of Beaufort to repair to the city of Bristol on 18 October and to raise part of the Gloucestershire militia to secure the city for the king, with similar instructions being sent to the Earl of Bath regarding the Devon militia securing Exeter.[95] Sir Robert Holmes informed Sunderland on 20 October that he could raise the Isle of Wight militia within 48 hours, but needed an extra £500 to pay for their provisions.[96] Holmes further stated that without this 'no great sum' it would be safest for all the 'arms, ammunition, and cannon' currently on the island to be withdrawn to the mainland so that the enemy could not make use of them. Sunderland replied on 25 October

88 NA: SP44/56, f.449.
89 NA: SP31/4, f.101; SP44/56, f.451.
90 NA: SP31/4, f.158
91 NA: SP31/4, f.106.
92 NA: SP31/4, f.94.
93 NA: SP31/4, f.112; SP44/56, f.457; SP44/97, f.7.
94 NA: SP44/69, f.236.
95 NA: SP44/56, ff.456–57; the Duke of Beaufort acknowledged the order on 20 October and confirmed he 'shall repair immediately to Bristol' (SP31/4, f.157).
96 NA: SP31/4, ff.151–53.

that the king had approved the supplies and funding for 400 militia and 'spare men' to be stationed in Yarmouth Castle and Hurst Castle.[97] The Lord Lieutenant of Lincolnshire, the Earl of Lindsey, advised St James Palace on 20 October 1688 that the Lincolnshire militia horse had been called out on the previous day, although he was 'very apprehensive' as to their order and conduct due to the length of time that had passed since their last muster.[98] While the militia appear to have had a limited involvement during the invasion, their use in replacing companies of regular soldiers in guarding key defences and towns allowed for an increase in the size of the English field army. A prime example of this was the order for the militia from the East Riding of Yorkshire to replace the regular companies guarding Hull, allowing those detached companies to rejoin their own regiment.[99] The Tower Hamlets militia in London were ordered on 15 November to be mustered for an additional duration of 30 days for the preservation of peace within the hamlets.[100] The two regiments of the militia had already been mustered for the maximum time allowed under the Act of Parliament and so needed royal approval for their muster to be extended and for the militia not to be stood down. Their duties, like so many other militia regiments within the country during this time, were to preserve the peace within their county or hundred. This duty of policing their counties resulted in the first action of the invasion when members of the Gloucester militia were killed and injured while intercepting Lord Lovelace and other gentlemen at Cirencester on their way to defect to William.[101] Although we have seen that the crown could not always be certain of the loyalty of all the members of the militia, they were not loyal to William either. On 20 November William instructed the Earl of Bath, Lord Lieutenant of Devon, who had previously declared Plymouth for the prince, to raise the militia of Devon and Cornwall. Bath's reply was that this request was 'somewhat impracticable and not serviceable to your Highness'.[102]

Scottish Regiments

In addition to raising new forces, James II utilised the troops under his command both in Scotland and Ireland, while also requesting the return of troops in Holland. While the Scottish and Irish forces were under his direct command, they were officially within the separate military establishments of Ireland and Scotland. James II ordered almost the entire Scottish establishment, which included the troop of Scots Horse Guards, Viscount Dundee's Royal Regiment of Scottish Horse, the Royal Regiments of Scottish Dragoons, six companies of the Scots foot guards, and Buchan's Regiment

97 NA: SP44/97, f.3.
98 NA: SP31/4, f.181.
99 NA: SP44/97, f.8.
100 NA: SP44/166, f.2.
101 NA: SP44/97, f.17.
102 NA: SP8/2, ff.58–59.

of Foot, to England. The Scottish army received orders on 24 September 1688 to proceed to the 'Louthians [Lothians]' and Marches in order that they 'may be ready to receive such further orders as We shall see fit to send from time to time', ensuring that they were ready to march into England.[103] James II ordered the Scots army to march into England three days later, as well as ordering that the Scottish militia be called out under the command of Sir George Monro. The army, under the command of Lieutenant-General Douglas, began its march south, heading first to Carlisle on its way to London.[104] By 20 October Major-General John Graham, Viscount Dundee, had reached Doncaster and advised Sunderland that his men 'wanted clothes' and that his horses 'will be mightily harrassed [out of condition]' before they reached London as ordered.[105] He begged leave to quarter his men 10–20 miles north of London to rest and recover their strength unless there was an immediate need for the regiments. Colonel John Wauchope's Regiment of Foot, which comprised Scottish troops returned from the Scots-Dutch brigade, was quartered around Clerkenwell (London) on 1 November 1688.[106] The rest of the Scottish army had arrived in London by the end of October and would later accompany the English army to Salisbury.

The transfer of troops from the Scottish to English establishment was the least problematic of the three groups. Firstly, they required the least logistical support and expense to be transferred onto the English establishment as they could simply march down to the south of England. They were also acceptable to the majority of the English population as they were Protestant, although Nonconformist as most of the troops within the Scottish army were either Presbyterian or Episcopalian. That said, although they would have been compliant with the Scottish Test Act of 1681, they would still have been non-compliant with the English Test Acts of 1673 and 1678.[107] While the first two provisions of these acts specifically impacted Catholics by asking for an oath of loyalty to the king and no other higher power (thus denying that the Pope was God's appointed representative on Earth) and to deny transubstantiation (the conversion of the substance of bread into the substance of the body of Christ, and wine to the blood of Christ), the third stipulation, to attend Anglican church services weekly, impacted all Nonconformists. Historians have taken it for granted that the Scottish troops who were transferred onto the English establishment were after all soldiers just following orders, but it is important to understand the loyalties of soldiers within this period. In reality, the officers' and common soldiers' identity and loyalty would have been multi-layered and interconnected, including issues of loyalty to the state, to the monarch, to their religion, loyalty to their regiment and their martial identity as a soldier. Enlisted soldiers would have identified with all these issues of loyalty and identity, with the additional factor of the need

103 C. Dalton, *The Scots Army, 1661-1688, With Memoirs of the Commander-in-Chief – Primary Source edition* (Edinburgh: William Brown, 1909), p.81

104 Dalton, *The Scots Army, 1661-1688*, p.82.

105 NA: SP31/4, f.155.

106 Dalton, *The Scots Army, 1661-1688*, p.82.

107 Harris, *Revolution*, p.28.

for survival, soldiering being their main profession and way of supporting themselves and their families, especially coming into winter, when day work would have been harder to find. As we will find following the disbandment of the English army on 11 December 1688, the soldiers understood their transfer to the English establishment was a temporary affair, based on a national emergency and their loyalty to the king, and that their loyalty to Scotland was never fully replaced by a loyalty just to the English state.

Irish Regiments

James II ordered four of the best-trained Irish regiments to be transferred from the Irish establishment to England, where they were then seconded onto the English establishment. While these troops were paid for by the Irish parliament, they were under the direct authority of James II and had sworn loyalty to him. These were therefore still 'domestic troops' and should not be considered as 'mercenary' or 'foreign' troops. The brigade transferred to England consisted of the following regiments: one battalion of the Irish foot guards (560 men), Lord Forbes' Regiment of Foot (650 men), Colonel Anthony Hamilton's Regiment of Foot (650 men), and Colonel John Butler's Regiment of Dragoons (500 men).[108] The brigade arrived in England at the port of Chester during September 1688. Some secondary sources state incorrectly that a fifth regiment, Colonel MacElligott's Regiment of Foot, arrived at the same time, however this regiment was raised in England with Irish soldiers returned from the Anglo-Dutch brigades. Due to the limited numbers of troops returning from Holland, the majority of its recruits came from England and the regiment was later strengthened with additional Irish recruits. On 18 September, the diarist Narcissus Luttrell recorded the arrival of 'another Irish regiment', which was Hamilton's regiment, which arrived after the first three regiments.[109] The numbers of troops arriving in Chester has been vastly over-emphasised, based on the full 'paper' strength of the regiments and not their actual strength. John Childs mentions a figure of 2,820 soldiers arriving in Chester from Ireland, which is far higher than even the paper strength of 2,360 men for the four regiments.[110] The figure quoted by Childs is not only far higher than the number of soldiers ordered to sail from Ireland, but it does also not account for regiments being under-strength. Lord Forbes' regiment was unacceptably understrength on arrival in Chester and needed to urgently 'drum up' recruits in the counties of Cheshire and Lancashire on its way south. The Irish foot guards lost most of their supplies during the crossing, with a new supply of arms, ammunition, and tents being ordered by Sunderland on 25 October 1688.[111] These regiments have always been described as either Irish, Catholic, or 'Popish' based on the assumption that all Irish regiments could only contain Catholic soldiers.

---

108 BL: Add MS 28938, 1679–89, Forces Ordered for Transport, October 1688, f.276.

109 Luttrell, *A Brief Historical Relation of State Affairs*, p.462.

110 Childs, *The Army, James II*, p.4

111 NA: WO55/335, f.97.

This assumption was based on what has been described as 'the great purge in Ireland' of 1685 and 1686.[112] The 'purge' was conducted by Richard Talbot, later 1st Earl of Tyrconnell, in order to create a Catholic army and shift the power dynamic from the Protestant population to the Irish and Catholic 'old English' population.[113] James II wanted to modernise the Irish army, which was considered to be the poorest and least disciplined when compared with the English and Scottish armies, with the army not being brought together for combined drills in over a decade and private soldiers being used as cheap labour on their captains' estates.[114] Tyrconnell's instructions resulted in thousands of enlisted soldiers being dismissed from the Irish army and militia, with 350 soldiers being dismissed from the Irish foot guards in July 1686.[115] Large numbers of these unemployed soldiers made their way over to England and would join the expanded English army in 1688, including making up the majority of the recruits for Colonel MacElligott's Regiment of Foot. These actions have led to the assumption that by 1688 the Irish army was constituted of entirely Catholic troops. They also increased the fears of James II's opponents within both the army and the wider English population that the king intended to do the same with the English army and only employ Catholic soldiers.[116] These fears were not only wholly unfounded, as this was never James's intention, but also completely impossible as there were not enough Catholics within England to emulate the events in Ireland.

As previously stated, Lord Forbes' regiment had an influx of English recruits upon its arrival, and although Cheshire and Lancashire had large Catholic populations, the regiment included both Catholic and Protestant recruits. While the regiment is always described as either 'Irish' or 'Catholic' in both contemporary and secondary sources, there were approximately 130 Protestant soldiers left within the regiment upon its disbandment in December 1688, including a small number of officers and NCOs.[117] The Irish Guards regiment, despite the 'Protestant' purges of 1686 and 1687, still contained a large number of Protestants within its ranks, including three captains, two lieutenants, and one ensign.[118] Following the end of hostilities and the disbandment of the English army, the four 'Irish' regiments were ordered to Portsmouth, where the Protestant troops were drawn into a new regiment for service with William.[119]

The suspected loyalty and intent of the 'Irish' regiments has been used to fuel 'Whig' and 'anti-Popish' propaganda and these claims are prevalent

112 Childs, *The Army, James II*, pp.56–83.

113 Childs, *The Army, James II*, p.59.

114 Henry Hyde, Earl of Clarendon, *The Correspondence of Henry Hyde, Earl of Clarendon, and his brother Laurence Hyde, Earl of Rochester: with the diary of Lord Clarendon From 1687 to 1690, Containing Minute Particulars of the Events Attending the Revolution And the Diary of Lord Rochester During His Embassy to Poland in 1676* (London: H. Colburn, 1828), vol. I, pp.440–5, Clarendon to Rochester, June 1686.

115 Childs, *The Army, James II*, p.61.

116 John Miller used the term 'almost wholly Catholic' in regard to the Irish army in 1688. Miller, *James II*, p.212.

117 Childs, *The Army, James II*, p.196.

118 Luttrell, *A Brief Historical Relation of State Affairs*, p.483.

119 HL/PO/JO/10/1405, f.46.

within previous historiography. Their reputation is partially based on the regiments' relationship with their English counterparts and the local communities where they were billeted. This relationship could be described as strained at best and overtly hostile at worst. There was a 'great rift' reported between two of the regiments garrisoned within Portsmouth, the Duke of Berwick's Regiment of Foot (English) and Colonel MacElligott's Regiment of Foot (Irish).[120] The disturbance was the result of reports of the 'Irish' soldiers firing their muskets into a Protestant church on 27 October 1688.[121] Further reports reached London in early November of further riots in Portsmouth between the English and Irish garrison. The reports were vague on both the cause and the number of casualties; the various reports quote between four and 50 fatalities on each side, however only two casualties can be confirmed. The riots were believed to have centred around an alehouse, presumably inflamed by drink as well as religious tension, and resulted in two officers being killed, who had been 'run through the body'.[122] The majority of the reports of disorderly conduct by the Irish regiments were simple anti-Catholic propaganda used to incite religious fear and continue a narrative that supported the Williamite cause.

Six captains of the English garrison at Portsmouth were famously cashiered and lost their commissions for failure to follow orders and take 'Irish' soldiers into their companies. The captains had been commissioned into Princess Anne of Denmark's Regiment of Foot, which was raised in June 1685 in response to the Monmouth Rebellion, with all the officers involved holding commissions from this date. The regimental colonel, James FitzJames, Duke of Berwick, also held the commission of the Governor of Portsmouth.[123] By August 1688, only six companies remained in Portsmouth, the other six companies having been posted to the Channel Isles.[124] On 4 September 1688 the Duke of Berwick ordered that forty 'Irish' soldiers should be incorporated into his regiment. These 'Irish' soldiers were originally to have been recruited into Colonel MacElligott's Regiment of Foot, which was over-strength, and were therefore to be used to fill vacancies within the duke's regiment. Where companies were at full strength, captains were ordered to dismiss any substandard soldiers in order to take these new recruits.[125] This should have been a simple issue of replacing 'substandard' soldiers with experienced ones that had previously served within the Irish establishment, but the officers refused this lawful order, presumably on the basis of the suspected religion of these new recruits. The officers refusing to take these soldiers were Lieutenant Colonel John Beaumont and captains Simon Packe, Thomas Paston, Thomas Orme, William Cooke, and John Port.[126] The officers

120 A. Coleby, 'Military-Civilian Relations on the Solent 1651-1689', *The Historical Journal*, 29.4 (1986), pp.959–61; F.C. Turner, *James II* (London: Eyre & Spottiswoode, 1948), pp.409–10.
121 BL: Add MS 41805, f.89.
122 Ferguson, *History of the Scots Brigade*, p.123.
123 Petrie, *The Marshal Duke of Berwick*, p.32.
124 NA: WO4/1, f.91.
125 E. Priestley and J. Beaumont, 'The Portsmouth Captains', *Journal of the Society for Army Historical Research*, 55.223 (Autumn 1977), p.155.
126 Priestley and Beaumont, 'The Portsmouth Captains', pp.155–56.

refused the order on 6 September 1688 and were subsequently ordered to appear at their court martial, held at Windsor four days later. The court was presided over by the commander of the army, the Earl of Feversham, with another fourteen senior officers including Lord Churchill, in accordance with the current army regulations. The officers were charged with refusing to obey orders of a superior officer. The punishment for this charge, according to the army regulations of the time, was that 'he shall be Cashiered, or suffer such Punishment as a Court Martial shall think fit'.[127] Following the court martial a further seven junior officers resigned their commissions in protest as a result of the orders to take 'Irish' troops and the subsequent prosecution of their captains. These officers were lieutenants Edward Berrisford and John Knyvett, along with ensigns John James, Ralph Mansell, William Campion, John Jodrell, and possibly George Butler.[128]

The four 'Irish' regiments brought over from the Irish establishment along with Colonel MacElligott's (Irish) Regiment of Foot have always been taken to contain only Irish and Catholic troops, when neither was actually correct. They did contain large numbers of Irish soldiers, but as previously mentioned, they also recruited troops within England, primarily from Cheshire and Lancashire. MacElligott's regiment was originally raised for Irish soldiers returning from service in Holland, but there was never enough returning soldiers to fill one regiment, let alone the three regiments commissioned to receive the expected English, Irish, and Scottish soldiers from both brigades. When we look at the number of officers returning from the Continent following James II's recall, additional officers were still required to fill vacancies in a number of companies. Five commissions were issued in late September to fill vacancies in Colonel Butler's Regiment of Dragoons, with an additional two commissions for the regiments belonging to Lord Forbes, and one for Colonel Hamilton's regiment.[129] Other than these isolated instances the 'Irish' regiments were successfully incorporated into the English establishment and proved to be some of the most loyal troops James II had.

Anglo-Dutch Brigade

The transfer of the regiments from the Irish and Scottish establishments was a simple matter for James, as he was the monarch of both Ireland and Scotland. The transfer of the Anglo-Dutch and Scots-Dutch brigades back to England required the approval of William of Orange and the States General and would be far more problematic. Ignatius White, the Marquis de Albeville pressed James to recall the Anglo-Dutch and Scots-Dutch brigades

---

127 Anon., *Rules and Articles for the Better Government of His Majesties Land-Forces in Pay during this present Rebellion: Published at His Majesties Command* (London: John Bill Deceased, Henry Hills and Thomas Newcomb, 1685).

128 Dalton, *English Army Lists*, p.138.

129 NA: SP63/340, ff.297–98, 301. Butler's dragoons received a captain-lieutenant, two lieutenants, and two cornets, Lord Forbes a captain and a lieutenant, and an ensign for Hamilton's.

from Dutch service in August 1687, while Tyrconnell is reported to have suggested the recall of both brigades in an audience with James II at Chester on 7 September 1687.[130] The formal petition to return the six regiments was presented by the Marquis de Albeville to the States General on 6 February 1688, with William of Orange receiving it the following day.[131] The request was made in relation to the convention of 1678 on English (and Scottish) troops regarding service in the United Provinces.[132] The formal request also included provision for the States General to pay all outstanding arrears and for the regiment to be able to 'bring away' their arms with them.[133] The reply from the States General was sent on 13 March, refusing the request, and went as far as denying the existence of the 1678 treaty, emphasising the treaties between Queen Elizabeth and the State (the United Provinces) between 1585 and 1598.[134] The reply further stated that the States General has been in:

> 1664 and 1665 to be plunged into a war with King Charles II., also of glorious memory, the English and Scottish regiments, at that time in service, were all entirely discharged from it, and the officers who had commanded the said regiments were dismissed, and that those of them who were again taken into service in course of time were never again considered or regarded as officers of English or Scotch regiments.

While the detailed reason for the refusal to return the two brigades in 1688 does appear at first glance to contradict the States General returning the brigades in 1685, this was due to the political situation and the realisation that while William had allowed the Duke of Monmouth to launch his attempt on the English crown from Holland, he did not fully support it. The regiments, however, did not play any part in the Monmouth Rebellion, arriving after Monmouth had been defeated, with James II ordering the regiments to return to the service of United Provinces. Not all the Scots-Dutch brigade arriving back in England in 1685 were loyal to James, as nine soldiers drank Monmouth's health during a review of the regiments on Hounslow Heath in late July 1685. Two of the soldiers were sentenced to death by firing squad, while a third soldier was sentenced to be 'flogged at the gallows'.[135] While James II was in negotiation with the States General for the return of 'his regiments', Colonel Tollemache was reported to have left England for Holland and to have been given the command of a regiment there, Colonel Thomas Tollemache's

130 Miller, *James II*, p.183; Childs, *The Army, James II*, p.131. The Marquis de Albeville was James II's envoy extraordinary and plenipotentiary to the United Provinces at the Hague between 1686 and 1688. (See Gary M. Bell, *A Handlist of British Diplomatic Representatives 1509-1688* (London: Royal Historical Society, 1990), p.16.)

131 Ferguson, *History of the Scots Brigade*, p.543.

132 Ferguson, *History of the Scots Brigade*, pp.550–51.

133 G. Hilton-Jones, 'The Recall of the British from the Dutch Service', *The History Journal*, 25.2 (1982), p.425.

134 Ferguson, *History of the Scots Brigade*, p.552.

135 Ferguson, *History of the Scots Brigade*, p.540. The diarist and historian Narcissus Luttrell reported on 10 February 1688 of the soldiers of the Anglo-Dutch and Scots Dutch brigade that William 'absolutely refused for them to return' (Luttrell, *A Brief Historical Relation of State Affairs*, p.432).

Regiment of Foot (of the Anglo-Dutch brigade).[136] William sent emissaries to each regiment in 1688, instructing them to reject the recall by James II and to continue their service for William.[137] William had purged all the Catholic officers from within the six regiments of the two brigades and replaced them with political exiles from England and Scotland, as well as with Huguenot refugees.[138] This was more to do with the questionable loyalty of these officers than with their religion, as Catholic officers and soldiers were free to serve within the Dutch forces. While the States General and William continued refusing to release all six regiments, individual officers were allowed leave to return to England. The exact numbers of officers and soldiers obeying James II's orders to return is questionable, although the general opinion is that 104 of the 234 officers from the Anglo-Dutch and Scots-Dutch brigades obeyed James II's orders to return to England, with just over half originating from the Scots brigade.[139] On arrival in England, the officers had to report to David Crawford, the chief deputy commissioner of musters, and satisfy him of their service and upon doing so were commissioned into three newly raised English regiments of foot and received full pay from the date they left Dutch service.[140] Each regiment was due to have 13 companies, including one company of grenadiers, each of 50 men. The position of common soldiers, however, was far more problematic as they were not given permission to leave, and men were faced with possible imprisonment for even requesting to leave Dutch service.[141] It was common military practice for officers to be allowed to give up their commissions, while enlisted soldiers always needed the authority of the regimental colonel to leave, or risked being charged with desertion. The three regiments were reported to be 'beating up', which was the standard term for regiments recruiting, in April 1688 as it would have been obvious that they would not be able to rely on troops returning from Holland to complete all the companies.[142] The English ambassadors to the United Provinces and Brussels had been instructed to assist all English and Scottish soldiers to return to England and to provide them with money and passage as required. Very few ordinary soldiers returned to England: 14 soldiers with a sergeant arrived via Flanders, with another 44 arriving via the Spanish Netherlands.[143] Another 15 'Irish' soldiers escaped via Antwerp and Nieuport with the help of a Jesuit father and the English envoy to Brussels.[144] The common soldiers, upon their arrival in England, were enlisted into Colonel John Hales's (English) Regiment of Foot and Colonel Roger MacElligott's

136 Luttrell, *A Brief Historical Relation of State Affairs*, p.434.
137 Hilton-Jones, 'The Recall of the British from the Dutch Service', p.426
138 Glozier, *The Huguenot Soldiers of William of Orange*, p.73.
139 Childs, *The Army, James II*, p.133; Pull, *William III*, p.532; Hilton-Jones, 'The Recall of the British from the Dutch Service', p.429; R. Manning, *An Apprenticeship in Arms: The Origins of the British Army 1585-1702* (Oxford: OUP, 2006), p.356.
140 Hilton-Jones, 'The Recall of the British from the Dutch Service', p.432; NA: WO24/8, Part 5, f.41.
141 Hilton-Jones, 'The Recall of the British from the Dutch Service', p.431.
142 Luttrell, *A Brief Historical Relation of State Affairs*, p.437.
143 BL: Add MS 41821, f.79; Childs, *The Army, James II*, p.134
144 NA: SP77/55, f.424; BL: Add MS 41821, A list of the Gentlemen, who have Served as Volunteers in the Brigade and are gone over in the Yacht, ff.38–39 and 42–43; BL: Add MS 41822, Middleton Papers, Vol. XX, A List of the Officers whom I had detained, and have now sent over, f.215.

(Irish) Regiment of Foot, although these soldiers made up the minority of recruits within both regiments.[145] Due to the lack of soldiers returning from Holland, Colonel MacElligott was forced to send officers and recruiting parties to Ireland as the regiment was so understrength, although it is highly unlikely that these recruits would have made it back to the regiment prior to the invasion.[146] After leaving the Anglo-Dutch brigade, Ensign Edward Powell received a commission in Colonel John Carne's Regiment of Foot, which was raised in South Wales and the Marches in support of James II.[147] Catholic soldiers returning from Dutch service were also recruited into Lord Forbes's Regiment of Foot, which had arrived understrength from Ireland and was recruiting in Cheshire and Lancashire. These recruits were either already NCOs or were promoted to corporals by James II on their incorporation into the regiment.[148]

The standard reason for soldiers heeding James II's recall is that they were Catholic, but this does not tell the whole story and ignores issues of loyalty to James II and the state.[149] Eleven officers returned to England but did not subsequently receive commissions with the army of James II, and a further eleven officers who were commissioned under James II later either defected to William following his arrival in England or held commissions in the English army after January 1689.[150] The officers include Ensign George Hamilton, who served William, where he achieved the rank of lieutenant-general, then switched his loyalties again, joining the 1715 Jacobite Rising, and was subsequently tried and hanged for treason. Ensign Simon Boonfoy or Boonsoy obeyed James II's recall and subsequently defected to William in December 1688, however he was not re-commissioned into William's army.[151] It is certain, however, that the majority of the officers returning to England were Protestant as they returned from the Anglo-Scots brigade and these regiments were almost entirely made up of Presbyterian and Episcopalian soldiers.

145 NA: WO4/1, ff.79–80.

146 NA: WO4/1, f.105.

147 J. Childs, *Nobles, Gentlemen and the Profession of Arms in Restoration Britain 1660-1688* (NL: SAHR, 1987), p.74; Dalton, *English Army Lists*, vol. II, p.193.

148 G. Davies, 'Letters on the Administration of James II's Army', *The Journal of the Society for Army Historical Research,* 29.118 (1951), p.76.

149 Childs, *The Army, James II*, p.132; Hilton-Jones, 'The Recall of the British from the Dutch Service', p.432.

150 J. Childs, *Gentlemen and the Profession of Arms in Restoration Britain 1660-1688: A Biographical Dictionary of British Army Officers on Foreign Service* (London: Society for Army Historical research, 1987), pp.15, 23, 43, 46, 55, 85, 86, 91; *CSPD: James II, 1687–89*, pp.166, 175, 180, 277, 284–85; Dalton, *English Army Lists*, vol. II, pp.138, 151–52, 162, 172, 189; Dalton, *English Army Lists*, vol. III, pp.47, 61, 65, 109; HL/Pl/JO/10/1/409, f.173; SP8.13, King William's Chest, f.179; SP/164, f.407.

151 *CSPD: James II, 1687–89*, p.180.

Army Discipline

Apart from the few recorded disturbances between English and Irish troops detailed earlier within this chapter, there does not seem to have been any increased dissent or desertions within the English army during the summer and autumn of 1688. A great disturbance was reported between the civil population of Falmouth and the garrison of Pendennis Castle in early August. During the disturbance, the soldiers from Captain George Aylmer's company killed one man and injured an unknown number of other civilians.[152] From the birth of the new Prince of Wales in June 1688 to William's landing on 5 November 1688 there were no increases in the numbers of desertions from within the army. The desertions continued to be reported in similar numbers to the first half of the year. Ensign Wynne (Prince George of Denmark's Regiment of Foot) was reported to have deserted the garrison at Berwick on 16 August and was tried by regimental court martial.[153] Two soldiers, Walter Finley (about 30 years old) and Robert Burnett (about 26), were both reported to have deserted from Prince George of Denmark's Regiment of Foot in the *London Gazette* of 6 September 1688.[154] Aware of an amplification of tensions within the country resulting from the increase in the size of the army, James II reissued orders regarding the billeting of troops within the community. The fears of dragooning during the Civil War were still fresh within the collective memory of the population and James II was keen to

James II Performing a Balancing Act while William of Orange Plays the Tune, Romeyn de Hooghe, Netherlands, 1689. (Rijksmuseum: RP-P-OB-55.187, Public Domain)

152 NA. WO4/1, f.94. Captain Aylmer's company was part of Sir Edward Hales's Regiment of Foot (BL: Add MS 75392, f.32).

153 NA: WO4/1, f.45.

154 *The London Gazette*, No. 2379, Monday, September 3 to Thursday, September 6 1688, p.2.

placate any fears of a repeat of this process.[155] The declaration was made at Windsor on 2 September 1688 and was printed in the *London Gazette* of 10 September 1688. It would have been distributed throughout the country through broadsheets and by being printed in other papers.[156] The declaration stated that the king was aware of breaches to his declaration of 25 August 1685 regarding the quartering of troops within private homes and inns. It further states that all billeting arrangements must be confirmed with the Chief Magistrate, Justice of the Peace, or the constable of the location where troops were to be billeted. It stated that the punishment for breaking this order would be a court martial for private soldiers and any officer guilty of ordering or permitting any offence was to be cashiered and discharged from the army. The declaration went on to further state that the king had received reports of soldiers impressing horses, wagons, and carriages, and that this practice should stop immediately and troops should pay owners of carriages and wagons the 'usual rate of six pence a mile'.

Last Minute Preparations for the Invasion

All the lord lieutenants of coastal counties from County Durham in the north to Cornwall in the south-west were advised on 30 October of the king's orders to remove all horses, oxen, and any cattle fit for burthen (able to be used as draught animals) to be withdrawn a minimum of 12 miles from the coast or any point where the enemy could land.[157] There was an exception for any animals being used in the lord lieutenants' service or in the defence of the realm. This order had not been implemented prior to the Monmouth Rebellion and as a result the duke had been able to obtain draught animals for his force upon his arrival in Lyme Bay. Embargoes on all ships leaving or entering English ports and rivers were issued by the Privy Council on 22 October, including ships at Dover, the Thames, and northward towards Berwick.[158] The embargo was lifted for shipping belonging to countries deemed to be friendly to England or to countries that were enemies of William and Holland, including from France, Portugal, and Spain, along with shipping from Africa, America, and Asia on 29 October 1688.[159]

A message was sent to the Duke of Newcastle advising him that additional intelligence had been obtained by the king that a large number of horses had been brought up to the coast for the use of the Dutch during the invasion.[160] The order stated that Sir Hugh Cholmley of Whitby had at least 30 horses within his stables that needed to be secured by the lord lieutenant of the county. English regiments were reported on 28 September to be marching from their normal quarters towards the coast, heading into Kent and also

155 Dragooning was the process of forced billeting of troops on the population, or on a portion of the population as an act of punishment or revenge for acts against the government or monarch.

156 *The London Gazette*, No. 2380, Thursday, September 6 to Monday, September 10 1688, p.1.

157 NA: SP.44/97, ff.6–7; NA PC 2/72, f.54.

158 NA: PC 2/72, f.56.

159 NA: PC 2/72, f.83.

160 NA: SP44/97, f.9.

towards the ports of Harwich and Portsmouth.[161] Without a standing high command for the army, commanders were appointed on an 'as needed' basis and by late September 1688 it was understood that the English army would be commanded by Lord Feversham, Lord Dumbarton, and the Count du Coy.[162] The command of the army was given to Lord Feversham, but Lord Churchill was promoted to his deputy over Dumbarton and du Coy. James issued commissions for five new regiments: three of foot – the Duke of Newcastle, Colonel Solomon Richards, and Colonel Henry Gage – along with two of horse – Lord Brandon, and the Marquis du Miremont.[163]

After consulting with his senior officers, James II issued orders to Lord Dartmouth, Master-General of the Ordnance Board, on 7 November that all the regiments of foot currently issued with matchlock muskets should be exchanged for snaphance (flintlock) muskets.[164] The order stated that the snaphance muskets should be delivered to 'several' regiments and exchanged for the similar number of matchlock muskets. The warrant was issued before James was made aware of William's landing and would have in any event taken weeks to complete due to the location of the regiments and the logistics involved and it is highly unlikely that these changes would have been in place prior to the army departing from Salisbury. On 13 October Lord Dartmouth was issued orders to equip all the workmen and sailors currently working within the port of Chatham with 'a sufficient quantity of arms' in order for them to defend the port and facilities.[165] In addition to 600 muskets and swords, along with 200 half-pikes, Dartmouth was ordered to supply 300 grenadoes for the defence of the port. He was also instructed to fit out twelve longboats with 'small guns' for the defence of the river.

The English army had been set on the equivalent of a war footing prior to the expected invasion of the Dutch forces by James II, with orders going out to the senior commanders. Orders were given to the Board of Ordnance to supply the necessary equipment to keep an army on the move during the winter, including ordering 20,000 tents and for a pontoon train to be assembled.[166] The government also issued orders to obtain the required supply of victuals, including 'soft bread' for the army on 16 October. The orders stipulated that they needed to be enough for 20,000 men to march for one week.[167] Additional orders for 10,000 shoes for foot soldiers to be forthwith made and dispatched with all expedition to the army were issued on 22 November; the shoes were to be of a design approved by Major-General Sackville.[168] By 30 November there were 2,000 pairs of shoes ready to be dispatched to the army; the other 8,000 pairs were never delivered.[169] Due to the numbers of soldiers being billeted in overcrowded quarters, because of

161 Luttrell, *A Brief Historical Relation of State Affairs*, p.463.
162 Luttrell, *A Brief Historical Relation of State Affairs*, p.464.
163 Luttrell, *A Brief Historical Relation of State Affairs*, p.464.
164 NA: SP44/165, f.135
165 NA: WO55/400, f.230.
166 NA. WO55/336, f.71r.
167 NA: WO4/1, ff.105, 113.
168 NA: WO4/1, f.110.
169 NA: WO4/1, f.116.

both the lack of suitable quarters and the need for complete regiments to be billeted within a small area, the levels of sickness within the army increased. Large numbers of soldiers falling sick and unable to report for duty were reported at Landguard Fort, Sheerness, and Rochester.[170]

Disposition of the Army

From August 1688 there was an increase in the movements and deployments within England of individual companies and troops as well as full regiments in the expectation of the invasion. The primary plan was for the forts, castles, and blockhouses around the country to be garrisoned, for London to be secured, and for a mobile field army to be formed up within 25 miles of London, in order for it to respond to the direction of march of any invading army.[171] The Princess Anne of Denmark's Regiment of Foot was ordered to send seven of its companies to Portsmouth for embarkation for the Channel Islands on 16 August; three companies were ordered to garrison Jersey, with another three companies destined for Guernsey, and one for the Scilly Islands.[172] Colonel Cornwall's Regiment of Foot was ordered to march to Chester and to undertake the garrison of that important port. The first two companies were ordered to march on 16 August, with orders for the remainder of the regiment following in the next couple of days, while one company was split from the regiment for garrison duty in Chepstow Castle.[173] Colonel Hales's Regiment of Foot was ordered to join the garrison of Sheerness on 30 August 1688, with the governor and Lord Dartmouth ordered to find suitable quarters for the regiment, even if it was within the garrison chapel.[174] The regiment was ordered to depart its current location of Salisbury and to travel via Winchester, where the regiment was instructed to have a day's rest.[175] Prince George of Denmark's Regiment of Foot was ordered to the town of Great Yarmouth on 12 September 1688 in order to defend the port against any expected invasion by William along the Norfolk coast.[176] The order also confirms a problem that the government had with the billeting of troops, especially whole regiments, stating that 'there may not be sufficient number of public houses for the quartering of that regiment'. With no permanent barracks other than in forts and castles, the army needed to quarter soldiers within the civil population. The order stated that the regiment would need to be lodged directly in the town and within 'those houses that receive the greatest benefit from the regiment'. The wording, while inconclusive, would suggest that the regiment needed to be billeted within houses where the occupiers' loyalty to the king was in question. While looking similar to the practice known as dragooning, which was publicly banned by the king on

170 NA: WO4/1, f.108.
171 Childs, *The Army, James II*, p.170.
172 NA: WO4/1, f.91.
173 NA: WO4/1, ff.90, 92.
174 NA: WO4/1, f.94.
175 NA: WO4/1, f.97.
176 NA: WO4/1, ff.96–97.

the same day, these residents were going to be paid by the regiment for the use of their houses as billets. Similar instructions went out to the mayors and magistrates of five local towns for the housing of the regiment. The Holland Regiment of Foot under Colonel Theophilus Oglethorpe was ordered to move the 9 miles from Rochester to Maidstone on 13 September, with two companies to be stationed in Tunbridge (Tunbridge Wells). The move was presumably a precaution in order both to cover the naval base at Chatham and the south coast.[177] On 5 October the Earl of Lichfield's Regiment of Foot received orders to send 30 of its men to the fleet and was ordered to march to Gravesend by no later than noon on Saturday, 9 October 1688.[178] With no dedicated marine regiment, companies or half companies of regular regiments of foot were used to support the navy by supplying troops. The Duke of Newcastle's Regiment of Foot received orders on 3 November to march from its accommodation in Newcastle to Berwick-upon-Tweed or other such place as the duke saw fit in order to defend Bridlington Bay or the north from Dutch invasion.[179] The second battalion of the foot guards was ordered on 6 November 1688 to Portsmouth with great speed, and in order to do this was advised that 'such carts as are appropriate for that purpose [are] at Guildford'.[180] The use of carts for the transport of regiments was not uncommon, but would normally be just for the regimental supplies and baggage.

Lieutenant-Colonel Hayford was ordered to take five troops of dragoons from his regiment, under the command of Colonel Robert Clifford, to Halesworth in Suffolk on 15 September, with the rest of the regiment staying in Lowestoft.[181] The Earl of Peterborough's Regiment of Dragoons was ordered on 22 September to return its two outlying troops to Northampton with the rest of the regiment.[182] The regiment was also ordered to increase the size of every troop by 10 men along with filling the vacancies notified in the regimental muster of 5 September. Colonel Butler's Regiment of (Irish) Dragoons was ordered to Colebrook, Devon (Colebrooke), on 25 October, with the order confirming that they had been entered onto the English establishment.[183] The Royal Regiment of Horse was ordered to Salisbury on 12 November, with an officer to travel to Winchester to collect armour for the regiment which had been left in the town by a previous regiment.[184] The second squadron of the Queen Dowager's Regiment of Horse, commanded by Sir John Talbot, was ordered to march to Salisbury on 22 November with their armour, with the Royal Regiment of Dragoons ordered to Portsmouth on the same day.[185]

177 NA: WO4/1, ff.97–98.
178 NA: WO4/1, f.103.
179 NA: WO4/1, f.108.
180 NA: WO4/1, f.109.
181 NA: WO4/1, f.99.
182 NA: WO4/1, f.102.
183 NA: WO4/1, f.107.
184 NA: WO4/1, f.109.
185 NA: WO4/1, f.110.

On 7 November James II issued commissions to officers filling the senior military posts required for an army to conduct operations.[186] These commissions included Colonel Edward Sackville to the position of Major-General of Horse and Henry, Lord Dover as a brigadier of horse. John, Lord Churchill was given the commission of lieutenant-general of all the English forces, horse and foot.[187] The following day commissions were given to Colonel Richard Werden to be promoted to lieutenant-general, and for Colonel Percy Kirke to be promoted to major-general, as well as to Sir John Talbot and Sir Charles Littleton to be brigadiers of horse and foot respectively.[188] Warrants for new regiments to be raised were still being issued as late as 8 November, with commissions being raised for Henry, Earl of Stafford to raise a new regiment of foot and to be the colonel of that regiment.[189] Unusually for new regiments being commissioned at this time, named commissions were raised for all the officers within the regiment.[190]

James II issued orders to the earls of Middleton and Tyrconnell on 8 November for an additional regiment to be despatched from Ireland and

The fleet of William III at Hellevoetsluis, 18 (28) October 1688, in a print by Daniël Marot, Amsterdam?, 1688–1700. (Rijksmuseum: RP-P-OB-23.126, Public Domain)

186 NA: SP44/165, ff.133, 136–37.
187 NA: SP44/165, f.135.
188 NA: SP44/165, ff.134–37.
189 NA: SP44/166, ff.5-6.
190 NA: SP44/166, ff.7, 8–9.

embarked for either the port of Chester or Liverpool without arms.[191] The wording of the order confirms the lack of certainty that James II had over the situation facing the country and also in his own decision making. Although he ordered Tyrconnell to dispatch the troops from Ireland on confirming that their arms will be waiting for them at Chester on Saturday 20 November, he also allowed Middleton to delay the order if he felt that the order was not in the king's service. Rumours circulated throughout the country during the last week of September 1688 that King Louis XIV of France had offered to send French regiments over to England to help with the defence of the country against the Dutch. These were countered by James II's supporters, stating that the king had refused the offer, 'resolving to trust his own subjects'.[192] While untrue, these rumours increased the fears that James II planned to turn the country Catholic and become an absolute ruler in the vein of Louis XIV. James II had been informed of William's landing in Torbay on 6 November when he informed Lord Langdale that even though an enemy force had landed in the South East, the defences of the citadel of Hull should not be neglected. This was due to the concern that the Dutch could possibly be able to conduct a second landing in the North East to disperse the English army.

191 NA: SP63/340, f.340.

192 Luttrell, *A Brief Historical Relation of State Affairs*, p.462.

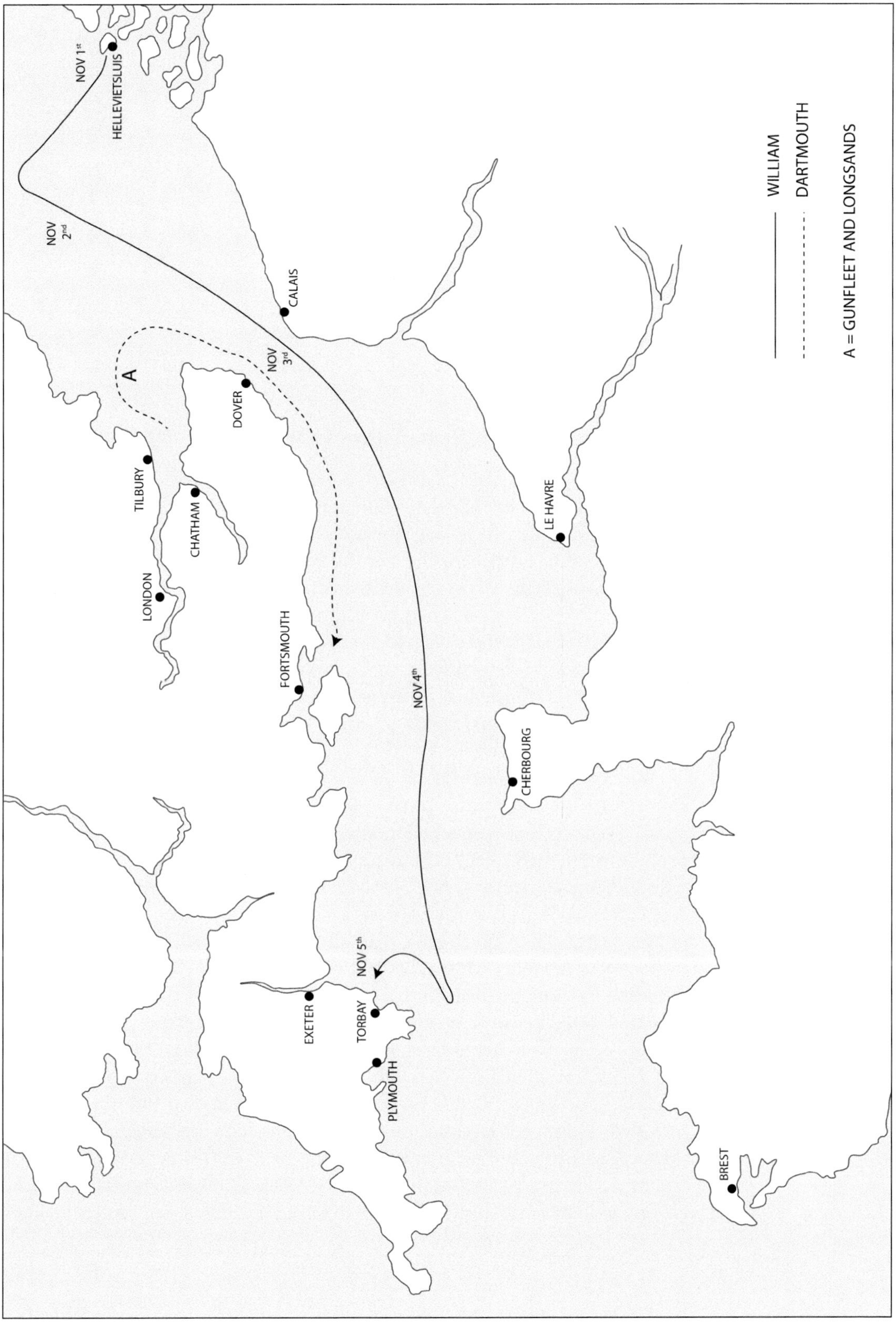

The sea route of the invasion fleet

4

The Invasion

1 November to 4 November 1688: Dutch Fleet Sets Sail

It was on 1 November 1688 that William III, Prince of Orange finally departed from Hellevoetsluis in South Holland. He was at the head of an invasion fleet destined to overthrow the rightful King of England and would change the course of English History. William's fleet had made a previous attempt to depart for England, but had been forced to return to port due to severe winter storms. Hellevoetsluis had been a good choice as the departure point of the fleet as it was a fortified town and major port able to accommodate the logistical needs of the fleet. The port had been the home port for admirals Maarten Tromp, Michiel de Ruyter, and Piet Heyn, along with a large part of the combined Dutch navy.[1]

William's fleet consisted of at least 50 good men-of-war along with some 5–10 fireships and between 300 and 400 merchant ships. The naval escort was far from just a ceremonial escort for William; it contained the pride of the Dutch fleet and was a powerful naval force. Although conflict with the English fleet was not William's aim, with the prince and his English supporters taking all available steps to avoid a naval battle, the force was both ready and able to engage any English fleet or vessels sent against it. The inclusion of fireships within the fleet confirms that William had the ability to attack the English fleet both at sea and while at anchor. The force that departed Hellevoetsluis on the first day of November was over twice the size of the Spanish Armada that had challenged England 100 years earlier and set off invasion fears throughout the country. There has been a lot of emphasis on the fact that William had organised for a printing press to be included within the supplies being carried over to England, accentuating the supposedly peaceful intentions of the prince. However, the force also contained almost 20,000 soldiers, with between 4,000 and 5,000 horses, and all the artillery and supplies required for an extended military campaign.

1 Fox, *The Four Days' Battle of 1666*, pp.184, 197.

This was not a force of revolutionaries setting sail into the North Sea; neither was this a force to support an English coup. This was an invasion force, and would have been seen as such by both the Dutch citizens viewing its departure from Holland and by the people on the south coast of England watching the progress of the fleet over the coming days as it sailed through the English Channel. It was viewed in a similar manner throughout Europe, both by William's own supporters and by Louis XIV of France and his allies.[2] After setting sail from Holland, the fleet headed north-north-west, taking advantage of the prevailing winds. Although the fleet would later turn south-west, it would have given the impression that the fleet was heading for the north-east coast of England and to one of the suspected landing sites. Norfolk and Hull had both been thought to be possible landing sites, but both were never really realistic invasion points as Norfolk was too remote and Hull was too far north, as well as having a large garrison and therefore likely to put up military resistance. Hull was specifically mentioned as the destination of the invasion in a letter to Sunderland on 17 October, when the Duke of Newcastle enclosed correspondence from his cousin who had just returned from Holland.[3] Any initial military action upon landing would both put the whole expedition in danger and destroy the pretence of 'coming to save the people from a dangerous King'.

Prince William III departs with the fleet from Hellevoetsluis, 1 (11) November 1688, in a print by Pieter Pickaert, northern Netherlands, 1689. (Rijksmuseum: RP-P-01938-1728, Public Domain)

2 J.R. Jones, *The Revolution of England in 1688* (London: Weidenfeld and Nicolson, 1972), pp.255, 259.
3 NA: SP31/4, ff.129–30.

Fleet review at the departure of William III from Hellevoetsluis, 1 (11) November 1688, in a print by Romeyn de Hooghe, northern Netherlands, 1688. (Rijksmuseum: RP-P-OB-79.448, Public Domain)

The fleet finally set sail from Hellevoetsluis on the evening of 1 November 1688, after a council of war was held on the *Leyden*.[4] William embarked on his ship, the *Brill*, between 3pm and 4pm, which then fired a number of its cannons, instructing the fleet to weigh anchor and set sail for England.[5] On the second day out of Holland, 2 November 1688, the Dutch invasion fleet turned south-south-west and with the help of the 'divine Protestant wind' passed the coast of Norfolk, passing Landguard Fort, which protected Harwich and the estuary leading to Ipswich. The fleet was heading towards the Thames estuary and Gunfleet Sands, where the majority of the English fleet was waiting at anchor. The fleet was sailing through the area of the North Sea where, during the Second Anglo-Dutch War, on 1 June 1666 a large Dutch fleet engaged a smaller English fleet in what was to become known as the Four Days' Battle of 1666. Nearly 200 ships fought over the four days, resulting in the destruction of large numbers of ships on both sides, including the *Royal Prince*, which was taken and burnt along with another nine ships that were lost forever.[6] One of the main concerns the English had was that the Dutch would repeat their successful attack of 1667, when they attacked the Medway, capturing Sheerness Fort and successfully attacking the English fleet anchored off Chatham, resulting in the loss of a number of English warships and the Dutch capturing the English flagship *Royal Charles*. In reality, this was never a realistic option. William was aware that the defences of the Medway and Thames had been increased by Charles II

4 Pull, *William III*, p.566.
5 Anon., *An Exact Diary of the Late Expedition*, p.28.
6 Fox, *The Four Days' Battle of 1666*, pp.271–74.

following the end of the Second Anglo-Dutch war to prevent a repetition of this attack. He would also have been informed that James II, in the lead-up to November 1688, had strengthened the garrisons and fortresses along the coast and the Thames estuary. In reality, although the garrisons had been strengthened, the buildings and artillery were in a sorry state of disrepair following years of neglect and a lack of money from Parliament. The prevailing winds sent the fleet north-east towards Hull, and then on 2 November the fleet turned south, passed Norfolk and the Thames Estuary and passed Gunfleet where the English fleet was anchored, unable due to the direction of the wind to depart and intercept the large Dutch fleet as it transited the North Sea towards the English Channel. The English navy consisted of 52 ships split between second, third, fourth, and fifth-raters, with an additional 17 fireships, and according to Lord Dartmouth moved from Gunfleet on 30 October and sailed to Longsands Head, where he was forced to stay until 4 November due to easterly winds.[7]

There had been speculation as to William's planned landing location, if not on the North Sea coast then at a port location on the south coast such as Tilbury, Dover, Southampton, or Portsmouth. However, these were never the target for the invasion. While Admiral Herbert, commander of the William's fleet, as well as William and his closest advisers, had always favoured the South West, they were not interested in landing at any of the main ports. All the main ports along the south coast were too well defended for such an undertaking and William understood that it could take days to unload the men and horses of his army, with even longer needed to unload the artillery and supplies. Therefore, he would need a safe landing zone that was easily

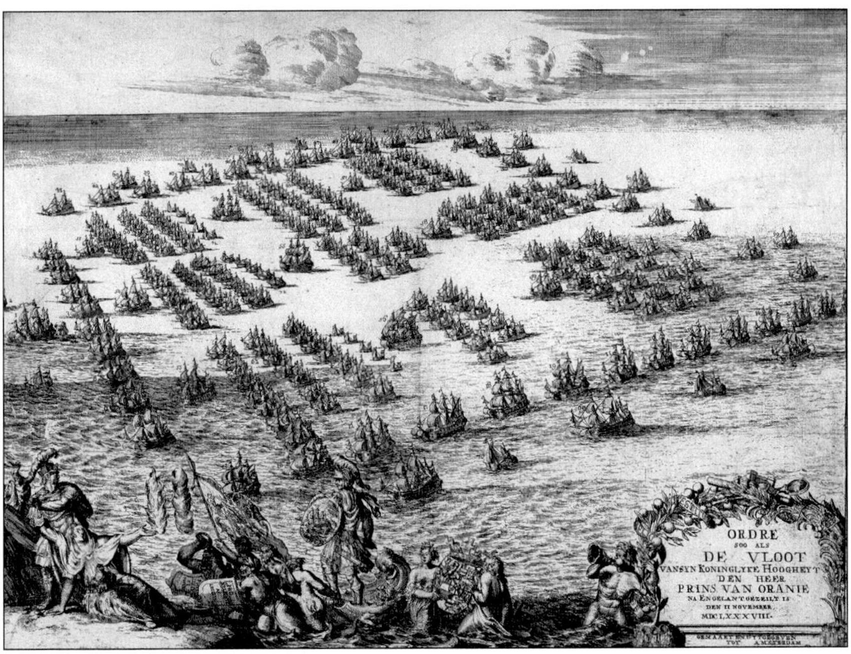

Formation of the fleet with which William III sailed to England, in a print by Adriaen Schoonebreek, Amsterdam, 1688. (Rijksmuseum: RP-P-OB-82.645A, Public Domain)

7 D. Ogg, *England in the Reign of James II and William III* (Oxford: OUP, 1957), pp.214–15.

secured and that was not defended and outside the immediate reach of English forces.

The potential landing locations included options as far north as Hull, a direct landing in London, and landing in Dover or Southampton. William Croker wrote to his father on 3 November 1688 that he believed that a fleet of 300 flat-bottomed boats filled with horses would land in the north of England.[8] William Bentinck produced a list of possible landing places for William. The documents listed the distance between towns and the number of rivers that needed to be crossed, and included notes on other difficulties.[9] The fleet transited through the English Channel on 3 November with those on board the ships spotting land, believed to be either Essex or Kent.[10] As the fleet passed between Dover and Calais, William ordered each vessel to fly all their flags and for the closest ships to the two ports to fire their guns in salute to the two towns. The people of both towns were reportedly 'amazed at the glorious sight' of the invasion fleet.[11] The fleet was reported in the *London Gazette* to be passing Dover, with the wind being described as a 'very fresh gale' from the east-north-east.[12] During the night, crew on the escorting warships reporting sighting signal fires along the English coast, alerting local towns to the fleet and presumably sending the news to London about the Dutch fleet and its imminent landing.[13] On 3 November, His Majesty's Ship *Swallow*, commanded by Captain Aymer, captured a Dutch tender and

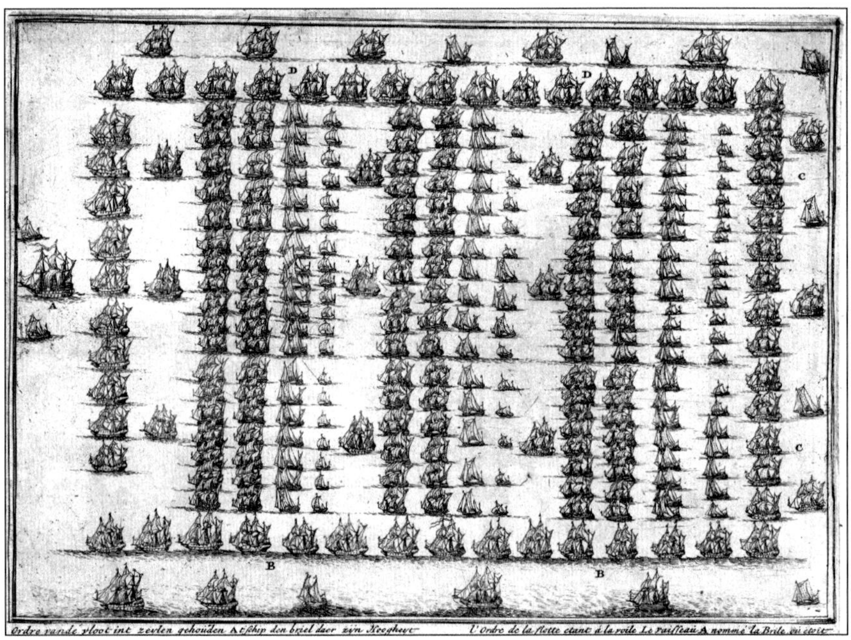

Order of the fleet with which William III sailed to England in 1688, in a print by Pieter Pickaert, Amsterdam, 1689. (Rijksmuseum: NG-1087-22, Public Domain)

8 EA: 312M/8/F/2.
9 NU: PwA2188/8.
10 Carswell, *The Descent on England*, p.167; Grew, *William Bentinck*, p.133; Anon., *An Exact Diary of the Late Expedition*, p.30.
11 Anon., *An Exact diary of the Late Expedition*, p.31.
12 *London Gazette*, Thursday, 1 November to Monday, 5 November 1688, p.2.
13 Anon., *An Exact diary of the Late Expedition*, p.32.

brought it into the Downs roadstead off the town of Deal, Kent. The ship was found to be transporting four companies of Colonel Babington's Regiment of Foot from the Anglo-Dutch Brigade.[14] These soldiers were subsequently arrested, imprisoned, and held until they were released in December 1688 following William's victory.

The fleet passed the Isle of Wight on 4 November, and although this was William's birthday and would therefore have been an auspicious day for a landing, it was not a realistic option due to the heavy fortifications of Portsmouth. Portsmouth had been on James II's list of prospective landing locations and the garrison had been strengthened by the addition of an Irish regiment and put under the command of his son, James, Duke of Berwick.[15] William, however, had chosen Torbay for the landing beach, with the fleet arriving on 5 November 1688, the anniversary of the failed Catholic plot to kill James I and to overthrow Protestant England. The invasion could not have got off to a more auspicious start, which exemplified William's propaganda and original claims that he was the saviour of Protestant England. However, this was not the planned invasion date and was in fact just a coincidence following the delay caused by the storm and the fleet having to return to Holland to undergo repairs and replace the killed and wounded horses. Had the fleet sailed on time, Whig propaganda would not have been able to link William's arrival with the Protestant holiday of defeating Guy Fawkes's plot to blow up Parliament and impose Catholic rule on the country, or the coincidence of William's arrival on his birthday.[16] As the first vessels of the fleet entered the bay, church bells were heard ringing, which was taken by

Prince William III landing, 5 (15) November 1688, in a print by Pieter Pickaert, Amsterdam, 1689. The print's caption says the landing site was Exmouth Bay rather than Torbay. (Rijksmuseum: RP-P-1939-54, Public Domain)

14 *London Gazette*, Thursday, 1 November to Monday, 5 November 1688, p.2.

15 Coleby, 'Military-Civilian Relations on the Solent', pp.959–61; Turner, *James II*, pp.409–10.

16 Wilson, 'Inventing Revolution', p.352.

the fleet as a good Protestant omen. However, they could equally have been warning of the imminent invasion, a practice that was common within the country.[17] The *Brill* entered the bay, attended by between three or four men-of-war, while the rest of the warships protected the rear of the fleet from any interference by any English vessels that might have been in the area.[18] Fear grew amongst the locals due to the unknown nationality of the large fleet anchored off Torbay, with some believing that the white division flags indicated that they were French forces invading England. However, the sight of William's large propaganda flag, which stated 'for the Protestant religion and Liberty', soon confirmed their nationality as the expected Dutch fleet.[19]

Arrival of Prince William III in England, 1688, a print by Johannes Jacobsz van den Aveele, northern Netherlands, 1691. (Rijksmuseum: RP-P-OB-82.555, Public Domain)

5 November 1688: The Landing

Whig propaganda would have people believe that the first troops to come ashore on that fateful day of 5 November 1688 were English soldiers from the Anglo-Dutch and Scots-Dutch regiments. This is indeed a fitting image for the narrative that William arrived in England as its saviour and to protect both the English people and the Protestant church from Catholicism and foreign intervention. Unfortunately, as is the norm for our understanding of these events, this was not the case. The first troops to land on the English

17 Anon., *An Exact diary of the Late Expedition*, p.34.
18 Anon., *An Exact diary of the Late Expedition*, p.36.
19 Anon., *An Exact diary of the Late Expedition*, p.34.

beaches were members of the Gardes te Voet, William's foot guards.[20] The Dutch troops disembarked from the warships anchored within the bay and, under the watchful eyes of the scared civilians on the shore, boarded ships' boats and rowed through the surf and onto the English beach. Dutch troops, in their distinctive blue uniforms with yellow cuffs and turnbacks, landed uncontested on English soil, supported by Dutch warships with their loaded guns trained on the town and bay. Nothing had ever been seen like this on English shores. The army was about twice the size of William the Conqueror's army of 1066 and would have been comparable to the size of the Spanish army if the Armada had been successful in 1588. It would have been hard for even William's English supporters to believe this to be anything other than an invasion by a foreign army. William arrived on land shortly afterwards, along with Marshal Schomberg and other senior officers, marching up towards the hill above the bay with all the pomp and circumstance of a victorious monarch, with flags flying in the wind accompanied by the sound of hautboys, trumpets, and drums.[21] Any invasion force is extremely vulnerable while they land until they have enough troops ashore to fully secure the beachhead and William would have been afraid that any English troops in the area would have been able to hold him in the bay or disrupt his landing. He was also concerned that the county militia would be raised and, at the very least, be able to disrupt his advance and supply parties. In reality, there were no troops near Torbay and the militia were not a factor during this first phase of the campaign. While various reports show that William landed at Brixham, the army would need sandy beaches to quickly land the vast number of soldiers and horses. In addition, Brixham is in effect a peninsula, cut off from Dartmouth and open country by the River Dart. William would not have wanted his army bottled up in an area without easy access to the wider countryside. The infantry regiments were the first to complete their offloading from the ships, along with William's regiment of horse guards, the Gardes du Corps. All the infantry regiments were discharged from the ships by the end of the first day. On the first night the army camped on the high ground overlooking the bay, with the Gardes te Voet camped in the primary position, as befitting their prestige and position within the army. They pitched their tents within a field surrounded by hedges and stone walls, with the Nassau Regiment camped within the adjoining field and Count Fagel's Regiment next to them.[22] The rest of the army camped in a continuing line, thus enabling a quicker departure in the morning as all the regiments were billeted in their marching order. Due to the possible threat of a counterattack, and still without any horse or artillery support (except from the ships at anchor within the bay), the army was ordered to stay at stand-to with their arms ready all through that first cold and frosty night.[23] Each regiment was allowed to send troops to forage for firewood in turn and to be allowed to make fires for warmth and to cook the food that they had arrived with. While

20 Anon., *An Exact diary of the Late Expedition*, p.37.
21 Anon., *An Exact diary of the Late Expedition*, p.37.
22 Anon., *An Exact diary of the Late Expedition*, p.39.
23 Anon., *An Exact diary of the Late Expedition*, p.39.

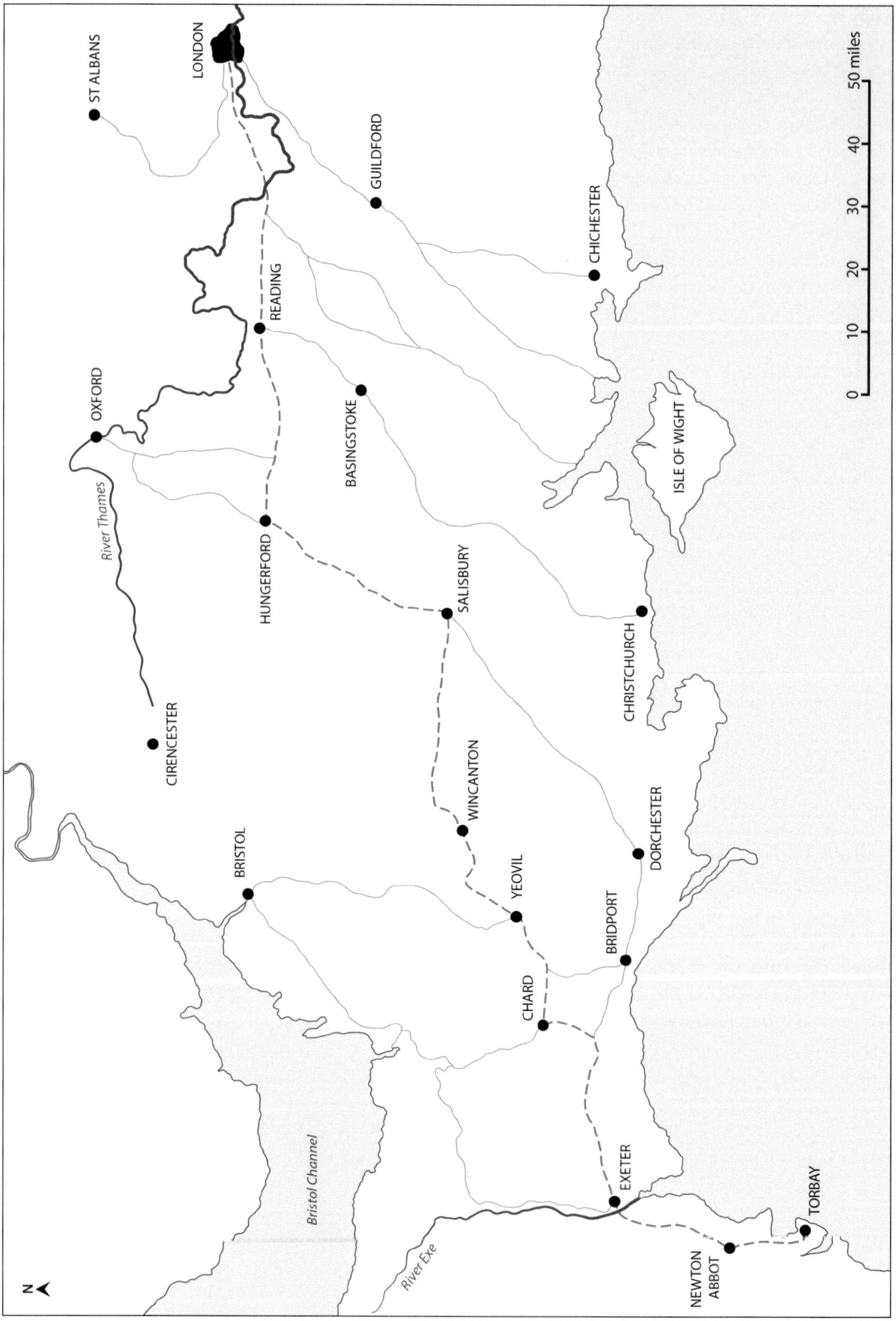

Map showing William's direction of march from his landing until he reached London. (Map ©Mark Shearwood, 2025)

the infantry regiments were standing on the hill in the cold, William, his staff, and at least one company of his guards were quartered within the fishermen's houses in the town. Despite the large numbers of foreign troops landing in such a small area, the day passed peacefully, although a number of Catholics had fled the area, and there were some false reports of muskets being fired at the prince when he arrived.[24] The invasion force included a large number of English and Scottish 'volunteers'. These included English lords who had been exiled from England and were living on the Continent, Protestant officers who had lost their commissions in the Irish army following Tyrconnell's purges, and survivors of the failed Monmouth Rebellion.[25]

6 November 1688

On the morning of 6 November William, escorted by his senior officers and his personal guard from the Gardes du Corps, rode up from his overnight accommodation within the town to review the army camped upon the hill, reviewing each regiment in turn. He then departed with his staff and escort and travelled the two miles to stay at Forde House, the home of Sir William Courtenay, outside of Newton Abbot. Courtenay had been the Member of Parliament for Devon between 1679 and 1685 and had held the rank of colonel in the Devon Militia Regiment of Horse. He was in too poor health to stand for re-election in 1688.[26] While Sir William Courtenay was willing to accommodate the prince and his staff at his house, he did not join William, give him any support, or encourage his tenants to join the Williamite expedition. However, in the week after William's stay at Forde House, two of Courtenay's sons had enlisted in William's army.[27] While William was inspecting his troops, on the beaches the operation to unload the horses was still being carried out with all speed, both due to the threat from the Royal Navy and to ensure the health of the animals. All the horses would need several days to recover from the sea journey as they were 'much out of order, and sorely bruised'. Scores of horses had died on the crossing, with these being thrown over the sides of the transport vessels.[28] The expedition had lost about 600 horses in total during the storm and crossing which would have to be replaced.[29] While the horses and the immediately required supplies were offloaded in Torbay, William ordered the artillery, along with the bulk of the ammunition and baggage, to be transported by ship to Exeter, where it would be unloaded after the army had arrived there. This decision to keep the artillery onboard, not accompanying the army, shows that William was

24 Anon., *An Exact diary of the Late Expedition*, p.37.

25 Beddard, *A Kingdom Without a King*, p.21. See BL: Add MS 41822, ff.230–31 for a full list of officers and others coming with the prince.

26 'COURTENAY, Sir William, 1st Bt. (1628-1702), of Powderham Castle and Ford House, Newton Abbot, Devon.', History of Parliament Online, < https://www.historyofparliamentonline.org/volume/1660-1690/member/courtenay-sir-william-1628-1702>.

27 'COURTENAY, Sir William.'

28 'COURTENAY, Sir William.'

29 Anon., *An Exact diary of the Late Expedition*, p.40.

far more concerned about the state of the roads and his current lack of draught animals than an immediate concern about having to face English troops or militia in battle. William had managed to gain a secure beachhead for his army, and had been allowed to dictate his own timeline rather than being forced to react to English actions. The Dutch invasion could not have had a better start, with the unopposed landing feeding into the propaganda narrative that William had arrived to protect English Protestants and to 'save the county from foreign enemies'. The ground and roads were described as 'very wet after so much rain and ill weather', which would have made them completely unsuitable for the army's heavy wagons and the heavy guns.[30] William had given orders to the army prior to its being disembarked from the ships that when in England all goods must be purchased at a fair price and nothing was to be stolen or acquired without consent.[31] These orders were to be repeated by the future Duke of Wellington prior to the British army entering Spain in 1808, when he ordered the commissariat to purchase all supplies at a fair rate and confirmed the death penalty for looting. Two Dutch soldiers were executed by hanging for stealing a chicken on 30 November 1688, as a deterrent to the rest of the army against any further thefts of English property or goods.[32] The army operated the camp for five days and during this time people from the surrounding countryside came to see both the army and William of Orange.[33] Whether the people were openly supporting William, or were just intrigued by this vast multinational force camped upon English hills, is unclear. However, the population certainly did not appear to be generally afraid of this foreign army.

7 November 1688

While some of the army stayed at the temporary camp until midday on Wednesday 10 November, the majority of the army was ordered to march to Exeter. The main part of the army left on 7 November. The order of march was set according to how the regiments were camped, with the Dutch foot guard taking the lead, followed by the Nassau Regiment, then Count Fagel's Regiment and then the English, Dutch, and Huguenot regiments, with the Scottish regiments bringing up the rear.[34] Although the army marched in three lines the progress was slow, additionally hampered by the troops being encumbered with extra equipment due to the lack of horses and the horrendous condition of the ground. While numerous locals had come to view William and the army, none had come to join, with William being disappointed that he had not been inundated with recruits from the area and from the militia, as the Duke of Monmouth had been three years earlier. He had been advised by his English supporters in the build-up to the invasion

30 Anon., *An Exact diary of the Late Expedition*, p.39.
31 Anon., *An Exact diary of the Late Expedition*, pp.37, 40.
32 Childs, *The Army, James II*, p.175.
33 Anon., *An Exact diary of the Late Expedition*, p.40.
34 Anon., *An Exact diary of the Late Expedition*, p.40.

that the men of England were just waiting and eager to join the fight against their Catholic monarch. The local population seemed to be afraid of any possible reprisals from the king and the Irish regiments with James II's army and also 'wanted no more' of conflict and the retributions inflicted on the West Country following the Monmouth Rebellion and the subsequent Bloody Assizes.[35]

When with the army, William and his staff were to be found in the prince's usual position when with his army on campaign, which was the rear of the middle column of march. The army marched through the rain into the evening and camped a few hours after the sun had set. The lanes from the coast were narrow and extremely rough, and were definitely not suited for the amount of traffic being forced down them. Although the main artillery and ammunition wagons were being transported by sea, the army still had numerous carts, wagons, and coaches with them.[36] On the night of 7 November William, his senior officers, and his personal guard billeted at Forde House, about two miles from the main camp and direction of march.[37] Despite the standing orders regarding only purchasing goods and to avoid any destruction of private property, the continued storms resulted in the troops cutting down hedges along the route of march, along with field gates and trees, for firewood both to keep themselves warm and cook their rations brought over from Holland (which consisted mainly of beef).[38] The weather and lack of tents were already taking their toll on these seasoned troops, with troops having to sleep under hedges. The following morning troops were ordered to discharge their muskets and reload them with dry powder to ensure that they would be ready in case of any contact with English troops.[39] These records give us a good idea of the issues and processes that an army on the march was required to deal with, including troops sleeping with loaded muskets on campaign and the practice of having to discharge potentially damp powder in order to clear their muskets.

The *London Gazette* reported that His Majesty's Ship *Woolwich* had captured a Dutch small pink and a Dutch fishing boat with 24 horses on board. The ships were taken below Hole Haven, which is a creek entering the River Thames between Corringham and Canvey Island.[40] The reports do not state where the Dutch vessels were captured, or if the fishing boat was just an innocent vessel caught up in hostilities. Other than this report of the captured ship, there were no reports of the invasion within the London papers, although the news had already reached the capital.

---

35 Anon., *An Exact diary of the Late Expedition*, p.41. For more on the assizes, see C. Trench, *The Western Rising: An Account of Monmouth's Rebellion* (London: Longmans, 1969) and D. Chandler, *Sedgemoor 1685: From Monmouth's Invasion to The Bloody Assizes* (Staplehurst: Spellmount, 1985).

36 Anon., *An Exact diary of the Late Expedition*, p.41.

37 Anon., *An Exact diary of the Late Expedition*, p.41.

38 Anon., *An Exact diary of the Late Expedition*, p.42.

39 Anon., *An Exact diary of the Late Expedition*, p.42.

40 *London Gazette*, Monday, 5 November to Thursday, 8 November 1688, p.2.

8 November 1688

Advanced units of the army arrived in Newton Abbot, which was crowded with people due to being market day. William's messenger read a declaration to the townspeople assembled in the market square. The declaration started that:

> William Henry, by the Grace of God, Prince of Orange, etc. Of the Reasons inducing him to appear in Arms in the Kingdom of England, for preserving of the Protestant religion, and restoring the Laws and Liberties of England, Scotland, and Ireland.[41]

These declarations were read out in each of the towns that the army passed through in order to persuade the population that this was not an invading foreign army, but here purely to defend the Protestant way of life. Meanwhile, the Reverend Dr Gilbert Burnet (18 September 1643 – 17 March 1715), who had accompanied the prince from Holland, travelled onwards into Exeter to arrange accommodation for the prince, with the cathedral deanery being chosen as the most suitable location. Reverend Burnet would later be consecrated as the Bishop of Salisbury in April 1689 and sworn in as chancellor of the Order of the Garter as a reward for his friendship and service to William. William stayed two or three nights with Courtenay, while the majority of his army spent the next two days marching the 16 miles into Exeter.[42] During the march from Paignton, the three columns of march had been further divided by the network of small lanes and each regiment was encamped within different towns or parishes. By the time that the invasion army arrived on the outskirts of Exeter, the soldiers were suffering from their exposure to the poor November weather, being described by some as having 'grown lame, and so marched slip-shod, which was irksome'.[43] Part of the army passed through Chudleigh, Devon, on 8 November and the army arrived in Exeter on 9 November 1688.

With the Dutch army close to the city of Exeter, the English army finally received orders to advance towards the enemy. Eight regiments of English cavalry received orders to leave their current quarters and march to the designated muster point for countering any invasion force advancing from the south-west. The regiments were ordered to advance to Salisbury; seven regiments were ordered to depart on 8 November, with the Queen's Regiment of Horse ordered to depart Maidenhead one day early on 7 November. Five of the regiments had been quartered in London and Westminster – these regiments were the Royal Regiment of Horse, the Earl of Peterborough's, Major-General Werdon's, the Earl of Arran's, and Colonel Hamilton's.[44]

41 Anon., *An Exact diary of the Late Expedition*, pp.43–44.
42 Anon., *An Exact diary of the Late Expedition*, p.46.
43 Anon., *An Exact diary of the Late Expedition*, p.46.
44 NA: WO55/335, f.105r.

William arriving in Exeter in a print by an anonymous print maker, northern Netherlands, 1688–89. (Rijksmuseum: RP-P-OB-82.588, Public Domain)

9 November 1688

William entered Exeter with all the fanfare his tired and exhausted army could muster. The army had only been in England for four days but needed to clean their uniforms prior to entering the city, due to the build-up of dirt and damage from the crossing and the bad weather. The first troops to enter the city were the six companies of Gardes te Paard (Gardes bleus or the Blue Guards), commanded by their colonel, Hans Willem Bentinck, and the single company of the Prince of Orange's horse guards, the Gardes du Corps, on their white horses. William had placed himself in the middle of these seven companies of horse guards, who entered the city with their colours flying, swords drawn, and with trumpets and kettle drums enthusiastically announcing their arrival. William was accompanied by some of his senior officers, including Marshal Schomberg, Count Solms, and Count Nassau, along with a number of English and Scottish officers and gentry, including the earls of Shrewsbury, Macclesfield, and Argyll, along with Colonel Sydney and Sir Rowland Guyn. The prominent position of these lords not only confirmed their status, but also sent a message that this was not a foreign invading army: it included English and Scottish troops and officers. The rest of the army followed behind the prince, although not all the army entered the city. The majority of the army was camped outside the city from Newton Abbot, and into the Teign valley at Chudleigh. This was both for tactical and logistical reasons. Exeter would not have the supplies or billets to house the entire army – normal procedure was to spread an army out in order for it not to overwhelm the local area – and tactically William needed to ensure that his army had room to manoeuvre in case of contact with the enemy.

The printing press brought over from Holland with the invasion force was set up in Exeter, along with the presses available within the town, to produce

Williamite propaganda justifying his landing and his message of freeing the English population from 'Popery and Slavery'.[45] This description of the army's arrival into the city differs in a number of aspects from the handbill later produced by William's propaganda machine and quoted in much of the literature on the Glorious Revolution. While the handbill is correct in a number of areas – for example, the prince was greeted with 'huzzas... ringing of bells... and such acclamations' – other aspects are nothing more than fantasy.[46] William was not accompanied into Exeter by 200 slaves from the Dutch West Indies, dressed in feathers and white furs, as the propaganda stated. While individual officers may well have owned slaves and even had them amongst their personal staff, there are no records of any slaves accompanying William in November 1688. Likewise, although there were troops from Switzerland and Scandinavia with the Dutch army, these were spread throughout the regiments and were not issued with bear skins and black armour, and the image of flaming swords is one straight out of myth and legends, and a direct reference to the Bible and to archangels Jophiel and Uriel.[47] The symbolism of William's troops carrying flaming swords would not have been lost on the English population: they would have clearly been able to link this imagery with ideas of divine protection and divine judgement and William's declared aim of being the protector of Protestant England. William made his way through the city to the cathedral, with soldiers armed with halberds clearing the way through the throng of citizens who had filled the streets in order to view this Prince of Orange who had entered their city at the front of a foreign army, stating that he had arrived in England to be their saviour.

William entered the cathedral and was conducted to the bishop's seat, flanked by his lifeguard. Dr Burnet, who was leading the service, read out William's declaration to the congregation, who were reportedly 'very attentive to the Doctor's reading', although a number of the attending clergy left the cathedral before the declaration was concluded.[48] Burnet used his sermon to push the message of William's divine quest to protect the English population and the Protestant religion. He recited Psalm 107, *Confitemini Domino* ('Confess to the Lord'), the second line stating, 'Let us give thanks whom the Lord hath redeemed: and delivered from the hand of the enemy.'[49] The psalm goes on to state that: 'Because they rebelled against the words of the Lord: and lightly regarded the council of the most Highest.' This clearly is referencing the fact of James II turning to the Catholic Church and rebelling against the Church of England. William's arrival in Exeter had not been welcomed by all the citizens. The Bishop of Exeter, Thomas Lamplugh, had

45 Beddard, *A Kingdom Without a King*, p.22.

46 Anon., *A True and Exact Relation of the Prince of Orange: His Publick Entrance into Exeter* (Exeter: NP, 1688); Anon., *An Exact diary of the Late Expedition*, p.47.

47 Genisis 3:24.

48 Anon., *An Exact diary of the Late Expedition*, p.48. This document gives the date as 11 November, however the first Sunday after William entered Exeter would have been Sunday, 14 November 1688.

49 B. Cummings (ed.), *The Book of Common Prayer: The Texts of 1549, 1559, and 1662* (Oxford: OUP, 2013), pp.571–73.

already departed Exeter as soon as he had confirmation of William's landing. He made his way to St James's Palace to inform the king of William's arrival.[50] On the evening of 10 November, a minister within the city was reported to have offered prayers for King James and for his son, the new Prince of Wales.

Reports arrived in Exeter of an English army heading to Salisbury comprising an estimated 35,000 men, along with a 'prodigious great train of artillery' being sent from the Tower of London, and that the king was planning to encamp the army around Sarum, where he intended to commit his army in battle.[51] Sarum, or as it is currently known, Old Sarum, is the site of an Iron Age fort on the north side of the town of Salisbury. Major-General John Fenwick, who was in charge of the defence of Gloucestershire, received orders to 'have the bridge at Canesham [Keynsham] broken down', with the lord lieutenant of the county, the Duke of Beaufort, along with his deputies, to assist him fully in all matters.[52] Keynsham is situated on the confluence of the River Chew and the River Avon and destroying the bridges there would protect the entry to Bristol. While the morale of the English army seemed to have been holding firm, at least one soldier, Henry Mason, was reported to have deserted from his regiment, Princess Anne of Denmark's Regiment of Dragoons, before being ordered to march.[53] Regiments are recorded as travelling between 4 and 14 miles each day between 9 and 12 November; however, the type and name of each regiment is not recorded. It has always been assumed that the cavalry regiments were covering the greatest distance, but for an infantry regiment to only cover 4 miles in a day shows the difficulty the army was having due to the November weather and the bad state of the road network. The surviving order of march paperwork does not always stipulate between movements that had already occurred and movements expected for that day, therefore there are always going to be differences within the interpretation of the timescale.[54] The English navy had still not engaged with the Dutch navy, with the English commander being ordered by James II on 9 November to use his discretion in engaging with the Dutch.[55]

'A True and Exact relation of the Prince of Orange His Public Entrance into Exeter,' Anon., Exeter, 1688. (Author's Collection)

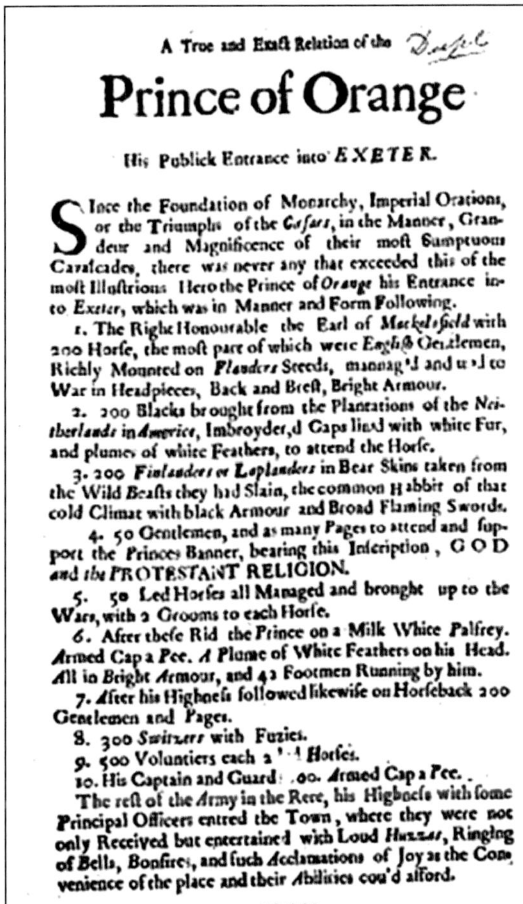
A True and Exact Relation of the

Prince of Orange

His Publick Entrance into EXETER.

SInce the Foundation of Monarchy, Imperial Orations, or the Triumphs of the *Cæsars*, in the Manner, Grandeur and Magnificence of their most Sumptuous Cavalcades, there was never any that exceeded this of the most Illustrious Hero the Prince of *Orange* his Entrance into *Exeter*, which was in Manner and Form Following.

1. The Right Honourable the Earl of *Mackelesfield* with 200 Horse, the most part of which were *English* Gentlemen, Richly Mounted on *Flanders* Steeds, mannag'd and u'd to War in Headpieces, Back and Brest, Bright Armour.

2. 200 Blacks brought from the Plantations of the *Netherlands* in *America*, Imbroyder'd Caps lin'd with white Fur, and plumes of white Feathers, to attend the Horse.

3. 200 *Finlanders* or *Laplanders* in Bear Skins taken from the Wild *Beasts* they had Slain, the common Habbit of that cold Climat with black Armour and Broad Flaming Swords.

4. 50 Gentlemen, and as many Pages to attend and support the Princes Banner, bearing this Inscription, GOD *and the* PROTESTANT RELIGION.

5. 50 Led Horses all Managed and brought up to the Wars, with 2 Grooms to each Horse.

6. After these Rid the Prince on a Milk White *Palfrey*. *Armed* Cap a *Pee*. *A* Plume of White Feathers on his Head. *All* in *Bright Armour*, and 42 Footmen Running by him.

7. *After* his Highness followed likewise on Horseback 200 Gentlemen and Pages.

8. 300 *Switzers* with Fuzies.

9. 500 Voluntiers each 2 [illegible] Horses.

10. His Captain and Guard [illegible]00. *Armed* Cap a *Pee*.

The rest of the *Army* in the Rere, his Highness with some Principal Officers entred the Town, where they were not only Received but entertained with Loud *Huzzas*, Ringing of Bells, Bonfires, and such *Acclamations* of Joy as the Convenience of the place and their *Abilities* cou'd afford.

FINIS

50 Thomas Lamplugh was made the new Bishop of York by James II on his arrival in London. He held the office under William III until his death in 1691.

51 Anon., *An Exact diary of the Late Expedition*, pp.59–60.

52 NA: SP44/97, f.15.

53 *London Gazette*, Monday, 19 November to Thursday, 22 November 1688, p.2.

54 NU: PwA 2206–2229.

55 Ogg, *England in the Reign of James II and William III*, p.215.

11 November 1688: First Action

The first skirmish of the invasion was not at Wincanton, as is normally stated, or even between the English army and the Dutch forces, but between Gloucestershire militia cavalry and English troops and gentlemen trying to defect to the Williamite forces. The skirmish happened at Cirencester, Gloucestershire, on 11 November 1688.[56] The English troops were under the command of Lord Lovelace who, along with a troop of between 70 and 100 men, some from his troop of horse, along with members of the county gentry, was on his way to defect to William of Orange.[57] Lovelace had been a long-term supporter of William and his invasion plans and had visited Holland numerous times to meet with Dutch officials, with his latest journey in September 1688.[58] The encounter on the 11th involved the Gloucestershire Militia Regiment of Horse, which had a maximum strength of 240 men and was under the command of the Duke of Beaufort and Major Loveage. Some records show Loveage with the rank of captain, although most sources state his rank as major.[59] When the militia encountered Lovelace, Beaufort and Loveage refused to believe Lovelace's story that he had been ordered to conduct a reconnaissance of the area.[60] Following what was described as a 'short, sharp engagement', the militia forced the deserting troops to either flee or surrender. During the brief engagement Major Loveage and his son were killed, along with five or six troopers, with about half a dozen more members of the militia being injured.[61] The king sent a reward to Loveage's family for their bravery as well as rewarding the surviving members of the militia.[62] Lovelace, along with thirteen members of his company, was captured by the militia with a further eight English deserters killed during the brief engagement, the rest of the company managing to retire and escape custody.[63] The numbers of deserting soldiers injured during the action is not recorded, although the king ordered that the wounded soldiers within Lord Lovelace's company should be held in Cirencester until they were able to travel. A detachment of horse and dragoons was dispatched to Cirencester to take Lord Lovelace and his thirteen companions into custody and transport them via Marlborough to Salisbury.[64] Lovelace was transferred into the temporary custody of the Duke of Beaufort at Gloucester, where he was later rescued and released from custody by a group of officers and civilians led by

56 See Harris, *Revolution*, p.295 for Wincanton being mentioned as the first skirmish.

57 NA: SP44/97, f.17.

58 Luttrell, *A Brief Relation of State Affairs*, p.464.

59 S. Lewis (ed.), *A Topographical Dictionary of England, 4 vols*, vol. 1 (London: S. Lewis, 1848), p.598.

60 NA: SP8/8, f.81

61 Childs, *The Army, James II*, p.186; Harris, *Revolution*, p.283.

62 NA: WO4/1, f.109; A. Hewitson (ed.), *Diary of Thomas Bellingham: An Officer under William III* (London: National Army Museum, 2010), pp.29–30 (Bellingham states there were thirteen English soldiers; this refers to the numbers taken prisoner, not the total number involved).

63 Luttrell, *A Brief Relation of State Affairs*, p.475; J. Miller, 'The Militia and the Army in the Reign of James II', *The Historical Journal*, 16.4 (1973), p.670.

64 NA: WO4/1, ff.109–10; NA: PC2/72, f.91.

Sir Richard Dutton. Lovelace would later enter Oxford with 300 Williamite horse on 8 December 1688 and read the Prince's declaration after destroying Magdalen Bridge.[65] William wrote to the Duke of Beaufort, pressuring him to release Lovelace and threatening to burn his home to the ground if he refused. William also imprisoned a number of English Catholics as hostages against Lovelace's release.[66]

Lord Cornbury's Regiment of Dragoons (the Royal Regiment of Dragoons) had been stationed with the English vanguard along with Princess Anne of Denmark's Regiment of Horse when Lord Cornbury and Lieutenant-Colonel Thomas Langston (Princess Anne of Denmark's Regiment) arranged between themselves to defect to William. In total, these two officers commanded almost 1,200 men. The two colonels invented fictitious orders for their respective regiments to advance towards Exeter and engage the Dutch vanguard, but with the actual intent of deserting to William with their regiments.[67] After covering the 50 miles to Axminster in under 24 hours, officers with the regiments became suspicious and, suspecting their colonel of treason, Major Robert Clifford demanded to see the regimental orders.[68] While a number of dragoon officers defected, a large body of troopers rode through the lines with Lieutenant-Colonel Langston to join the Williamite forces, while the majority of both regiments returned to Bridport, still in the service of the king.[69] Upon arriving in Bridport, the Royal Regiment of Dragoons was apparently only missing their colonel and ten men, including one lieutenant and two cornets. A number of deserters arrived in the Williamite camp in Exeter on this day, including Richard, Lord Colchester of the Fourth Troop of Horse Guards, which has been previously mistaken as only containing Catholic troops. Other troops arriving in Exeter that day included William Jephson (later

'The Army going over to ye Prince of Orange,' playing card, Anon., 1689. (Author's Collection)

65 Luttrell, *A Brief Relation of State Affairs*, pp.481, 484; J. Israel, 'General Introduction', in J. Israel (ed.), *The Anglo-Dutch Moment: Essays on the Glorious Revolution and its World Impact* (Cambridge: CUP, 2003) pp.15–16.

66 Luttrell, *A Brief Relation of State Affairs*, p.477; LOVELACE, Hon. John (c.1642-93), of Water Eaton, Oxon. And Hurley, Berks.', History of Parliament Online, < https://www.historyofparliamentonline.org/volume/1660-1690/member/lovelace-hon-john-1642-93>.

67 Anon., *An Exact diary of the Late Expedition*, p.52; Childs, *General Percy Kirke*, p.126.

68 NA: SP44/336, f.315; Childs, *General Percy Kirke*, p.127.

69 *London Gazette*, Thursday, 15 November to Saturday, 17 November 1688, p.1.

chaplain to Sir Edward Dering's Regiment of Foot) and Charles Godfrey, who would go on to later raise a regiment of horse for William in December 1688.[70]

12 November 1688

Reports reached London that the Williamite artillery had begun to be unloaded at Topsham on the estuary of the River Exe and that all of the houses within the city of Exeter were full of Dutch soldiers.[71] Williamite propaganda printed in England under the title of *A letter from a gentleman in Exeter to his friend in London* states that William's artillery train consisted of over 120 field guns, which was close to six times its actual size.[72] This letter was just one of a series that were published by either William or his supporters to undermine James II's government and proved just how effective William's propaganda campaign was. A large show of force was arranged in London following a series of riots over the previous days, with both the army and the London Trained Bands present in what was described as 'massive guards' at a number of important or vulnerable sites around the city, including Whitehall and St James's Palace, as well at several Catholic chapels.[73] The riots turned deadly on the 12th when seven or eight of the rioters were killed when soldiers opened fire on the 'rabble' as they approached Whitehall.[74] By 12 November James II had become impatient with the inaction of the Royal Navy and the seeming uncontested movement of the Dutch fleet. He ordered Dartmouth to attack the Dutch 'wherever he might find them'. However, the English fleet was still forced to shelter in the Downs due to bad weather until the 16th.[75]

15 November 1688

A group of noblemen from Devon arrived in Exeter to join William, including Lord Delamere, the earls of Devonshire and Stamford, Sir Scroop How, and Sir William Russel. While these arrivals were welcomed by the prince, the numbers of noblemen and soldiers arriving in Exeter were far less than expected, although more were on the way to join William. Lord Cornbury arrived in Exeter with the small number of his officers that had chosen to accompany him. Some reports state that Lord Cornbury arrived with about 100 dragoons from his regiment, although the exact numbers are impossible to confirm. Rather than being warmly welcomed by the Williamite forces, Langston's troopers found themselves being treated as prisoners-of-war,

70 Dalton, *English Army Lists*, vol. III, p.71; Childs, *Nobles, Gentlemen and the Profession of Arms*, p.36.
71 *London Gazette*, Monday, 12 November to Thursday, 15 November 1688, p.2.
72 Anon., *A Letter from a Gentleman in Exeter to his Friend in London* (London: NP, 1688), p.2.
73 Miller, 'The Militia and the Army', pp.475 76.
74 Miller, *James II*, p.201.
75 Ogg, *England in the Reign of James II and William III*, p.215.

with William being unsure of their loyalty and true intentions.[76] Childs puts the numbers of deserters as 100 troopers from the Royal Regiment of Dragoons and most of Princess Anne's Regiment, along with between 30 and 50 men from the Royal Horse Guards, while Smith puts the total number as 178 men.[77] These defections were expected by William, who had stationed Colonel Thomas Tollemache's Regiment of Foot from the Anglo-Dutch Brigade in Honiton in order to receive the regiments and to arrange quarters for the deserters.[78] The presumption is that the English deserters would be less intimidated by English troops and therefore these Anglo-Dutch troops would reduce the risk of any conflict between the deserters and Williamite troops. Lord Feversham arrived in Salisbury with the bulk of the English army, along with the artillery train and baggage. The army had taken longer to reach the town than expected due to the bad weather and the appalling state of the roads, with the army having to struggle through mud and ice.[79] The army would need several days to recover from the arduous conditions during their advance and to become anywhere near fit and ready to engage the Dutch army.

16 November 1688

A plot to commit regicide by Whigs and Williamite supporters was uncovered by the Earl of Middleton, with the plotters who had intended to kill James II being sent into the custody of the Keeper of Newgate Prison on 16 November.[80] The plotters included Major Ventris Colenbine and Captain Thomas Norgate, along with four lieutenants, four ensigns, and three gentlemen without rank. All were charged with the high treason.[81] The charges against all these supposed conspirators were dropped on 5 December, with the Keeper of Newgate Prison being ordered to release all the men concerned.[82] Although the plot was a complete fabrication, it does confirm the uncertainty within the country and the extreme levels of paranoia amongst the king's supporters. With reports of large numbers of senior officers deserting James, it is clear to see how easy it would have been to believe that William and his supporters could have instigated an assassination attempt. William's later actions confirmed that he had never had any intention of having his father-in-law assassinated. The actions and plans of his supporters, however, cannot be confirmed with the same certainty.

William ordered the local constables of Exeter and the surrounding countryside to go from house to house accompanied by a guard of two Williamite soldiers to assess the quality of all oxen and carriages within the parish. He was desperately short of draught animals and was in urgent need

76 Childs, *General Percy Kirke*, p.127.
77 Childs, *General Percy Kirke*, p.127; Smith, *Armies and Political Change*, p.114.
78 Childs, *General Percy Kirke*, pp.127–28.
79 Childs, *The Army, James II*, p.183.
80 NA: SP44/338, f.142.
81 NA: SP44/339, f.26.
82 NA: SP44/139, f.37.

of additional animals in order to convey his baggage train and artillery train to Honiton.[83] William proposed that any gentlemen of the parish who had teams deemed fit for service would receive the amount of 4 shillings a day for a team of four oxen, and six shillings a day for teams of six oxen. All teams should be available within the city by 20 November and the drivers would need to bring yokes and enough lanes (harnesses) for their needs.

17 November 1688

James II left Whitehall at about 3pm and travelled to Windsor with Prince George of Denmark, where he would stay the night before continuing on towards Salisbury on the morning of 18 November. James left standing instructions that in his absence the Privy Council 'shall meet for the dispatch of all affairs as occasions requires'.[84] The Earl of Abingdon is reported to have passed through Dorchester with a party of 50 horse on their way to defect to William of Orange.[85] In early November James had announced that he was willing to call a free Parliament, with elections in January, but he now summoned his council to advise them that he could no longer call Parliament due to the foreign army upon English soil.[86] Eighteen of the council members signed a petition urging the king to accept that a free parliament such as this was the only way forward for the king to avoid bloodshed and placate William and his supporters. The petition was rejected by the king. With the increasing fear of uprisings within the capital, and of attacks by 'Papists', Protestants, and Williamite fifth columnists, seven companies from the regiments of the London Trained Band were ordered to stand on duty around the city, including at the Jesuit Chapel in the Savoy.[87] London seemed to be a powder keg, with the fear of insurrection by all elements of the population, and seemed to be heading towards martial law with soldiers patrolling the city.

William reviewed the forces stationed in and around Exeter, Dutch regiments as well as the newly arrived English officers and troops that had deserted to join him. The Dutch were still concerned about the location and intentions of the English navy, with the Dutch fleet still vulnerable to attack due to its proximity to the English coast. Admiral Herbert had been keeping a watch on the English fleet and dispatched a letter from his headquarters at Torbay to William, giving details of the location of James's fleet. While Williamite forces were constrained in and around Exeter, his supporters in the Midlands were declaring cities in William's name, with Derby declaring for the prince on the 17th, Nottingham on the 20th, and York on the 22nd.[88]

---

83 NU: PwA 2251.

84 *London Gazette*, No. 2401, Saturday, 17 November to Monday, 19 November 1688, p.2.

85 Luttrell, *A Brief Relation of State Affairs*, p.476.

86 D.L. Jones, *A Parliamentary History of the Glorious Revolution* (London: HMSO, 1988), p.3.

87 Miller, 'The Militia and the Army', pp.675–76.

88 Speck, *Reluctant Revolutionaries*, p.87.

Plate A. Regiment Ginkel
(Illustration by Marco Capparoni © Helion & Company 2026)
See Colour Plate Commentaries for further information.

Plate B. Regiment s'Gravemoer
(Illustration by Marco Capparoni © Helion & Company 2026)
See Colour Plate Commentaries for further information.

Plate C. *Gardes Dragonders* (Eppinger)
(Illustration by Marco Capparoni © Helion & Company 2026)
See Colour Plate Commentaries for further information.

Plate D. Regiment Grobën
(Illustration by Marco Capparoni © Helion & Company 2026)
See Colour Plate Commentaries for further information.

Plate E. *Gardes te Voet*
(Illustration by Marco Capparoni © Helion & Company 2026)
See Colour Plate Commentaries for further information.

Plate F. Regiment Holstein-Norburg
(Illustration by Marco Capparoni © Helion & Company 2026)
See Colour Plate Commentaries for further information.

Plate G. Colonel Henry Sidney's Regiment of Foot
(Illustration by Marco Capparoni © Helion & Company 2026)
See Colour Plate Commentaries for further information.

Plate H. Colonel Hugh Mackay's Regiment of Foot
(Illustration by Marco Capparoni © Helion & Company 2026)
See Colour Plate Commentaries for further information.

18 November 1688

A number of senior members of the aristocracy and government defected to William on 18 November, either in person or by declaring their support and loyalty to the Prince of Orange. The Earl of Bath informed William on 18 November 1688 that he had defected to the prince and that he would accept all further instructions and orders from the prince rather than from James II.[89] The king's daughter, Princess Anne, sent William her 'best wishes' and informed him that her husband, Prince George of Denmark, who was one of King James's Privy Councillors, would be defecting to him.[90] The news of James's daughter and her husband defecting to William would send the king into a melancholy mood, instigate nosebleeds, and shake the king's resolve, resulting in him returning to London.

19 November 1688

James II arrived in Salisbury on the evening of 19 November 1688 in order to view the English army assembled in the area.[91] The king was described by the Earl of Middleton as being in 'perfect health' and rode on horseback on 20 November to view the country. While with the army, James II issued a number of commissions, including replacing Colonel Henry Cornwall as colonel of his regiment of foot with Colonel Oliver Nicholas.[92] In addition, James II promoted a number of senior officers within Prince George of Denmark's Regiment of Foot, including Richard Baggott to lieutenant-colonel, George Littleton to major, and William Pierson to the position of senior captain of the regiment. James II's initial plan for the English army was for the entire force of cavalry to advance and take the towns of Axminster, Chard, and Langport, which would then form a defensive line and confine the Williamite forces to the south-western counties of Cornwall, Devon, and western Somerset.[93] The king eventually failed to issue the orders for the cavalry to take the three towns. This was in part due to his growing fears regarding the loyalty of the army and the perceived risk of the cavalry regiments deserting him for William. In addition, James had been advised that William's army was already on the march and that the terrain was not suitable for cavalry, which meant that a substantial force of foot would be needed to accompany the horse to hold the ground for the king. The English navy, finally free from the storms that had disrupted its progress, arrived off Torbay with 22 ships only to find the entire Dutch fleet still at their anchorage within the bay. Dartmouth, realising that he was greatly outnumbered and outmatched, retired eastwards towards St Helen's without engaging the Dutch.[94]

89 NA: SP8/2, ff.56–7.
90 NA: SP8/2, ff.152–3.
91 Harris, *Revolution*, p.294.
92 NA: SP44/166, f.10.
93 Miller, *James II*, pp.201–02.
94 Ogg, *England in the Reign of James II and William III*, p.215.

20 November 1688: Skirmish at Wincanton

Advanced parties of the Williamite army had reached as far as the town of Wincanton by 20 November, when a forward command of 26 soldiers belonging to the Dutch army encountered elements from the English army.[95] Troops from the Scots-Dutch brigade belonging to Colonel Hugh Mackay's Regiment of Foot entered the town with orders to secure additional horses from the town for the army. The troops were commanded by the newly promoted Lieutenant Campbell, who had been informed by some of the townspeople of Wincanton that an advanced element of the English army was approaching the town.[96] Campbell then ordered his detachment into defensive positions in order to ambush the English patrol. The English troops consisted of about 70 troopers from the Fourth Troop of Horse Guards, 50 troopers from the Fourth Troop of Horse Grenadiers, and 50 men from the Royal Consort, The Queen's Regiment of Dragoons.[97] The English detachment was under the command of Lieutenant and Lieutenant-Colonel Patrick Sarsfield, with the grenadiers commanded by Lieutenant Henry Luttrell and the dragoons by Cornet John Webb.[98] The Dutch troops took up their defensive positions and prepared an ambush between Flingers Lane and Ireson Lane, to the north of the town. Twenty men were stationed behind a hedge to protect them from view of the advancing cavalry; in the corner of the field was a gate and a weaker dead hedge. A small detachment of six men had been stationed within a garden on the opposite side of the road, with the troops protected from the cavalry by another hedge. The Dutch troops allowed the English cavalry to advance down the lane until they came within musket range of the troops in their ambush positions. Unsure whether the troops were friendly to William, Lieutenant Campbell issued a verbal challenge rather than ordering his men to open fire. The confusion regarding the loyalty of these advancing troops was due to instances of English soldiers deserting to the Dutch army, as men of Lord Cornbury's Regiment of Horse had done in the preceding days.

Campbell moved from his position behind the hedge and into the line of sight of the advancing English cavalry, shouting out 'Stand, stand, for who are ye for?' Patrick Sarsfield as commander of the English troops replied to the challenge by answering, 'I am for King James, who art thou for?' Campbell replied by stating, 'I am for the Prince of Orange,' to which Sarsfield replied, 'God damn you! I'll Prince thee!' At this moment Campbell ordered the Dutch troops to open fire, with fire being immediately returned by the mounted English troops. The first casualty of the engagement was the commander of the Dutch troops, Lieutenant Campbell, who was shot

95 Anon., *An Exact diary of the Late Expedition*, p.50.

96 BL: Add MS 28053, f.355; P.A.C. Wauchope, *Patrick Sarsfield and the Williamite War* (Dublin: Irish Academic Press, 1993), p.37. Lieutenant Campbell had spent 12 years as a sergeant within the regiment and had only recently been promoted to the rank of lieutenant.

97 The numbers of troops varied depending on the source; *An Exact diary of the Late Expedition* (p.56) states that there were 150 English troops and not 120, as quoted in most secondary sources. Wauchope, *Patrick Sarsfield*, p.37.

98 BL: Add MS 75392, f.2; SP44/164, ff.256, 326.

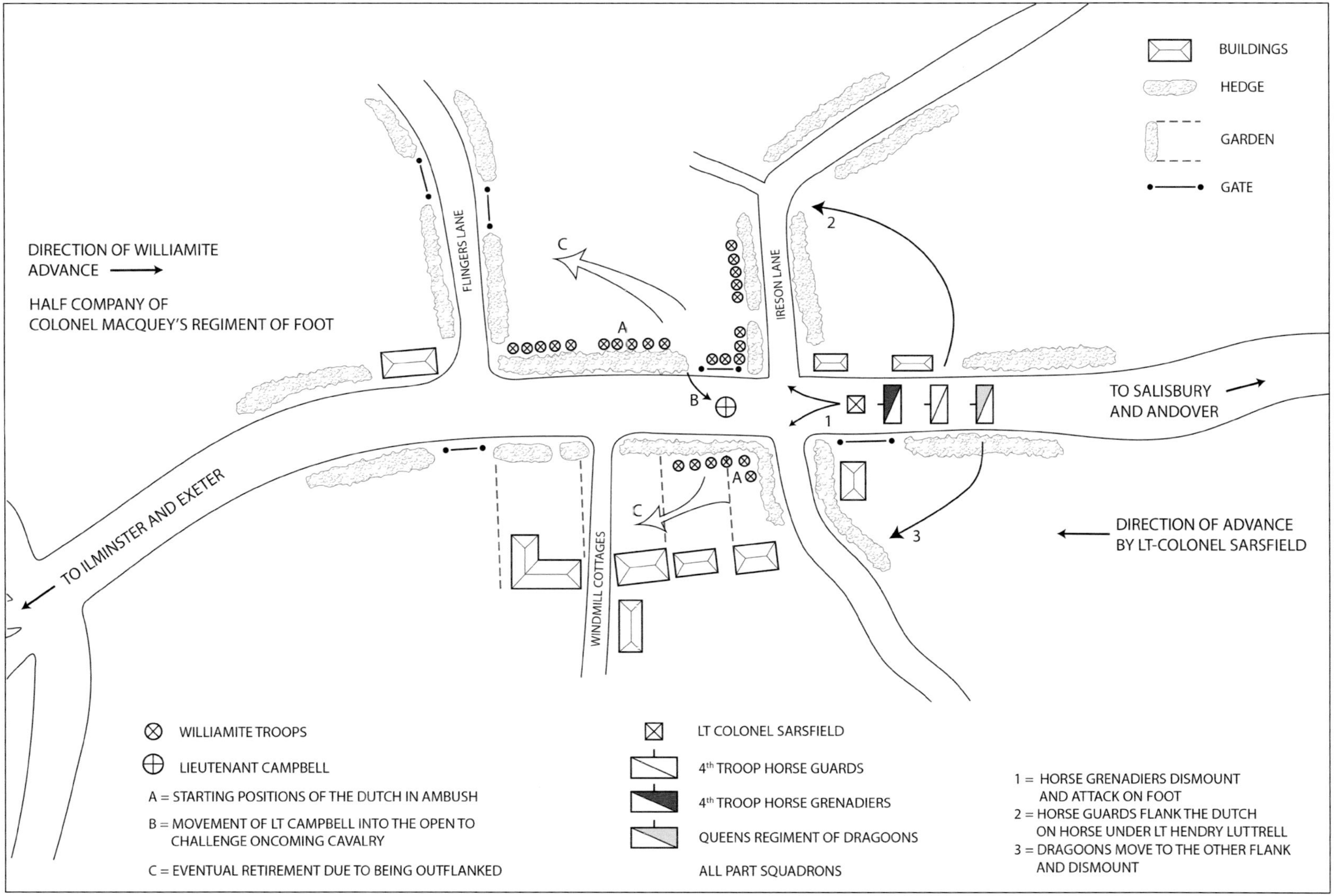

The action at Wincanton, 20 November 1688

in the head and died instantly.[1] Although the Dutch troops had lost their commanding officer, they held their ground as they were experienced troops, having served at Loo, Nijmegen, Spankeren, and Brabant in the previous three years. The opening volley from the Dutch troops killed and wounded several English troops, forcing the English horsemen to dismount and find cover. While both the Dutch and English troops were armed with muskets and swords or bayonets, the horse grenadiers were also armed with hand grenades for use in close assaults against enemy infantry and positions. The English troops regrouped after the first volley and fought on foot, returning the Dutch fire and throwing grenades at the Dutch troops within their defensive position. Under cover of the firefight and frontal assault, Sarsfield ordered Lieutenant Henry Luttrell to take some of the troopers that were still mounted and outflank the main Dutch force defending the hedge lines, breaking through the hedges in the upper end of the field.[2] The Dutch troops knew that they were badly outnumbered, fighting five times their numbers, but they continued to hold their defensive position. They would have known that it was only a matter of time before the English cavalry outflanked them, cutting off their retreat, and negated the advantage of their defensive position.[3] Even knowing that they could be outflanked at any time, the remaining soldiers of Mackay's regiment refused an offer to surrender and even the English troops recognised that they had defended themselves as well as they possibly could 'for such a handful against so many' enemy.[4] In the end the Dutch troops were saved from being overrun, not by additional Williamite troops coming to their aid, but by the local miller, who falsely advised Sarsfield that he had overtaken a 'strong force of cavalry belonging to the Prince of Orange' who were just about to enter the town, shouting, 'The Dutch! The Dutch!' and 'Away with your lives!'[5] Hearing this news, Sarsfield ordered the English troops to withdraw from the town, resulting in a technical victory for the Williamite forces, although they had lost over half of their force, with six men captured and a total of 12 men including Lieutenant Campbell killed in the engagement.[6] Patrick Sarsfield's command lost at least 15 soldiers killed during the action and a greater number injured. Included in the injured was Cornet John Webb of the Queen's Regiment of Dragoons, who would later change his allegiance from James II to William III and accept a commission as captain in the First Regiment of Foot Guards in William's reformed English army in April 1689.[7] The dead soldiers were buried within two mass graves, one containing the 15 soldiers who had died for James II and a smaller grave for the eight Dutch soldiers who had died during the skirmish, the remainder of the Dutch dead dying later from their wounds.[8] Reports in the *London Gazette* stated that the English forces had

1 Anon., *An Exact diary of the Late Expedition*, p.57.
2 Wauchope, *Patrick Sarsfield*, p.38.
3 Anon., *An Exact diary of the Late Expedition*, p.58.
4 Anon., *An Exact diary of the Late Expedition*, p.58.
5 Anon., *An Exact diary of the Late Expedition*, p.50; Wauchope, *Patrick Sarsfield*, p.38.
6 Anon., *An Exact diary of the Late Expedition*, p.50.
7 SP44/164, f.164; SP44/165, f.150; Dalton, *English Army Lists*, vol. III, p.42.
8 Anon., *An Exact diary of the Late Expedition*, p.59.

only lost four soldiers killed and two wounded, including Cornet Webb, who was stated incorrectly to have been mortally wounded.[9] Harris mentions a follow-up action where the Duke of Schomberg refused to offer quarter to English troops encountered on the outskirts of Dorchester, resulting in the Williamite forces killing 53 English soldiers.[10] Harris's is the only account of this 'massacre of English troops', in which the wording suggests that the English troops were trying to surrender to the Williamite forces when they were killed. The author has been unable to find any further mention of the Dorchester incident, either in any of the references quoted by Harris or in any other letters, journals, broadsheets, or documents. The only reasonable conclusion is that the 'Dorchester incident' is a rare occasion of pro-James II propaganda intended to vilify the Williamite forces. This, however, was not anywhere near successful as the Williamite 'scare tactics', including the infamous 'Irish Fright' of December 1688.

When the news of the skirmish reached Exeter, William ordered his staff to obtain as many extra wagons and horses as possible and to purchase them from both the city merchants and from the farmers in the surrounding area. Normal practice with any army on the march was for local farmers and drovers to be employed to drive the army's wagons and oxen, with two companies of foot being detached from the main army as a wagon guard. The guard, comprising about 100 soldiers, was commanded by a captain, and presumably also had at least one lieutenant and ensign. The troops within the city were put on alert and ordered to keep themselves and their arms in good order in case the skirmish was an indication of the English army going on the offensive, with William's personal guard being increased as a precaution.[11] William arranged for supplies for the army to be purchased from local traders. The sudden activity does seem to suggest that William was not expecting any encounters with the English army, or that he had been focused on holding the audience within Exeter and not on the surrounding area or the military situation. William was forced to leave a large quantity of supplies in Exeter as he was unable to purchase or hire the required number of draught animals and left the city with a Williamite garrison. All of the Anglo-Dutch and Scots-Dutch regiments were able to recruit replacements while in Exeter and were able to continue the campaign at full strength.[12] It is unclear how many recruits were needed and if they all came from the civilian population, or if they were experienced solders who had previously served with the county militia or were defecting English soldiers. Two new English regiments were recruited for William, Sir John Guye's Regiment of Foot and Sir Robert Peyton's Regiments of Foot, both of which were reportedly recruiting up to full strength.

The Earl of Bath handed over the Royal Citadel of Plymouth to the Prince of Orange on 20 November 1688, with Edward Russell and Lord

9 *London Gazette*, Thursday, 22 November to Saturday, 24 November 1688, p.2.

10 Harris, *Revolution*, p.295.

11 Anon., *An Exact diary of the Late Expedition*, p.50.

12 Anon., *An Exact diary of the Late Expedition*, p.50.

Leven's regiment taking the citadel's surrender.[13] In a letter received by the prince a week later, the earl states that he had dismissed all 'Popish' officers and soldiers from the garrison and imprisoned the colonel of the regiment stationed within the city, the Earl of Huntingdon. The regimental command was given to Ferdinando Hastings, who had been the lieutenant-colonel of the regiment, who was described as 'who deserves extremely well for his great zeal, fidelity and prudent conduct in your service'.[14] The letter confirms that all the 'Protestant' officers were convened on 23 November and after the earl read the prince's declaration, all the officers and men declared for the Prince of Orange and that without any bloodshed the Royal Citadel of Plymouth, the island of St Nicholas, and Pendennis Castle had been secured for His Highness.[15] The officers and soldiers of the Plymouth garrison deserted James II and declared their loyalty to William after listening to his Declaration of Reason being read aloud, followed by them throwing up their hats and shouting 'huzzah'; similar events also happened at nearby Falmouth.[16] In addition to controlling the citadel, the Royal Navy ship *Newcastle*, a fourth-rater commanded by Captain George Churchill (1654–1710), after entering Plymouth harbour supposedly to 'undergo repairs', declared for the prince after hearing the news regarding the fall of the port.[17] Churchill, the brother of Lord Churchill, was also a member of the Treason Club, so it is uncertain whether the reason for arriving in Plymouth was for actual repairs or an excuse to declare for William without raising the suspicions of his officers or crew. Viscount Cornbury attempted to defect to William with three regiments of horse that departed Salisbury and marched through Dorchester towards Axminster. The regiments believed they were following legitimate orders to advance towards the enemy, but when it became apparent that the senior officers were actually attempting to defect with the regiment, most of the troops returned to Salisbury.[18]

21 November 1688

The Earl of Middleton reported in a letter to Lord Preston that King James had suffered three or four occasions of 'blooding of the nose' on the afternoon of 19 November, which resulted in the king taking to his bed with an herbal remedy.[19] The king was reported to have woken in good health but had decided not to travel to Warminster to inspect the forward elements of the army. Reports reached the king's party that day regarding the skirmish that

---

13 Carswell, *The Descent on England*, p.194.

14 NA: SP8/2, f.58.

15 NA: SP8/2, ff.58–59.

16 L. Schwoerer, 'Propaganda in the Revolution of 1688-89', *The American Historical Review* (82.4), p.856.

17 The *Newcastle* was commissioned in 1653 as a 44-gun fourth-rater, but later had her armament increased to 54 guns in 1677. George Churchill served as a Lord Commissioner of the Admiralty between 1699 and 1702.

18 Hewitson, *Diary of Thomas Bellingham*, p.30.

19 NA: SP44/97, f.19.

had happened the previous day in Wincanton, which resulted in Middleton stating that, 'The war is prosperously begun, I pray God the end may answer it.'[20] This statement by Middleton is the first mention that England, or at least the ruling elite, believed the country to be at war with William and, by default, with the state of Holland. William stayed within the city of Exeter until 21 November; this stay of twelve days has always seemed strange to some historians as it allowed James II to organise his army. However, there are a number of reasons for this delay, including William waiting for the expected large numbers of soldiers from the standing army and militia, along with volunteers from the gentry and general population. This large-scale influx of new soldiers never happened at Exeter, or any other location. The other main reason for the delay was to give his army time to recover from the crossing and the appalling weather since they arrived. William set up in the Blue Maid's Hospital (now the Maynard School on Denmark Road, Exeter), with 156 men being initially admitted to the hospital.[21] Two-thirds of the men listed were identified as coming from Holland or Gelderland, but the records also show soldiers from Brandenburg, England, Flanders, France, Germany, Greece, Poland, Prussia, Scotland, Sweden, and Switzerland. Most men were recorded as being admitted for fevers or violent coughs, presumably as a result of the combination of the conditions on board the ships and the bad English weather. Many of the patients were not well enough to depart with the army as it left Exeter in late November, with most being discharged by early January 1689. At least twelve succumbed to their illness and died at the hospital, including: James Clements, 24, from Scotland, Martin Falke, 58, from Prussia, and Jacob Justus, 40, from Holland from consumption; and Joris Hallerton, 25, and Isaac Kanenbergh, 17, both from Holland, due to fever. The patient records both confirm the range of nationalities of the soldiers within William's army and the wide range of their ages. On 21 November William departed Exeter and resumed the march towards London. Orders were given for the army to march in three columns, with the first column marching as far as St Mary Ottrie and being quartered for the night in and around the village. William travelled from Exeter to Honiton with elements of Dutch cavalry, covering a distance of just over 17 miles.[22]

22 November 1688

On the morning of 22 November 1688, the first Williamite column marched into Axminster, where they were joined by William, while the second column continued its march to St Mary Ottrie.[23] The Dutch troops were still suffering on the march and having to deal with the constant rain and bad

20 NA: SP44/97, f.19.

21 P.M.G. Russell, *A History of the Exeter Hospitals, 1170-1948* (Exeter: Exeter Post-Graduate Medical Centre, 1976); Historical Manuscripts Commission, *Report on the Records of the City of Exeter* (London: His Majesty's Stationery Office, 1916), pp.219–24.

22 Anon., *An Exact diary of the Late Expedition*, p.53; NA: SP44/97, f.22; NU: PwA 2235.

23 Anon., *An Exact diary of the Late Expedition*, p.53; NU: PwA 2235.

weather. Troops were marching along flooded roads, wading in water up to their knees for up to half an hour at a time, only to be billeted in 'very poor quarters' when they reached the town.[24] James II's health was still of concern to his closest advisers, who believed that the king was still overworking himself, inducing 'so much toil that it might prove prejudicial to his health'. The Earl of Middleton reported in his letter to Lord Godolphin that the king had had two further instances of bleeding a little from his nose.[25] Middleton continued to state that the king had been seen by his doctors and that they believed these issues have been caused by 'a ferment of the blood' caused by 'too constant and anxious application to business'.[26] Middleton confirmed to Lord Preston that most of the English foot regiments, as well as the majority of the artillery, had started to move from their current positions towards Salisbury and the enemy.[27] Sir John Talbot's Regiment of Horse was ordered to march for Farnham on 22 November; the order specifically stated that they were to bring their armour with them.[28] A hundred troopers from the Royal Regiment of Dragoons were ordered to be diverted from the regiment's march to Salisbury to head towards Portsmouth to guard the king. Danby, who had been one of the 'Immortal Seven' and who had also declared that he was going to raise a regiment of foot for James, instead seized the city of York for William on 22 November and declared for a free parliament. He also declared York for the Protestant religion and that it was free of 'popery'.[29] The king, along with his senior commanders, held their daily council of war, where James decided not to stand and fight William at Salisbury, but for the English army to retire towards London.[30]

23 November 1688

Colonel Hans Willem Bentinck advanced with 1,200 horse and dragoons, including elements from the Gardes te Paard and the Gardes Dragonders (also known as Eppinger Dragoons), towards the town of Sherborne on the way to Wincanton.[31] As the vanguard entered the town from the south-west, elements of English horse were entering the town from the other direction.[32] The English troops were, however, not willing to engage the larger Dutch force and, having located the direction of march of one column of William's force, retired back towards Sarum, Salisbury, and the safety of the main English army. The English army was still not sure of the intended direction of the main element of the Williamite army, there still being a possibility that William intended to capture the port city of Bristol. Capturing Bristol

24 Grew, *William Bentinck and William III*, p.141.
25 NA: SP44/97, f.21.
26 NA: SP44/97, f.21.
27 NA: SP44/97, f.22.
28 NA: WO4/1, f.114.
29 Harris, *Revolution*, p.285.
30 Turner, *James II*, p.430.
31 NU: PwA 2235. (This move by Bentinck is sometimes quoted as happening on 24 November.)
32 Anon., *An Exact diary of the Late Expedition*, p.54.

would give the invading army access to the military stores held within the city as well as giving access to a deep-water port. Bristol would also be an ideal base for further operations towards the Midlands and Wales.[33] Most of the English foot and artillery was still in the camp at Salisbury on the morning of the 23rd and broke camp prior to midday, departing with the intention of following the king's orders to return to defend London. Lord Churchill's grenadier company, which had been located with the forward elements of the English army in Warminster, was reported to have deserted the king and defected to William. Colonel Maine of the Third Troop of Horse Guards received orders to pursue the deserting troops and bring them back before they could reach Williamite positions. [34] A high level of uncertainty and suspicion permeated the English army and within James II's inner circle of advisers. Middleton was unsure of Maine's actual intention: was he actually trying to stop English troops from deserting to the enemy or could his pursuit be a clever subterfuge, with his real intentions to join Colonel Maine and defect to William, while covering the defectors' flank from other English troops trying to intercept them. There is no doubt that the defection of 23 November had a major impact on James's confidence in his ability to trust, with three of his closest and most trusted advisers and family members all defecting. These included his nephew, the Duke of Grafton, and his son-in-law Prince George of Denmark. In addition, Lord Churchill had been reported missing from Winchester and was also believed to have defected to William along with a whole brigade of foot. Churchill left a letter for James II explaining the reasons for his defection, concluding it that he was 'His Majesty's most obliged servant'. This was more to do with the correct etiquette for signing off a letter to a monarch than showing the king his loyalty.[35] The brigade that was suspected incorrectly of defecting consisted of three regiments: Her Majesty the Queen Dowager's Regiment of Foot (commanded by Colonel Percy Kirke), Her Majesty the Queen Consort's Regiment of Foot (Commanded by Colonel Charles Trelawney), and the Queen's Regiment of Dragoons, along with part of the Third Troop of Horse Guards. There was a supposed plot to kidnap the king and hand him over to William along with these three regiments. Middleton confirmed to Lord Preston that when James II had been planning to leave Salisbury for Warminster he was due to meet with Lord Churchill and inspect the regiments of Kirke and Trelawney and that the king's nosebleeds had saved him from being seized by the defectors.[36] The plan to kidnap the King included Colonel (Ambrose) Norton and Captain (Cornelius) Wood of the Second and Third Troops of the Life Guard, who were both outriders to the king's carriage and were implicated in a plot of regicide if loyal forces attempted to rescue the king.[37] Churchill was also implicated within this plot, which might help explain William's distrust of him during the following year and his general exclusion from operations

33 NA: SP44/97, f.22.

34 NA: SP44/97, f.23.

35 R. Holmes, *Marlborough: England's Fragile Genius* (London: Harper Press, 2008), p.152.

36 NA: SP44/97, f.23.

37 Wauchope, *Patrick Sarsfield*, p.40.

in Ireland. The plot to kill James II, if true, would not have been instigated by William, who was well aware that the belief the divine right of kings was still prevalent within England. William would have been mindful that if James II had been assassinated by his supporters, it might have had the effect of uniting the country (including the army) against him and forcing the country into an unwanted civil war. James's continued uncertainty was compounded by numerous and often unsubstantiated rumours of officers and men deserting him for William. Having originally ordered all foot to march to London, James II ordered Kirke along with Trelawney and all the remaining foot still at Warminster to march to East Lavington in order to prevent any surprise attack by the enemy.[38] Most of the officers, along with approximately 200 solders, from Charles Trelawney's battalion deserted the regiment on 24 November, leaving Major Zachariah Tiffin in charge of the regiment, supported by one captain and the lieutenants and ensigns from six of the companies.[39] One of the reasons for the large numbers of officers and men deserting from Trelawney's regiment compared with other regimental desertions was the number of the regimental officers who were members of the Treason Club. They also belonged to the group known as the 'Tangier Club', officers who had served together in Tangier and who had developed close social ties as well as political bonds.[40] A large number of the soldiers within the regiment were veterans of the Tangier campaign and had developed a close relationship with their officers. It would have also allowed the officers to understand the underlying loyalties of their men.

James II convened a council of war where he decided that the army should retire over the River Thames to Reading. Orders were given to ensure that all regiments were to avoid using the Basingstoke Road, as this route had been designated exclusively for the artillery to use.[41] The artillery received orders to march 'in such manner and with such rest as you shall see fit' in order to take sufficient care of the train while on the road. The army's order and morale had deteriorated dramatically since their march to Salisbury. Reports of a 'great disorder' committed by the Royal Regiment of Fusiliers on their march from Salisbury to London resulted in orders given on 23 November for the officers of the regiment to be called in for questioning regarding the events and their lack of discipline within the regiment.[42] While this episode seems isolated, it does confirm the breakdown of discipline within the English army. The troops had first been ordered to march towards the enemy, with the real prospect of having to engage with a well-disciplined and experienced enemy force, and then subsequently been ordered to retire without making a stand. The foot guards were ordered to be stationed at or near Whitehall in London in preparation for the arrival of the king while the train of artillery was ordered to continue its march towards London.[43] The English regiments of

38 NA: WO4/1, f.110.

39 Dalton, *English Army Lists*, vol. II, p.27; Childs, *General Percy Kirke*, pp.130–31.

40 Smith, *Armies & Political Changes*, p.108.

41 NA: WO4/1, f.111; Harris, *Revolution*, p.295.

42 NA: WO4/1, f.113.

43 NA: WO4/1, f.113.

horse and dragoons were ordered to shadow the Williamite forces but to keep out of immediate range of the enemy. It is unclear if this order was designed to reduce the possibility of the regiments suffering unnecessary casualties or to reduce the chance of any troopers or officers deserting to the enemy. The increased number of desertions by English troops to William forced the king to issue a proclamation pardoning all English subjects that had taken arms up against him, providing that they returned to his service within twenty days.[44] The proclamation also offered pardons and protection to all foreign nationals that left the service of William and joined James II's cause.

Meanwhile, the Dutch fleet was reported to be running low on supplies as it was still being kept on station off the English coast, with the Dutch admiral remaining in Torbay. William arranged for as many supplies to be sent to the fleet as he could spare, which comprised 165 barrels of biscuits, 141 hogsheads of beer and 14 barrels of brandy. Lord Bath and the Governor of Exeter gave assurances that further provisions would be sent to the Dutch fleet.[45] The exact location of the English fleet was not known to the Dutch but Admiral Herbert suspected that it was being held to the east of the Isle of Wight.

24 November 1688

The persistent fears of Catholic massacres and atrocities resurfaced throughout the City of London and the surrounding areas when rumours spread about guns being trained upon Protestant London. The rumours were instigated by the actions of the Catholic Governor of the Tower of London, Sir Edward Hales, who had removed mortars from the Ordnance stores and placed them within the Tower and had them trained upon the city. Rumours spread through the city that Hales intended to use the artillery not to defend London, but against the Protestant houses and population surrounding the Tower in an act of revenge against the population and their support for William. Hales, in reality, was probably just preparing to defend the fortress from any approaching Williamite army and from any civilian attack against the Tower. While this may have been a legitimate military action in preparing the defences of the fortress, the optics of training artillery on London when it was in a state of fear caused both alarm in the city and anger from the king. Hales had ordered the placement of the mortars without the king's permission and he was dismissed from his post as governor three days later on 27 November 1688.[46]

The entire Williamite field army was on the march towards London and due to both its size and the state of the road network, it was forced to take three roughly parallel routes and was spread over a vast swathe of the English countryside. The army is recorded as being billeted in 21 towns and villages on the night of the 23rd. Wherever possible, Williamite commanders spread the

44 Luttrell, *A Brief Relation of State Affairs*, p.478.
45 Grew, *William Bentinck and William III*, p.141.
46 Miller, 'The Militia and the Army', p.475.

accommodation requirements of the army over as large an area as possible to enable the troops and horses to obtain enough supplies without stripping the countryside completely of food and animal fodder. The extended disposition of the Williamite army would suggest that William and his generals were not concerned about any immediate attack by the English army.

25 November 1688

The rumours regarding the defection of colonels Kirke and Trelawney on 23 November had been proved to be unfounded. While both colonels were indeed members of the Treason Club, secretly supported William, and would eventually defect to over the prince, both officers were confined to their quarters in Warminster on 24 November. Colonel Theophilus Oglethorpe confirmed the news to Middleton when he arrived in Andover on the morning of 25 November.[47] Oglethorpe held the rank of colonel in the Holland Regiment of Foot and in the First Troop of Horse Guards as well as brigadier of all forces and was fiercely loyal to James II – he would eventually follow James II into exile in France.[48] Oglethorpe confirmed that the actual number of desertions was far less than originally reported, with only some of the missing men actually defecting to William. The majority of enlisted soldiers deserting their regiments during this period never actually re-enlisted in the Williamite forces but decided not to serve in either army. Figures provided by Oglethorpe show that only 30 enlisted men had deserted to William – 20 dragoons and 10 grenadiers – although another nine officers from Colonel John Berkeley's Regiment of Dragoons had also deserted on the same day. The officers were Colonel Berkeley, as well as four of his captains, one lieutenant, and three ensigns. Apart from the men defecting to William, an additional 10 grenadiers had apparently deserted the army overnight but without any apparent intention of fighting for William. This information regarding the intent of deserting soldiers was obtained by speaking with soldiers within their companies and troops. Although there had been confusion regarding the numbers of enlisted men who had defected to William, it was confirmed by Oglethorpe that both the Duke of Grafton and Lord Churchill had broken their oaths to the king and defected to the enemy. New suspicion fell upon Churchill's troop of horse guards and grenadiers, with orders sent by Middleton to arrest two of his lieutenants, John Cole and Fraser Rogers, along with the clerk of the troop.[49] James II issued Lord Lichfield with a new commission giving him command of the foot guards in place of the now disgraced Duke of Grafton while Colonel Thomas Maxwell

47 NA: SP44/97, f.24

48 NA: SP44/165, f.137; SP44/166, ff.148, 405; Anon., *A View of the Court of St Germain: Since the Year 1690 with an Account of the Entertainment Protestants meet with there* (Dublin: Andrew Cook, 1696), p.8; F. Wright, *The Layburnes and their World Circa 1629-1729, The English Catholic Community and the House of Stuart*, Unpublished doctoral thesis, University of St Andrews, 2002, p.205.

49 NA: SP44/97, f.25.

was promoted from lieutenant-colonel of Berkeley's Regiment of Dragoons to colonel of the regiment.

Most of William's cavalry and dragoons were stationed around the towns of Crewkerne and Sherborne, with the infantry battalions between Over Compton, Nether Compton, Mudford, and Marston. For a full order of the Williamite order of march, please see Appendix II.

26 November 1688

After being originally cleared by Oglethorpe of attempting to defect to William, Trelawney and all his officers deserted James on the 26th and defected to William, along with most of the officers of Cannon's Regiment of Dragoons.[50] These desertions brought Kirke's name back to prominence; Middleton again questioned whether his loyalty was to the Williamite cause rather than to James. In order to ascertain Kirke's loyalty, Middleton ordered the Earl of Feversham to arrest Kirke on 26 November and to arrange transport for him to Whitehall, where he was required to answer the charges directly before the king.[51] The order shows that even at this stage of the invasion, Kirke's loyalty was still very much in question; the main evidence against him at this time was his close association with Churchill and Trelawney (which would later be shown to be correct). The warrant therefore states that 'yet he is to be used with all civility and his baggage permitted to come along with him and no convenience to be denied him'.[52] Kirke would be acquitted of all charges and released from custody in early December.[53] The king informed Lord Feversham that he was departing in his coach for London on Friday 26 November; he also ordered Feversham to ensure that there was enough money available in Maidstone for when the army arrived.[54] James II learned that his daughter Princess Anne had left her residence and was planning on joining her husband, Prince George, who was currently with William of Orange. The King was reported to be in 'perfect health' on his arrival in London.[55] William spent the day on the road and covered almost 13 miles before stopping for the night in Crewkerne.

27 November 1688

On Monday 27 November William had marched as far as Sherborne, with the first line of the Dutch army as far west as Wincanton, a mere 37 miles from the main English army camped at Salisbury.[56] While the advanced

50 NU: Pw A 2235.
51 NA: SP44/338, f.145.
52 NA: SP44/338, f.145.
53 Luttrell, *A Brief Relation of State Affairs*, p.483.
54 NA: WO4/1, f.112.
55 *London Gazette*, Monday, 25 November to Thursday, 29 November 1688, p.2.
56 The 25th, according to *An Exact diary of the Late Expedition*, p.55.

elements of William's army had reached as far as Wincanton, the majority of the army was spread over too large a geographical area to even think about engaging the English army at this point. In addition, the distance between the two armies, even at its closest point, was still a three to four-day march based on the current weather conditions, along with the state of the road network, and the fatigue of the Dutch army.

While William was arriving in Sherborne, back in Whitehall James II had summoned an expanded Privy Council, with around forty peers. During the meeting James was advised by his councillors that he needed to summon a 'free parliament, grant a general pardon for all those currently in arms against the king', to adhere to the terms of the treaty of Nijmegen, to dismiss all Catholics from office (both military and civil) and to send a commission to William.[57] While the majority of these proposals were seemingly acceptable to James, he was fervently against the notion of dismissing all English Catholics from service. The commission would consist of Halifax, Nottingham, and Godolphin and would travel to William with the king's amended proposal, stating that he would call a parliament on 15 January 1689; the proposal also called for the immediate cessation of armed conflict.[58] While William's declared intention was to persuade James to summon parliament and to direct England onto a more 'Protestant path' under his rule, he could never accept the king's proposals. William's reputation, along with his ability to defeat Louis XIV's France, depended on his ability to dictate the actions of the English army and navy by becoming England's monarch.

28 November 1688

James II took the extraordinary step of ordering the Earl of Craven to publish the Articles of War in a number of broadsheets as well as in handbills. James also ordered all the troops under his command to retake the Oath of Fidelity to the king.[59] This had been the second time that the king had requested this, as he had ordered the entire English army when it was at Salisbury, waiting to engage William, to reconfirm their oaths of fidelity and loyalty. While at Salisbury, the act was accomplished by each regiment laying down and then picking up their arms; the distrust in late November resulted in the Oath having to be said aloud. The act of laying down arms was the equivalent of a solder swearing an oath of loyalty to the new monarch. When there was a change of monarch (i.e. from Charles II to James II), a regiment would lay down their arms to signify that they no longer served the old king and then pick them up, confirming their loyalty to the new monarch. The actions of James II confirmed the distrust and uncertainty he felt for his senior commanders, army officers, and the army in general. The Williamite fifth columnists had succeeded in reducing the effectiveness of the English army and the trust James II had in his army. These actions helped to ensure that

57 BL: MS Egerton 2717, f.413.

58 Beddard, *A Kingdom Without a King*, p.25.

59 NA: WO 4/1, f.114.

William's invasion would succeed without any serious engagements between the two armies, and the narrative of a 'peaceful' transition could continue. It would also help to instil both James II's and William III's reputations.

English intelligence reported that the Williamite army was approaching Chippenham and that several nobility and gentry in the 'Western Parts' of the country were in arms and supporting William.[60] While the main focus of the events of November and December 1688 was in the South West and on the road to London, there were uprisings and rebellions throughout the country. While these events may not have been instigated by Williamite troops, or even on William's direct orders, they were organised by his supporters with the explicit aim of destabilising both the country and James II's monarchy. A detachment of two troops of Colonel Butler's Regiment of Dragoons received orders to return to Chester with the greatest speed.[61] Butler's dragoons were sent to Chester to secure the city for the king against Williamite supporters and stop any insurrection from starting. James II ordering an Irish 'Catholic' regiment to a city with a large Catholic population confirms the king's concern for the safety of his Catholic subjects and also the insecurity he felt with of some of his Protestant officers and soldiers. While the prevailing narrative propagates anti-Catholic propaganda and the violence against the Protestant population, either real or imagined, in reality the Catholic population felt at risk and under attack. Attacks against Catholic chapels were well reported in London, but attacks on Catholics and Protestant supporters of the King throughout the country were becoming more widespread, resulting in a climate of fear and persecution reminiscent of the reigns of Henry VIII and Queen Elizabeth I, and under the protectorate of Oliver Cromwell.

29 November 1688

King James's confidence regarding the loyalty of the English army and in his ability to defeat William had been weakened sufficiently that he started to look for a diplomatic solution to the Dutch invasion. The Earl of Feversham was instructed to request that William of Orange send over blank passports in order for the king's commissioners to travel to William to 'treat with him'. Passports were commonly used to allow individuals to travel through opposing forces' lines of control. The request also asks for the names of any commissioners appointed by the prince that would need passports to be issued for their safe travel.[62] In addition to the diplomatic overtures of sending commissioners to William, James countermanded his previous orders regarding transporting additional Irish regiments into England, although he did yield to a request by Colonel Roger MacElligott to raise 150 Irish volunteers for his regiment and transport them to England.[63] Despite the diplomatic overtures, James II's commanders were still conducting military

60 NA: WO4/1, f.116.

61 NA: WO4/1, ff.116–17.

62 NA: SP8/2, ff.60–61.

63 NA: SP63/340, ff.313–14.

operations and arranging for supplies as normal. The Earl of Feversham requested a supply of ammunition to be delivered to Maidenhead, which is described as the central location of the army. This request was passed on by James II to Sir Henry Sheeres, of the Board of Ordnance, with instructions to carry out the request. James issued a royal warrant calling for Parliament to be reconvened on 15 January 1689, in accordance with his peace proposal to William.

The morale and order of the English army continued to decline as the army marched towards London. Acts of disorder are reported within Colonel Gage's Regiment of Foot, with the officers of the regiment using 'reprehensible and insolent words against the protestant soldiers within the regiment'.[64] The King ordered the two most senior officers present within the regiment, Lieutenant-Colonel William Molyneux and Major Cunningham, to take charge of 'their' regiment and restore order and that he was aware of a disagreement between the major and the Governor of Chester. The Governor of Carlisle reported disturbances within the city and surrounding county and noted the poor state of the garrison in the city and that the governor had refused the county militia entry to the city of Carlisle.[65] This action by the governor confirms the breakdown in trust between members of the aristocracy and in the loyalty of the army and the militia. The king confirmed his faith in his 'dearly beloved' governor in a letter dated 4 December and gave his approval to barring the militia's entry into Carlisle without orders from the king. This act by the king, barring English militia from entering the county town, confirms the deep levels of trust and uncertainty within the country and the effectiveness of the Williamite fifth column's actions and propaganda.

1 December 1688

The Privy Council arranged for a commission of lords to visit William of Orange to negotiate the conditions for the removal of the foreign army from English soil, along with the terms for ending all hostilities. The commission included Lord Halifax, Lord Nottingham, and Lord Godolphin. Lord Feversham sent messengers to William, asking him to provide safe conduct for the commissioners; however, it would take until 3 December for William to issue passports for the three lords to travel through Dutch lines.[66] The remaining elements of the Dutch fleet that had previously been anchored off Torbay entered Plymouth Sound on 1 December and dropped anchor under the protection of the guns of the Royal Citadel.[67] William received news from the north of the country that the lords Danby, Devonshire, and Lumley were marching south with their supporters to join his forces. While William had been advised that large numbers of Englishmen were eager to throw off

64 NA: WO4/1, ff.115–16.

65 NA: WO4/1, f.117.

66 Anon., *An Exact diary of the Late Expedition*, p.53; All Souls College, Oxford, f.viii.

67 NA: SP 8/2, Part 2, ff.63–4.

the yoke of Catholic James and rise in the defence of Protestant England, the lords would bring relatively few men with them. William also received word regarding the imprisoned Lord Lovelace. Lord Delamere informed the prince of Lovelace's release from his prison cell in Gloucester by a citizen mob and that he would be joining him in the near future.

2 December 1688

William Cavendish, the 4th Earl of Devonshire, who had been one of the 'Immortal Seven', informed William that James's daughter, the Princess Anne, wished to defect to him and join her husband, Prince George of Denmark, who had already defected over to Williamite cause .[68] Cavendish also informed William that he had 'raised a force of about a thousand horse', which would have been the equivalent of three full regiments of horse. This figure was a gross overestimation of the numbers actually raised by the earl; he was in reality only able to raise one regiment of horse and one regiment of foot. Despite raising regiments from his estates in Derbyshire and the surrounding countryside, the earl struggled to find prospective troopers who owned suitable horses, or with the financial resources to purchase the required horse and saddle. The earl was forced to organise the procurement of mounts and tack and then leverage their pay to recover the debt. William received word from Lord Shrewsbury concerning his capture of the city of Bristol for William and the apparent rejoicing of the local population after being freed from 'Popish' rule. While the message stated that the city had been captured, there had not been any military action to 'take' the city, just the dignitaries declaring for William and James II's supporters discreetly retiring from the port.

4 December 1688

When William entered Salisbury, he was greeted by John Hill, mayor of the town, along with a delegation of the town's aldermen.[69] The Prince of Orange was welcomed with bonfires and peals of church bells proclaiming to the population that he had 'been invited to restore their liberties, and preserve their religion'. As with his arrival into Exeter, it was not his English or Scottish regiments that entered the town first but his regiment of foot guards, the Garde te Voet, commanded by Count Solms. The foot guards were followed by the horse guards, both the Gardes te Paard and the Gardes de Corps on their white steeds. This was designed to show both the strength of the Dutch army and act as a victory parade as Salisbury had until recently been where the main English army was camped, with the majority of its officers having quarters within the town. The fact that William had managed

68 NA: SP 8/2, Part 2, ff.67–8, 69–70.

69 NU: PwA 2231; other documentation gives the date of entry into Salisbury as 6 December 1688. Anon., *Great News from Salisbury, The Sixth of December 1688* (NL: NP, 1688).

to secure this important town without a fight proved the power of his army, but also the effect of his disinformation campaign and the importance of the disruption caused to the English army by the Williamite fifth column, the Treason Club.[70] Unlike Exeter, William did not enter the city with his advisers who had accompanied him from Holland, but with senior members of the English royal household. In a show aimed to legitimise his arrival in England, William rode through the streets with Prince George of Denmark riding on his right hand and the Duke of Ormond riding on his left.[71] Following the army's arrival in Salisbury the reports show that the weather changed for the better and the roads and ground were far more suitable for the advancing army, allowing the Dutch army to cover more ground each day. The army was still divided into three divisions.

Even though the English army was retreating from Salisbury and there was a large number of defections to William in addition to general desertions from the army, the Board of Ordnance was still able to act efficiently and as normal. James instructed Lord Dartmouth, Master General of the Ordnance, and his deputy to order as much of the ammunition and stores currently being held within London to be sent to the town and garrison of Kingston Upon Hull that would be able to fit into such vessels available for their immediate transportation.[72] Additional stores were also sent to Staines (Middlesex) in anticipation of the arrival of the English army and the attached train of artillery. The stores were to consist of 200 barrels of fine corn-powder, two tuns of carbine shot, two tuns of pistol shot, and 2,000 unfixed grenado shells.[73] The English army, which was reported to consist of about 4,000 foot and 2,000 horse, was reported to be in Reading and in the process of fortifying the Staines Bridge over the River Thames.[74] Additional ammunition and stores were issued to Colonel John Carne's Regiment of Foot, and to Captain John Sibley's Independent Company of Foot.[75] Colonel Cornwall relinquished his commission as colonel of his regiment of foot to the king, along with two regimental captains and five other officers.[76] The act of relinquishing their commissions confirms that they still felt the need to abide by their oaths of loyalty to the king, even if they felt that they could no longer service within the army. The collective memory of the late civil war was still at the forefront for a large number of soldiers and their greatest fear was that the current events would be the spark for a new full-scale civil war within the country, as would later happen in Ireland. The regimental command was given to Colonel Oliver Nicholas, who was instructed to bring the seven companies of the regiment currently quartered at Greenwich and Dartford back into military order. The Irish Guards were ordered to

70 Anon., *An Exact diary of the Late Expedition*, p.61.
71 Anon., *An Exact diary of the Late Expedition*, p.61.
72 NA: SP44/165, f.147.
73 NA: SP44/165, f.152. A barrel held 26¼ imperial gallons, while a tun held eight times the volume of a barrel (210 imperial gallons).
74 Luttrell, *A Brief Relation of State Affairs*, p.483.
75 NA: SP44/165, f.153.
76 NA: WO4/1, f.117.

Gravesend (Kent), with the first two companies (100 men) arriving on 5 November, with the rest of the regiment over the next day or so.[77]

5 December 1688

William stayed at his camp in Salisbury, where he received Lord Oxford, who had just arrived from London. William sent troops from the Garde te Voet to Andover with orders to escort the delegation from the House of Lords, which consisted of Lord Godolphin, Lord Halifax, and Lord Nottingham, to Hungerford, with instructions that the three lords were to wait there for His Highness's arrival. Lord Herbert of Cherbury and Sir Edward Harley, along with a large number of the gentry from the counties of Herefordshire and Worcestershire, entered the city of Worcester accompanied by a 'large body of horse' and declared the city for the Prince of Orange.[78] Lord Herbert would in the next few days depart Worcester and seize Ludlow Castle and in the process capture Sir Walter Blunt (7 March 1646 – 12 May 1717), the Catholic Sheriff of Worcester (1687–88). Blunt had fled Worcester for the presumed safety of Ludlow and would be imprisoned in the castle by Lord Herbert.

6 December 1688

William arrived in Collingbourne Kingston from Salisbury, where he set up the headquarters for his army. The Williamite army was quartered in the following locations on 6 December:[79]

Name of Officer or Regiment	Location
Headquarters	Collingbourne Kingston
Marshal Schomberg and Staff	Collingbourne Ducis (Collingbourne St Andrews)
One Guards Battalion	West Everleigh
Prince van Birkenfeld	Chute
Three Guards Battalions	North Tidworth, South Tidworth, and Haxton
Birkenfeld's Brigade	Appleshaw, Shoddesden, Kimpton, and Thruxton
Sydney's Brigade	Amesbury
General Nassau and one Brigade	Great Bedwyn

77 NA: WO4/1, ff.117–18.

78 Anon., *Great News from Salisbury*, p.1.

79 NU: PwA 2221. Locations are stated with the modern spelling; any entry ending with a ? is the most probable location based on the original spelling in the entry.

One Battalion of Wynberg's Brigade	Little Bedwyn
Two Battalions of Wynberg's Brigade	Burbage
Lord Macclesfield	Overton
English lords and volunteers	Ludger Shall
Scottish lords	Amport
Refugee Officers	Boscombe
Corps of Guards	Wilton
Horse Guards	Beechingstoke and Wilsford
Cornbury's Dragoons	Marlborough
Langston's Dragoons	Marlborough
Cannon's Dragoons	Preshute and Clatford
Coning's Infantry	Wootton Rivers?
Eppinger's Dragoons	Tidcombe, Wexcombe, Marton, and Shaibourne
Marwitz's Dragoons	Ham, Buttermere, Harding Farm, Great Bedwyn?
Waldeck and Lype [Lippe]	Stoke
William Bentinck and Hyde	West Grafton
Loppenbrock	East Grafton
s'Gravemoer	Milton Lilbourne?
Nassau	Easton Royal
Ginkel	Draycot Fitz Payne
Oye and Riedt Ecsel	Pewsey
Flodroff and Opdam	Manningford Abbots
Zuylenstein and Schack	Wilcot
Montpouillan	Manningford Bruce

7 December 1688

William accompanied the army on its march from Collingham Kingston to Hungerford, where the commissioners dispatched by James II and the Privy Council were waiting. The prince spent the evening meeting with Lord Halifax, Lord Godolphin, and Lord Nottingham.[80] Godolphin's loyalty to James II was complex and his reasons for being appointed to the commission are questionable; he was a close friend and ally to John Churchill and would later serve under both William III and Queen Anne. During his service for William he, along with John Churchill, continued a secret correspondence with James II, supposedly sharing intelligence on William's planned action

80 NU: PwA 2231.

against Brest. While William stayed in Hungerford, advanced elements of the Williamite force under Waldeck moved towards the town of Newbury, Berkshire.

8 December 1688

By 8 December the advancing line of the Dutch army had reached as far as Newbury, with the second and third lines near Hungerford and Collingbourne Kingston, when during the night an alarm went through the army that enemy horse were approaching. Messengers were dispatched between two of William's infantry regiments that were in forward positions; the message from Colonel Fagel's regiment advised Colonel Sydney's that the English were about to assault the Dutch artillery train.[81] In reality, the Williamite pickets had seen returning tradesmen riding home after attending Hungerford market, and not advanced scouts of the English army. Although the reports turned out to be false, the alarm demonstrates the heightened level of fear and tension throughout the country, even amongst the Williamite forces.

The Privy Council commission was received a second time by William at his lodgings at the Bear Inn in Hungerford and informed the prince of James II's proposals, stating that they were sent to discuss the requirements for the 'freedom of elections and the security of Sitting [of Parliament]'.[82] The commissioners informed William that James II was willing to immediately enter into a treaty with the prince and that as part of this treaty, the Dutch army should hold its positions and not advance any further towards the capital. William replied to the commissioners on the following morning with seven demands of his own, these being:[83]

> 1. That all Papists and not qualified by law [the Test Act], be disarmed, disbanded, and removed from all employment, civil and military.
> 2. That all proclamations which reflect upon Us [William, Prince of Orange], or any that have come to us, or declared for us, be re-called; and that if any person for having so assisted, have been committed, that they be forthwith set at liberty.
> 3. That for the security and safety of the City of London, the Custody and Government of the Tower be immediately put into the hands of the said city [militia]. [There had been rumours that the current governor of the tower had trained artillery on the city.]
> 4. That if His Majesty shall think fit to be at London during the sitting of the parliament, that we may be there also, with equal number of our guards. Or if His majesty shall please to be in any place from London, at whatever distance he thinks fit, that we may be at a place of the same distance. And that the respective armies do remove from London, Thirty Miles, and that no more Foreign Forces be brought into the Kingdom.

81 Anon., *An Exact diary of the Late Expedition*, pp.63–64.
82 Anon., *An Exact diary of the Late Expedition*, p.65.
83 Anon., *An Exact diary of the Late Expedition*, pp.65–66.

> 5. That for the Security of the City of London, and their Trade, Tilbury Fort be put into the Hands of the City [Militia].
> 6. That to Prevent the Landing of French, or other Foreign Troops, Portsmouth may be put into such Hands, as by your majesty and Us shall be agreed upon.
> 7. That some sufficient part of the Public Revenue be assigned Us, for the Maintaining of our Forces, until the Meeting of a parliament.

While some of William's demands mirrored the proposals from the king and the commission regarding the removal of Catholics from the army and civil positions and the pardoning of all those citizens who joined the Dutch forces, most were the demands of a victorious power. The demands for William to be treated as an equal to James II for the opening of the Parliament and for all English troops to be banned from coming within 30 miles of London would be the equivalent of the king admitting defeat. Items 3 and 4 of the counter-proposals confirm that William and his staff had confidence that the London Trained bands (militia) would be loyal to his cause, and not to that of James II. This confidence was partly due to the lack of involvement of the militia following the invasion and partly to reports from his supporters within London. The mention of no more foreign forces only referred to James and was in relation to additional Irish troops being dispatched, as well as European Catholic states sending support. While the English crown or Parliament did not immediately start paying for the subsistence of the invading army, England did pay for the whole invasion force following William and Mary's investiture in 1689.[84]

While the commissioners were waiting for William's reply to James II's proposals and his offer for an immediate cessation of hostilities, James II informed the Earl of Feversham, commander of the English army, of his immediate intentions to retire to London. When Feversham heard that his king and the army were retiring to London, he sent a message to William stating that he would not make any offensive action against the Dutch to 'so prevent the effusion of blood'.[85] This message to William would be the prelude to Feversham ordering the disbandment of the English army. William ordered the first division of his army to march from Newbury to Reading. While on the outskirts of Reading in the village of Tylehurston (Tilehurst) Colonel Cutts, who was commanding Colonel Sydney's Regiment of Foot, was informed (incorrectly) that 'the Irish' had put Kingston-upon-Thames to the sword and that Basingstoke would be their next target.[86] These reports would later to be known as the 'Irish Fright' and would become a common feature during this phase of the invasion. The rumours included a mixture of deliberate anti-Catholic propaganda, along with the repetition of historical events and folklore. These were designed to propagate fear, based upon historical and imagined murders, massacres, and destruction of property by Catholics within England, Ireland, and Europe that were still within the collective memory of the English population. These reports would continue

84 *House of Commons Journal*, Volume 10: 7 February 1689, pp.20–22.
85 Anon., *An Exact diary of the Late Expedition*, p.66.
86 Anon., *An Exact diary of the Late Expedition*, p.68.

until 15 December, with the last large-scale supposed event being reported by the Governor of Chester, who reported that 8,000 to 9,000 'Papists' were coming to burn Chester to the ground.[87]

The English artillery train had reached Brentford in Middlesex and was ordered to set up quarters there and to await further orders. This order infuriated James II, whose displeasure was shown in his orders instructing the train to immediately move to Hounslow Heath. The orders stipulated that the full train of artillery must depart Brentford no later than the following day (9 December 1688).[88]

'The Fight at Reading,' playing card, Anon., 1689. (Author's Collection)

9 December 1688: The Battle of Reading

The main conflict of the invasion was on Sunday 9 December 1688 in Reading, which was being held by forces loyal to King James. Accounts of the skirmish vary enormously both in contemporary sources and in recent works on the period. Henry and Barbara van der Zee state that the Irish forces defending Reading were '600 Irish dragoons.' This account is impossible as the only Irish dragoon regiment was Butler's dragoons, and it would not match this number at full strength, even without two of their troops currently stationed in Chester.[89] It may be the case that these 'Irish dragoons' were mistaken for English dismounted cavalry, or Irish infantry operating in a 'mounted infantry role' (using horses to transport them between towns). William was in Hungerford when he received a message from some of the inhabitants of Reading advising him that there were troops loyal to James within Reading and that they planned to hold the town for the king.[90] Reading was garrisoned by a regiment of foot and a regiment of horse, with about 1,000 men in total defending the town. The garrison consisted of Colonel Hamilton's (Irish) Regiment of Foot along with Sir John Lanier's Regiment of Horse. Some reports also state that there were 'some' companies of the Scots foot guards in Reading.[91] If elements of the Scots guards were in Reading then

87 BL: Add MS 38695, f.104; J. McElligott (ed.), *Fear, Exclusion and Revolution: Roger Morrice and Britain in the 1680s* (Aldershot: Ashgate, 2006), p.93.
88 NA: WO4/1, f.118.
89 H. and B. van der Zee, *1688: Revolution in the Family* (London: Penguin, 1988), pp.187–88.
90 Prof. W.M. Childs, *The Story of the Town of Reading* (Reading: W.C. Long, 1905), p.181.
91 Childs, *The Army, James II*, p.194.

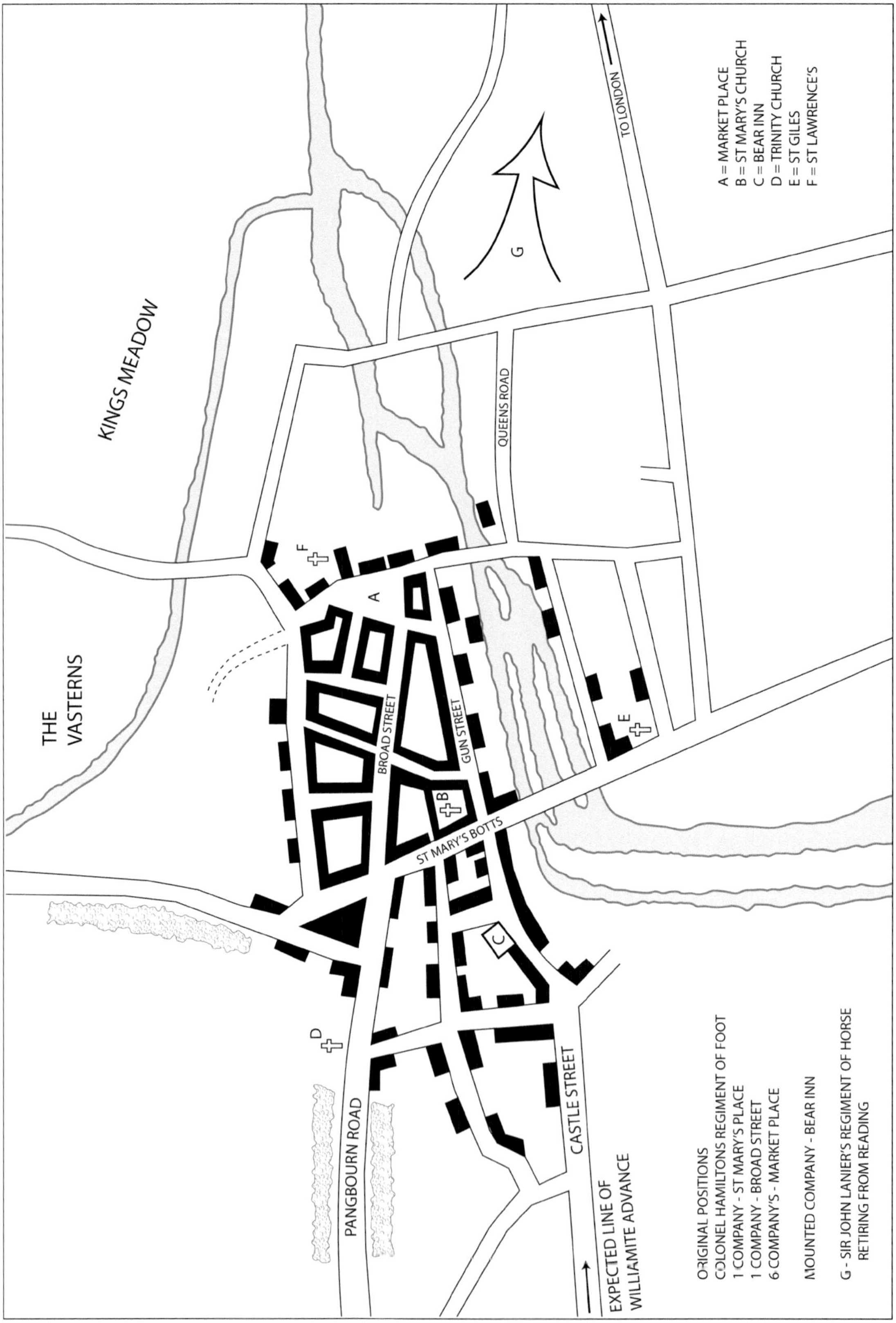

The Battle of Reading 9 December 1688 phase one

they must have retired from the town along with Lanier's horse prior to the Williamite attack as they are not mentioned either during the attack or in any of the casualty lists. When Sir John Lanier heard that an advanced force of between 250 and 300 Dutch horse was about to enter Reading, he withdrew his regiment of horse from the town with the intent of allowing William's troops free passage. The likelihood is that the Dutch troops about to enter the town belonged to either the Regiment Nassau-Zuylenstein or the Regiment Nassau-Saarbrücken; this assumption is based on the reports that they were commanded by 'Nassau'.[1] It is unknown if Lanier's regiment's withdrawal was due to their colonel's collusion with William, as he was a member of the Treason Club, or if he just believed that the situation was lost and he was only interested in avoiding bloodshed. Later Whig propaganda stated that 'but they never a man drew sword but went civilly to make room for the prince's forces'.[2] This account of Lanier's actions and the reference to their 'civility' and peaceful departure is an attempt by the Whig author to show the links between the English army and the Williamite forces and to place blame for the assault and later bloodshed on the 'Irish' and James II and not on the English army. The Irish regiment was still fiercely loyal to James II and to the country and continued to follow the king's orders to defend the town against the advancing enemy force. Hamilton's regiment were warned of the approaching Williamite force and organised their defence around Castle Street and the Market Place. A troop of horse has been reported to have been stationed in the yard of the Bear Inn on Castle Street.[3] This could have been a troop from Lanier's Regiment of Horse, an unrecorded independent company of horse, a company of unidentified dragoons, or a company of mounted infantry; however, they did not play any active part in the skirmish. Hamilton placed at least one company of foot in St Mary's churchyard, with sentries within the church belltower. The churchyard covered the corner of St Mary's Butts and Gun Street. An additional force of at least a company was located slightly to the north in Broad Street, while the rest of the regiment were stationed to the north-east, around the town's market place.[4] The posture of the defenders was in response to the belief that the Williamite forces would be advancing along Western Road from the direction of Hungerford and the main Williamite army.[5] The Williamite force had, however, been warned of the defensive positions adopted by James's troops by sympathetic townsfolk and entered Reading further to the north of the town, via Pangbourne lane. This lane held the advantages of having high hedges that covered the Dutch advance, allowing for a clandestine approach and a shock attack on the Irish forces. This change of direction by the Dutch forces away from the expected line of advance resulted in the defenders' strong positions being avoided, leaving the Irish troops both surprised and disoriented. The result of this unexpected line of attack resulted in the defending troops stationed along Broad Street

1 Carswell, *The Descent on England*, p.203.
2 Childs, *The Army, James II*, p.194.
3 Childs, *The Story of the Town of Reading*, p.181.
4 Childs, *The Story of the Town of Reading*, p.181.
5 Childs, *The Story of the Town of Reading*, p.182.

and Castle Street being unable to stand up to the Williamite onslaught, which resulted in the Irish troops being forced out of their positions, routed, and driven into the Market Place. The outlying companies found themselves crashing into the main body of their regiment, who were being held in the Market Place, disordering the whole regiment. As a result, the regiment was unable to put up any form of cohesive or meaningful defence against the Dutch cavalry and they too were forced to retire. Reports state that Hamilton's regiment fled the city in great disorder, with the local residents showing their support for William by firing on the departing troops from their houses. The skirmish, though minor and over in a short period of time, was deemed to be a great victory for William, with one English regiment failing to put up any form of defence and departing from the town, and Hamilton's Regiment of Foot being routed with ease. Although the regiment had been forced to retire from Reading, it did not disintegrate and was able to regain its cohesion and discipline. When looking at the outcome of the skirmish, the actual number of casualties caused varies depending on the source used. Taylor reports that the hostilities resulted in 29 fatalities and an unrecorded number of injured.[6] Another record states that the Dutch cavalry entered the town and put the Irish regiment to flight within a few minutes, with the result of 20 Irish dead and only one Dutch casualty, the officer that was leading the charge.[7] A contemporary broadsheet gives the casualties at 'several persons' but goes on to state that there were 'horses, lying dead upon the road (they say) to the number 200'.[8] The largest claims regarding casualties come from Childs and Harris, with reports of 50 soldiers from Hamilton's regiment being killed, as well as five Dutch soldiers. [9] The majority of the reports suggest that the Irish casualties were between 20 and 30 killed, with an unknown number or soldiers either wounded or captured. Several of the soldiers killed are buried in St Giles's churchyard in Reading.

While English regiments were having issues with morale, discipline, and desertion (either to William, or just from the army), the Irish regiments brought over by James still had generally good morale and were unshaken in their loyalty to the king. As soon as Hamilton's Regiment of Foot arrived in Maidenhead, they were immediately ordered to start to fortify Maidenhead Bridge and the adjacent houses. The houses between the bridge and the town were fortified by making port-holes (loopholes) within the walls for both their artillery and for musket fire.[10] Two field pieces were placed in the centre of the bridge to cover the access to the bridge. The Irish troops were in a strong defensive position that could have potentially resulted in large numbers of Dutch casualties, if the Dutch had been forced to assault the fortified position. Near midnight the Irish troops were able to hear large

6 S. Taylor (ed.), *The Entring Book of Roger Morrice, Volume IV, The Reign of James II, 1687-1689* (Woodbridge: Boydell Press, 2007), p.375.

7 Anon., *An Exact diary of the Late Expedition*, p.69.

8 Anon., *An Account of Last Sundays Engagement BETWEEN His Majesty's, and the Prince of Orange's Forces, in the Road between Reading and Maidenhead, amongst which, its said, a Blue-Garter fell. With a True Account of some Occurrences at Portsmouth* (London: W.D., 1688).

9 Childs, *The Story of the Town of Reading*, p.182; Harris, *Revolution*, p.295.

10 Anon., *An Exact diary of the Late Expedition*, p.69.

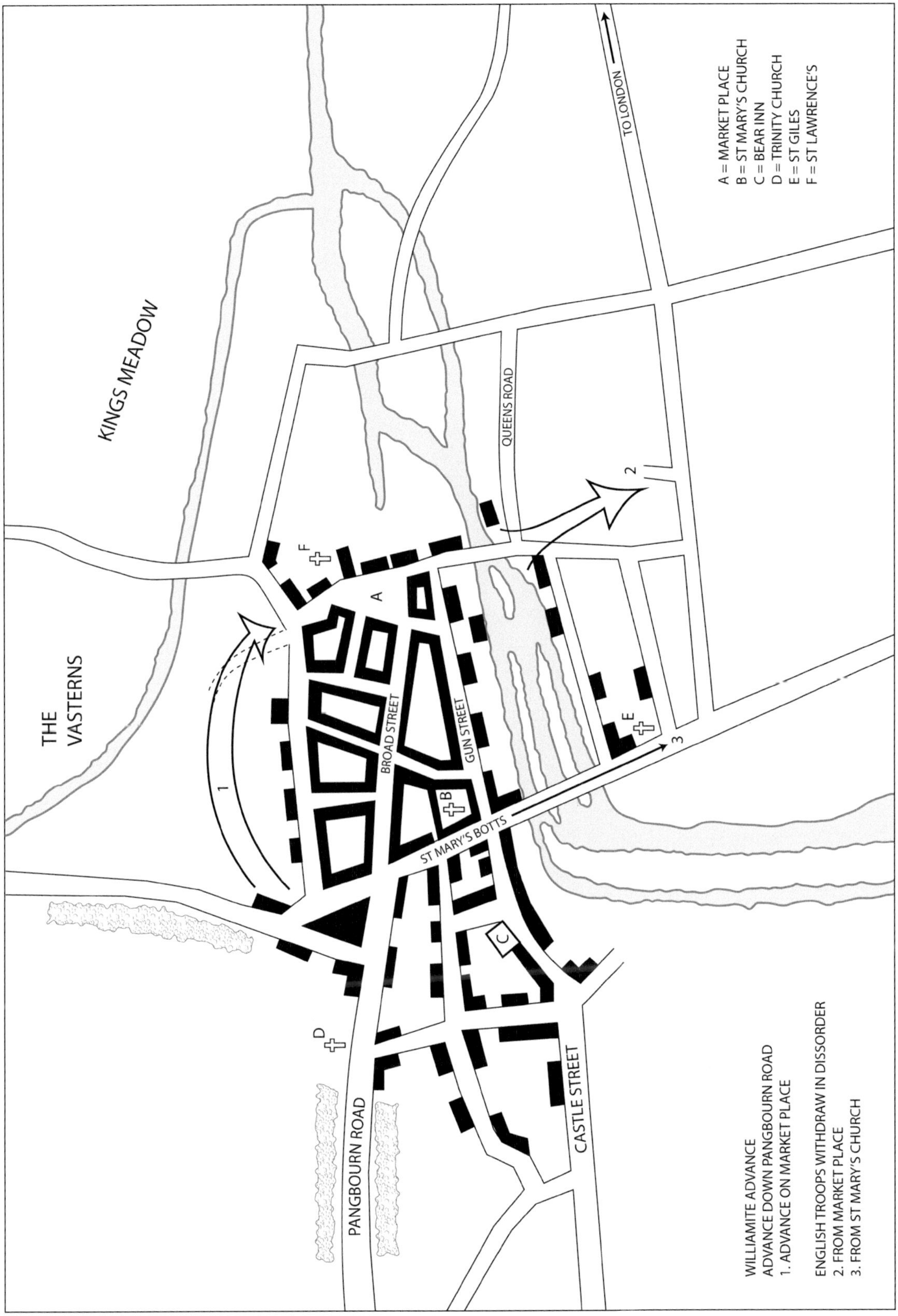

The Battle of Reading 9 December 1688 phase two

numbers of voices as well as Dutch marching music echoing through the night. The defenders, fearing that the Dutch were about to launch a full-scale night assault and without support from other English regiments, withdrew from their defensive position without a shot being fired in anger. The advancing 'Dutch' were in fact local citizens who had taken matters into their own hands and when the Dutch forces arrived the following morning, they were able to secure all the artillery left by the retreating Irish troops.[1]

10 December 1688

James II, sensing his inevitable defeat, ordered his wife, Queen Mary, along with their son, James Francis Stuart, to France and the safety of Louis XIV.[2] This action confirms his fears regarding the safety of both himself and his son and his commitment to protect his line of succession. With both his daughters now committed to the Williamite cause, the only safe line of succession was his Catholic son, James. All other options would have been seen to be a complete defeat. Dutch records show English regiments raised specifically for service in William's army being identified in the daily orders of march for the first time. These records confirm English regiments of horse and dragoons encamped at Lambourne and advancing to Wallingford, which is north-east of Newbury. These newly raised regiments were in addition to the two regiments of foot raised by William in Exeter, Sir John Guye's Regiment of Foot and Sir Robert Peyton's Regiment of Foot. Dutch dragoons under Waldeck had advanced as far as Reading while Bentinck had advanced east to occupy Streatley. William received news from Nassau, who was still in Reading, confirming that 500 men from the Scots guards had defected to William. The deserters were led by a sergeant and two corporals who had previously served William in Holland. The three NCOs were given commissions as ensigns within the Williamite army the following day (11 December 1688).

'Mortar Pieces put upon the Tower,' playing card, Anon., 1689. (Author's Collection)

1 William, Prince of Orange, *By the Prince of Orange, a Declaration* (Savoy, London: Ede and Jones, 1688).

2 Jones, *A Parliamentary History of the Glorious Revolution*, p.5.

11 December 1688

News reached the army in and around London and Uxbridge that James II had fled Whitehall on the evening of 10 December or the next morning and was planning to leave the country for France.[3] The king left London accompanied by Sir Edward Hales, along with two servants, with the intention of heading to the Isle of Elmley to take a boat to France. In the early hours of the morning of 11 December, as James II was rowed down the Thames, he threw the Great Seal of England into the river. This act would later be used by the convention held by members of the Lords and Commons to confirm that the king had deliberately abdicated the throne of England, allowing the vacant throne to be offered to William and Mary. James travelled by river as far as Vauxhall before continuing his journey on horseback on his way to Kent and freedom from William.[4] In the end the monarch's attempted flight from the country would result in him getting only as far as Faversham in Kent before he was identified, and then later returned to London under the escort of his guards.[5] James's party was intercepted by English seamen who were on the hunt for escaping Jesuit priests, with one of the seamen recognising Sir Edward Hales; James II was only recognised the following day.[6]

The news of the king's attempt to abandon the country shocked both the military and the civil authorities. Ten senior army officers wrote to the prince stating their great surprise at the king's departure and being left without any orders. They informed William that they would endeavour to keep their regiments together and to preserve the peace while they waited for His Highness's commands and requested his favour and protection.[7] The head of the army, Lord Feversham, informed the prince that he had received a communication from the king informing him of his departure from the country and instructing him to 'make no opposition against anybody' in order to stop the 'effusion of blood'. Feversham ended his communication with William by stating that he had sent an order to all the regiments and units under his command advising them that this was the last order they would receive from him. This was interpreted by the officers receiving the order that Lord Feversham was instructing the army to disband.[8] The letter stated:

> Having received this morning a letter from his Majesty with the unfortunate news of his resolution to go out of England and that he is actually gone, I thought myself obliged, being the head of his army, having received his Majesty's order to make

3 Beddard, *A Kingdom Without a King*, p.34.
4 Miller, *James II*, p.205.
5 Anon., *An Exact diary of the Late Expedition*, p.68.
6 Miller, *James II*, p.206.
7 NA: SP31/4, f.203. The ten officers included seven colonels, the Earl of Craven, Lord Brandon, John Hales, Robert Werden, Edward Villiers, Solomon Richards, and Richard Bynns, and three captains, William Selwyn, Henry Slingsby, and Robert Hodges.
8 NA: SP8/2, Part 2, ff.79–80; Taylor, *The Entring Book of Roger Morrice, IV*, p.378.

> no opposition against anybody, to let your Highness know it, with the advice of all the officers that are here as soon as it was possible to hinder the misfortune of effusion of blood. I have sent order already to that purpose to all troops that are under my command, which shall be the last order they shall receive from, sir, your Highness' most humble and most obedient servant.

James II's instructions to Lord Feversham regarding the royal army were vague to say the least. It is unsure if the king intended for the whole of the English army to disband, or for just the forces under Feversham to disband, or if his intent was just to ensure that the army stayed in place and did not engage the Dutch forces.[9] Feversham sent a second letter to William, countersigned by eight other army officers, advising the prince that the Irish forces within England were 'very ready and willing' to lay down their arms and submit to the orders of the prince.[10] The letter went on to request that the regiments be put under the prince's protection and that they requested permission to 'retire separately or otherwise as your Highness shall think fit for their safety'. William was apoplectic when he received this news, as although William did not want to engage the English army, he did not want it disbanded. As previously stated, one of the main aims of his invasion was to be able to command the English army in his campaign against Louis XIV and the disbandment of the army was the last thing that he had intended.

In addition to the English army disintegrating, with regiments collapsing and soldiers taking the opportunity to go home, William received an additional communication from the senior officers of the Scottish regiments. The lords Livingstone, Dunmore, and Dundee asked the prince on 11 December for his permission for their regiments to return home to Scotland.[11] The request stated that as the king had left the kingdom, the Scottish soldiers believed their duty and obligations to the king had been fulfilled. They informed the prince that they were concerned that without receiving any wages, their soldiers might commit disorders or be attacked by the civilian population as they were strangers within the land. This reference regarding being strangers is presumably a concern that the Scottish soldiers would be mistaken for 'Papists' or 'Irish' soldiers due to the heightened tensions and the large number of soldiers wandering the country. The three lords requested an audience with the prince in order to give a further account of their circumstances and to gain the prince's approval.[12] While William was still a long way from the centre of power, both geographically and politically, England was within his reach. He had secured a victory over James II without any major bloodshed and with his army intact.

---

9 Childs, *The Army, James II*, pp.194–95.

10 NA: SP8/2, Part 2, ff.75–6.

11 NA: SP8/2, Part 2, ff.77–8.

12 NA: SP8/2, Part 2, ff.77–8.

The Second Interregnum

With the belief that the king had left the country, England entered its second interregnum since the Civil War, with the country being run from the Guildhall in London by the Lords Spiritual and Temporal. The first meeting of the interregnum government was held on 11 December 1688 and consisted of 27 Lords Spiritual and Temporal, comprising six bishops and 21 peers of the realm. The lords issued a declaration at the Guildhall that they were going to send the Earl of Pembroke, Lord Weymouth, the Bishop of Ely, and Lord Culpeper to immediately attend the Prince of Orange with a declaration that they supported the prince and call for free Parliamentary elections.[13] England had in all effect capitulated to William and the Dutch Republic. Additional declarations were sent to the Earl of Craven, the Lord Lieutenant of Middlesex and London, to raise the militias of Middlesex, Westminster, and Southwark in order to prevent any disorder within the city.[14] The lords also ordered Feversham to remove all English forces from the capital to 'distant quarters or by any other way' that his lordship thought fit to prevent any hostilities between the English army and either the civilian population of London or the Williamite forces. Similar orders were sent to Lord Dartmouth, commander of the English navy, to prevent any act of hostility between the Dutch fleet and the English fleet.[15] The orders to the navy also included the instruction to remove all 'Papist' officers from their respective commands, although the mechanism for how this was to be achieved was left up to Dartmouth and Samuel Pepys. The lords also sent a rather vague order to the Lord General of the Army (Feversham) that all 'Catholics' are to be 'got together in arms about Hounslow [Heath]' and that all 'Roman Catholics' should be disarmed.[16] While the latter order stipulates the 'Irish regiments', the first order does have such a stipulation and has been interpreted as referring to all the English Catholic soldiers still serving within the army. If this was the actual intention of the order, it would have been a serious logistical challenge, with regiments spread throughout the country and in a state of disorder. Presumably, all these 'Catholic' soldiers would have needed to be escorted to Hounslow.

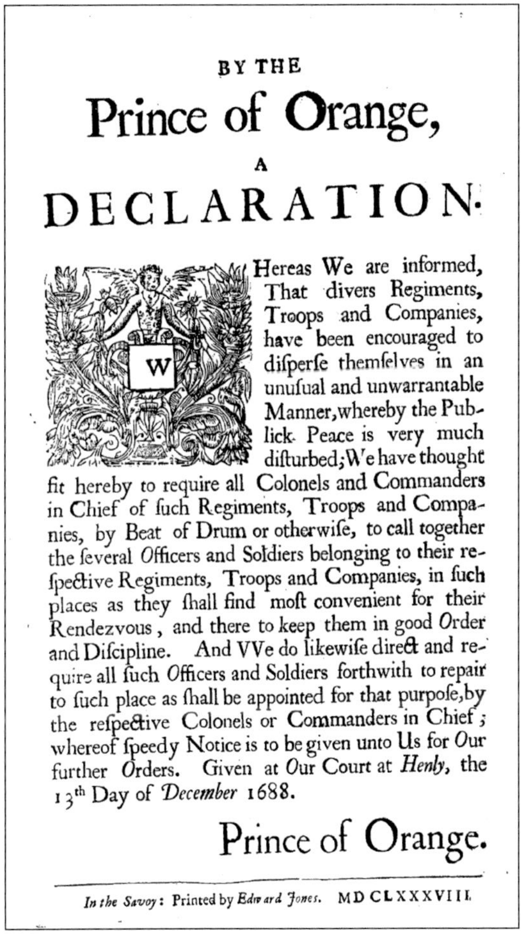
BY THE

Prince of Orange,

A

DECLARATION.

Whereas We are informed, That divers Regiments, Troops and Companies, have been encouraged to diſperſe themſelves in an unuſual and unwarrantable Manner, whereby the Publick Peace is very much diſturbed; We have thought fit hereby to require all Colonels and Commanders in Chief of ſuch Regiments, Troops and Companies, by Beat of Drum or otherwiſe, to call together the ſeveral Officers and Soldiers belonging to their reſpective Regiments, Troops and Companies, in ſuch places as they ſhall find moſt convenient for their Rendezvous, and there to keep them in good Order and Diſcipline. And We do likewiſe direct and require all ſuch Officers and Soldiers forthwith to repair to ſuch place as ſhall be appointed for that purpoſe, by the reſpective Colonels or Commanders in Chief; whereof ſpeedy Notice is to be given unto Us for Our further Orders. Given at Our Court at *Henly*, the 13th Day of *December* 1688.

Prince of Orange.

In the Savoy: Printed by *Edward Jones*. MDCLXXXVIII.

'By the Prince of Orange A Declaration,' instructing the army to reform and return to quarters, London, 1688. (Author's Collection)

13 *London Gazette*, No. 2409, Monday, 10 December to Thursday, 13 December 1688, p.1; NA: SP8/2, Part 2, f.86.

14 NA: SP8/2, Part 2, ff.83–4.

15 Beddard, *A Kingdom Without a King*, pp.68–69.

16 Beddard, *A Kingdom Without a King*, p.69.

12 December 1688

General disorder broke out in various parts of the country, with William's and the Whig anti-Papist propaganda resulting in riots and looting within the capital. The Spanish ambassador's house was ransacked and the queen's chapel was looted and then set on fire by the mob.[17] The lords issued emergency orders for the militia of London, Middlesex, and Surrey to patrol the city and offer all assistance to the Justices of the Peace to suppress the ongoing riots that could not be suppressed by the civil officers and 'Protestant' constables and deputies along with the *posse comitatus* (citizens summoned to keep the peace).[18] The English artillery train, which consisted of 22 artillery pieces, was ordered from its current location of Hounslow Heath to the Tower of London. The artillery train progressed through the crowded London streets to the Board of Ordnance stores located within the Tower.[19] The anti-Catholic riots were still causing concerns to the lords, who issued additional orders to officers of the First Regiment of Foot Guards, who were billeted in central London, to keep the peace. Lieutenant-Colonel Charles O'Hara and Lieutenant-Colonel Anthony Hastings were ordered to 'keep together their Protestant soldiers under their respective commands' and to aid and assist the civil magistrates in upholding law and order.[20] Following reports of a 'rabble threatening the Palace of St James' the lords issued orders for the guard to be 'called out' to protect the palace and surrounding area. The three senior officers of the regiments located within Whitehall and at the palace confirmed the number of men they had 'in arms'.[21]

> Colonel William Selwyn, First Regiment of Foot Guards 400 men
> Lt-Colonel Richard Baggott, Prince George of Denmark's Regiment of Foot 400 men
> Brigadier Edward Symms, First Troop of Horse Guards 160 men
> (Symms confirmed that he had 80 men at St James's Palace and 80 men at Whitehall, although only half were mounted, the rest being on foot.)[22]

Three hundred men along with three pieces of artillery were ordered to be situated within Whitehall, with the artillery sited before the gates. The Second Troop of Horse Guards were ordered to attend St James's Palace as soon as possible. News of the rabble threatening to burn down Catholic chapels reached Catherine of Braganza, the Queen Dowager, who requested extra protection in the form of a regiment of city militia to be stationed near her home of Somerset House, along with an additional 30 horse (guards) to

17 *London Gazette*, No. 2409, Monday, 10 December to Thursday, 13 December 1688, p.2.
18 NA: SP31/4, f.207.
19 Luttrell, *A Brief Relation of State Affairs*, p.486.
20 Beddard, *A Kingdom Without a King*, p.75. Beddard incorrectly identifies the identity of Lieutenant-Colonel Hastings, who he suggests is Lieutenant-Colonel Ferdinando Hastings of the Earl of Huntington's Regiment of Foot.
21 Beddard, *A Kingdom Without a King*, p.80.
22 NA: SP44/71, f.235; Dalton, *English Army Lists*, vol. II, p.115.

be stationed outside the building. Lord Feversham, along with the 30 horse guards, presumably from the second troop, were sent by the lords to protect the Queen Dowager.[23] The 'Protestant' rabble never reached the Queen Dowager's residence due to the increased security around Somerset House and attacked less-well defended targets.

The flight of King James II, 1688, from a print by Pieter Pickaert, Amsterdam, 1689. (Rijksmuseum: RP-P-1910-1701, Public Domain)

13 December 1688

Following James II's attempt to flee the country, the political and military situation within England was still uncertain and William was aware of the fact that the army and the country were on a knife-edge. William's hope of controlling the country without any serious military action or major loss of life was almost within his grasp, but the order for the army to disband had resulted in fear and chaos spreading across the country. In an effort to regain control, William issued an order to the English army on 13 December 1688 to reform; the order stated that all officers and soldiers should 'repair to such places as shall be appointed for that purpose by their respective colonels or commanders in chief'.[24] The order was printed in handbills and distributed throughout the country as well as being published in papers.

In an incident reminiscent of Charles I's flight and his later imprisonment by Parliament during the Civil War, the council members (20 Lords Spiritual and Temporal) of the interregnum government informed William that James II was still in Faversham. The council informed the prince that they were

23 Beddard, *A Kingdom Without a King*, p.81.

24 William, Prince of Orange, *By the Prince of Orange, a Declaration* (Savoy, London: Ede and Jones, 1688).

sending four lords to the king as well as a guard of six score horse guards (120 men) and fifty grenadiers to attend His Majesty's person.[25] The reason given by the lords for this action was that they intended 'to secure the monarch from the insolence of the number of people who may press upon him' and that they were hoping that their actions would have met with his 'Highness approbations'.[26] Despite the diplomatic wording of the letter, the horse guards and grenadiers were there to ensure the return of the king and for James II to be held until instructions were received from William of Orange. These orders effectively made the king a prisoner of the interregnum government and his son-in-law, the Prince of Orange.

The Duke of Grafton, now in the service of William, entered London at the head of the Regiment of English Foot Guards (later the Grenadier Guards). He would survive an assassination attempt the following day (14 December) outside Somerset House.[27] The attempt, by an English dragoon, failed when the assassin's pistol misfired when he was next to the Duke, resulting in the dragoon being killed by the foot guards.[28] Further English regiments were ordered to be stationed in and around London in order to secure the city for William and to prevent any further episodes of unrest. The Royal Regiment of Fusiliers, under the command of Major Thomas Soaper, received orders to be stationed with the Hamlets of the Tower of London.[29] The three Scots regiments belonging to Lieutenant-General Douglas, Colonel Wauchope, and Colonel Buchan were ordered to muster in and around Colnbrook (Berkshire). William was well aware that the army needed to be paid in order for order to be recovered, so he ordered the Paymaster-General to pay subsistence money for all soldiers obeying the orders of the new government.[30] The colonel of the Royal Regiment of Horse, Colonel Henry Slingsby, advised their lordships that while his regiment was quartered in Smithfield they were in danger from the London rabble and Trained Bands and that a large number of his regiment were Catholics who had 'gone away', leaving him only three troops available for service.[31] The colonel was subsequently ordered to quarter his three troops in the inns between St Giles's Pound and Holborn Bar and the he must ensure that all the inn landlords were paid in full, and that his troops 'behave themselves civilly'. With the exception of the companies of foot guards sent to escort the king back to London, the rest of the regiment received orders to retire to their normal winter quarters within London. The fact that a colonel of a regiment of horse was concerned enough by potential conflict with the city militia that he felt obligated to notify the lords confirms the lack of trust and uncertainty within the military and the country.

William, in an attempt to gain control of the country, sent a letter to James II's Secretary of War, William Blathwayt, requesting information regarding

25 Beddard, *A Kingdom Without a King*, pp.94–95.
26 NA: SP8/2, Part 2, ff.87–88.
27 Luttrell, *A Brief Relation of State Affairs*, p.487.
28 Taylor, *The Entring Book of Roger Morrice, IV*, pp.393–94.
29 NA: SP44/165, f.112.
30 Beddard, *A Kingdom Without a King*, pp.86–87.
31 Beddard, *A Kingdom Without a King*, pp.88–89.

the exact numbers and locations of all the troops within the kingdom.[32] The letter informed Blathwayt that he, William, would be at Windsor on the next Friday, 24 December, and he required the details delivered to him on that evening. William goes further, stating that the list was required so that he could give orders to the English army for the security of the country. The Williamite forces are divided between four commands: William who was at Henley-on-Thames; Waldeck in the advanced position at Brey; Sydney covering the rear, still at Reading; and Nassau, who was north of the main advance and ended the day south of Oxford in Warborough.

14 December 1688

A fifth column of armed 'Williamite' supporters, the majority having served with the county militia, seized the military governor of Chester on 14 December and subsequently declared the city for William by reading the prince's declaration.[33] The 'militia' managed to not only disarm the governor but also a regular English regiment garrisoned within the city and two troops from Colonel Butler's (Irish) Regiment of Dragoons in the process. The reports do not state if this action resulted in any casualties (wounded or killed) on either side, or if the change of support happened peacefully and without the loss of any blood. The interregnum government ordered all Irish soldiers to disarm and to repair back to their regiments; any soldiers not doing so would be apprehended as vagabonds.[34] The order states that the regiments would receive subsistence pay as long as they were peaceful and that this would continue until other provisions were made or they were further employed. The subsistence rate was confirmed by William to be 6d a day for a private soldier; the regular pay for a private in a foot regiment was 8d a day during this period.[35] The Irish regiments were then ordered to repair to their respective bodies and to be quartered in Barnet, in the county of Hertford.[36] One of the last regiments to be raised by James II was Colonel Solomon Richard's Regiment of Foot, who as an entire regiment laid down their arms on this day, finishing their service to James II, and subsequently picked up their arms as a sign of their new loyalty and service to William of Orange.[37] The lords were still concerned about the growing threat from the London rabble and ordered the following troops posted as guards in the following locations:[38]

First Regiment of Foot Guards
One and a half companiesSt James Palace
Two companies Tilt Yard

32 Beddard, *A Kingdom Without a King*, pp.96–97.
33 *The London Courant*, No. 4, 18 December to 22 December 1688, p.1.
34 NA: SP31/4, f.208.
35 NA: WO24/12, ff.1–6; BL: Add MS 15897, f.88.
36 Beddard, *A Kingdom Without a King*, p.107.
37 Morrice, p.395.
38 Beddard, *A Kingdom Without a King*, pp.107–08.

Two companies	Scotland Yard
Two companies	The Savoy
Three companies	Somerset House
Two companies	The Mews

Third Troop of Horse Guards	Horse Guards
Twenty men from the Third Troop	Somerset House

Royal Regiment of Horse (to be on mounted patrol at night)

One troop	Leicester Fields
One troop	St James Square to Berkeley House
One troop	Southampton Square to Great Russell Street

The Duke of Berwick, governor and commander of the garrison of Portsmouth, sent Sir George Berkeley, lieutenant-colonel of Sir Edward Hales's Regiment of Foot, to the Earl of Middleton with a letter stating that he was willing to hand Portsmouth over to William of Orange.[39] This was on the condition that that the officers and soldiers under his command were given free passage and allowed to return to their homes, either in England or Ireland. William ordered the Duke of Grafton to secure Tilbury Fort for the Williamite forces with two battalions of English foot.[40] William stayed in Windsor while he took command of the country following James's flight to France and was informed of James's arrest at Faversham. Most of the Williamite forces stayed in their current positions, although the forces under General Ginkel moved to Great Marlow and Sydney's command advanced into north Hampshire.

James II being recognised in Faversham, in a print by Pieter Pickaert, Amsterdam, 1689. (Rijksmuseum: NG-1087-11, Public Domain)

39 Beddard, *A Kingdom Without a King*, p.109.
40 Smith, *Armies and Political Change*, p.120.

15 December 1688

Lord Feversham had arrived in William's headquarters on the 14th with a letter for the prince stating that King James II had been arrested on his way to France and was in custody in Rochester. It is unclear what Feversham's motives were in delivering the letter in person, although from William's reaction it can be assumed that Feversham did not offer his loyalty and service as William had Feversham arrested and placed into custody the following day. William dispatched William Nassau de Zuylenstein to Rochester with instructions for James to stay in the town and away from London until he received further instructions from the prince. Unfortunately, James had already left the town when the envoy arrived and was on his way back to the capital. Captain Jeremiah Bubb of Colonel Henry Cornwall's Regiment of Foot declared Carlisle for William along with other pro-Williamite elements of the garrison.[41]

16 December 1688

James II arrived back in London and tried to resume governing the country, offering some concessions to the Privy Council. The interregnum government would not meet again until on 21 December, when 65 Peers of the Realm attended St James's following a summons issued by William of Orange on 20 December.[42] Accounts suggest that the king was welcomed back into the city with mixed feelings, some stating he was welcomed with cheering crowds, while one 'eyewitness' states that James II was received with 'much gaping, but no rejoicing'.[43] One of the king's first acts on his return to St James's Palace was to attend a Mass in the palace chapel. The service was to give thanks for his safe return which, while understandable, was possibly insensitive and without thought. The act was subsequently used against the king as confirmation that his intent was still to convert the country to the Catholic faith and his recent overtures to Parliament were merely a subterfuge.[44] In reality, James was surrounding himself with subjects and advisers who he could completely trust, both Catholic and Protestant. In addition to meeting his priest, James also met with the Archbishop of York, and the bishops of Peterborough, Rochester, and Ely.

James FitzJames, Duke of Berwick formally surrendered the city of Portsmouth with its garrison of almost 3,000 troops to Colonel Thomas Tollemache, with the troops allowed to follow the norms of honourable surrender.[45] While a minor point, the fact that the Williamite forces were

41 Dalton, *English Army Lists*, vol. II, p.139; Childs, *The Army, James II*, p.192.

42 Beddard, *A Kingdom Without a King*, pp.121–23.

43 Speck, *Reluctant Revolutionaries*, p.89.

44 Beddard, *A Kingdom Without a King*, p.55.

45 Petrie, *The Marshal Duke of Berwick*, pp.43–44. Thomas Tollemache had previously held a commission as Lieutenant Colonel of the Royal Regiment of Fusiliers until he sold his commission on 1 May 1686 in protest against James II commissioning Catholic officers. He

following the normal rules of warfare, including with how troops were allowed to surrender, would suggest that they believed that they were 'at war' and not putting down a rebellion. The Williamite army concentrated its advance on London, with Nassau turning back from his previous advance towards Oxford and Sydney suspending his southerly advance to turn back towards the capital. William received notification of James's return to London while at Windsor; in a supposed fit of anger, William ordered the arrest of Feversham.[46] The two most probable reasons behind the arrest were either that William was still furious that Feversham had ordered the disbanding of the English army or that William found it incredulous that the king had been arrested and had subsequently been allowed to return to London and carry on as if nothing had changed.

17 December 1688

William was in Windsor Castle where he issued instructions for James II to be removed from London by the Dutch Blew Garde, issuing the following order:

> We doe desire you, the Lord Marquis of Halifax, the Earle of Shrewsbury, and the Lord Delamer, to tell the King that it is thought convenient, for the greater safety of his person, that he doe remove to Ham, where he shall be attended by guards, who will be ready to preserve him from any disturbance. Given at Windsor, the 17 [th] day of December 1688.
>
> G. Prince d'Orange [47]

The rest of the Williamite army had been ordered into position surrounding London, taking control of the surrounding towns of Acton, Chiswick, Ealing, Fulham, Hounslow, Richmond, and Twickenham. Advance companies of the Dutch Gardes te Voet under the command of Count Solms entered Whitehall and surrounded St James's Palace, effectively imprisoning James II for a second time.[48] The Dutch troops entered London late in the evening, securing St James's Palace prior to moving on towards Whitehall. The Dutch foot guards entered into a standoff with James II's personal bodyguard from the English Regiment of Foot Guards (some reports state that the guard also contained troops from the Coldstream Regiment of Foot Guards), who were at first unwilling to allow the Dutch troops entry into the king's quarters. Unwilling to cause further bloodshed and violence, King James ordered his bodyguard to stand down and allow the Dutch troops to take post guarding the palace.[49] The Dutch had full control of the palace by 10pm, with James

came over with William of Orange's force in November 1688 and was rewarded with the colonelcy of the Coldstream Regiment of Foot Guards in November 1689. NA: SP44/164, f.311; SP44/167, f.8.

46 Beddard, *A Kingdom Without a King*, p.51.
47 BL: Althorp MSS, Halifax Papers, p.g/I.
48 Miller, *James II*, p.208.
49 Israel, 'The Dutch Role', p.127.

II put under guard. James II went to sleep surrounded by Dutch soldiers, a prisoner within his own royal palace. At 1am on 18 December, the lords Delamere, Halifax, and Shrewsbury arrived with an ultimatum from William for James to leave London immediately for Ham House.[50] William needed James to leave London in order for him to secure the capital and country and to isolate James and negate any possible attempt to marshal English forces in his defence. After James objected to being sent to Ham House due to its small size and lack of status, William conceded to allow James to depart for Rochester in Kent.

Reception of Prince William III in London, 1688, in a print by Pieter Pickaert, Amsterdam, 1689. (Rijksmuseum: NG-1087-26, Public Domain)

18 December 1688

James II left London for the final time under Dutch guard and under the control of William of Orange. James was to leave London again by river, entering his barge around 11am, and was attended by three of his Lords of the Royal Bedchamber, the earls of Aylesbury, Arran, and Dumbarton. William ordered Lord Halifax, Lord Shrewsbury, and Lord Delamere to accompany the king to Rochester. The king travelled to Gravesend via boat accompanied by a company of the Dutch Garde te Voet and was then escorted to Rochester by 100 Dutch horse. James arrived in Rochester about 11 in the morning of 19 December, where he was received by Sir Richard Head.[51] William entered the capital a few hours after James's departure, accompanied by Marshal Schomberg, Major-General Mackay, and four regiments of foot, including elements of the Anglo-Dutch and Scots-Dutch brigades. William was received at St James's Park by the sheriffs of London and Middlesex, who

50 Miller, *James II*, p.208.

51 NA: ADM77/3, f.62.

welcomed the prince on behalf of the City of London. William then entered St James's Palace around midday, where the Dutch troops were still standing guard. William had to all intents secured England and the crown. The diarist and social commentator Roger Morrice witnessed that the Prince of Orange was welcomed with 'universal joy and acclamation' and that 'his entrance was like that of the restoration'.[52] He also stated that numerous women greeted the prince by crying: 'God Bless you, you come to redeeme our religion, lawes, liberties, and lives. God reward you.'

William's grip on the army was still not certain, as shown when Lord Craven's Regiment of Foot refused to obey orders given on behalf of William on 19 December. Rather than obeying their orders to march for Rochester, the regiment laid down their arms instead, which was a traditional sign for a regiment believing that their duty was done.[53]

20 December 1688

Colonel Thomas Tollemache's Regiment of Foot entered the City of London to take control of the Tower of London from the militia and English troops who had been billeted within the fortification. The Anglo-Dutch troops entered the tower without any resistance. William held a council on the evening of 20 December in St James's Palace, where he ordered Lord Churchill and Colonel Percy Kirke to start to 're-model' the English army by disbanding all regiments that they thought unfit.[54] Units were deemed to be unfit if they had been raised by a Catholic colonel, had not been fully raised, or if the loyalty of the regiment was in question. Any solders thought fit to serve within the 'new' English army from these units would be transferred to a 'fit' regiment. Although William had entered London and Dutch troops were in charge of the city, the rest of the country was still in a state of flux. Chester formally declared for William on 20 December and informed the prince that Lord Molyneux's Regiment of Foot had been disarmed along with two 'Irish' regiments.[55]

21 December 1688

The disbanding of the army had resulted in a large amount of arms, equipment, and stores going missing and being absorbed into the general civilian population and economy. The civil population were ordered on 21 December 1688 to return all arms to any officers or soldiers who demanded their return. The order went further, stating that any person with military arms or equipment still in their possession should return them to the

52 Taylor, *The Entring Book of Roger Morrice IV*, pp.377–78.
53 NA: ADM77/3, f.62.
54 *CSPD: James II, 1687–89*, p.382.
55 *CSPD: James II, 1687–89*, p.382.

Ordnance officers at either Uxbridge, Hounslow, or the Tower of London.[56] William was still unsure of the numbers of English troops and their current locations so he ordered all the English regiments to repair to designated locations where a full muster would take place. This order gives us a good understanding of the number of regiments within the English army at the end of the year.[57]

Regiments of Horse and Dragoons

First Troop of Horse Guards[(a)]	Maidstone, Kent
Second Troop of Horse Guards	Chelmsford, Essex
Third Troop of Horse Guards	St Albans, Hertfordshire
Fourth Troop of Horse Guards[58]	Epsom and Ewell, Surrey
Royal Regiment of Horse	Northampton
Queen's Regiment of Horse	Cambridge
Earl of Peterborough's Regiment of Horse (late)[(b)]	Bedford
Sir John Fenwick's Regiment of Horse	Dorking and Reigate, Surrey
Lieutenant-General Werdon's Regiment of Horse	Newbury, Berkshire
Earl of Selkirk's Regiment of Horse	Stamford, Lincolnshire
Major-General Hamilton's Regiment of Horse	Fenny-Stratford, Buckinghamshire
Princess of Denmark's Regiment of Horse	Reading, Berkshire
Queen Dowager's Regiment of Horse	Guildford and Godalming, Surrey
Marquis de Miremont's Regiment of Horse	Aylesbury and Wendover, Buckinghamshire
Lord Brandon's Regiment of Horse	Bishop Stafford, Hertfordshire
Colonel Henry Slingsby's Regiment of Horse	Buckingham and Winslow, Buckinghamshire
Colonel Holmen's Regiment of Horse (late)	Sevenoaks, Kent

56 *London Gazette*, No. 2412, Thursday, 20 December to Monday, 24 December 1688, p.1.
57 *London Gazette*, No. 2411, Monday, 17 December to Thursday, 20 December 1688, p.1; No. 2412, Thursday, 20 December to Monday, 24 December 1688, p.1.
58 *London Gazette*, No: 2413, Monday, 24 December to Thursday, 27 December 1688, p.2.

Earl of Salisbury's Regiment of Horse (late)	Sevenoaks, Kent
Royal Regiment of Dragoons	Farnham and Alton, Surrey
Queen's Regiment of Dragoons	Dunstable, Bedfordshire
Princess's Regiment of Dragoons	Burford, Oxfordshire

Regiments of Foot

First Regiment of Foot Guards	Portsmouth, Hampshire, and Tilbury, Essex
Coldstream Regiment of Foot Guards	Rochester, Dover, and Maidstone, Kent
Royal Regiment of Foot	Oxford
Queen Dowager's Regiment of Foot	Wallingford, Berkshire
Prince George of Denmark's Regiment of Foot	Hartington, Derbyshire
Holland Regiment of Foot	Chesham and Amersham, Buckinghamshire
Queen's Regiment of Foot	Hartford, Cheshire
Royal Regiment of Fusiliers	Herefordshire
Princess Anne of Denmark's Regiment of Foot	Southampton
Colonel Nicholas's Regiment of Foot (late)	Worcester
Earl of Bath's Regiment of Foot	Canterbury
Earl of Lichfield's Regiment of Foot (late)	Banbury, Oxfordshire
Earl of Huntingdon's Regiment of Foot	Plymouth
Sir Edward Hales's Regiment of Foot (late)	Hampshire
Colonel Tufton's Regiment of Foot	Berwick-upon-Tweed
Colonel John Hales's Regiment of Foot	Milton and Sittingbourne, Kent
Colonel Billingoff's Regiment of Foot	Chichester
Colonel Richard's Regiment of Foot	Suffolk
Colonel Gage's Regiment of Foot (late)	Chesham

Duke of Newcastle's Regiment of Foot	Hull and Berwick-upon-Tweed
Colonel Stolton's Regiment of Foot	Newport Pagnell, Buckinghamshire
Colonel Archibald Douglas's Regiment of Foot	Stony Stratford, Buckinghamshire
Scottish Regiments	
Troop of Horse Guards	Birchester?, Oxfordshire
Scottish Regiment of Horse	Abingdon, Berkshire
Scottish Regiment of Foot Guards	Thame, Oxfordshire
Colonel Wauchope's Regiment of Foot (late)	Woodstock, Oxfordshire
Colonel Buchan's Regiment of Foot (late)	Witney, Oxfordshire
Earl of Dunmore's Regiment of Dragoons	Oxfordshire [town]
Irish Regiments	
Irish foot guards[59]	Lewes, Sussex
Lord Forbes' Regiment of Foot	Hertford, Hertfordshire
Colonel Hamilton's Regiment of Foot	Lewes, Sussex
Colonel Butler's Regiment of Dragoons	East Grinstead, Sussex

(a) Each troop of horse grenadiers were located in the same location as their corresponding troop of horse guards.

(b) The inclusion of (late) indicates that the colonel of the regiment had either given up or lost their commission and that a new colonel has not yet been commissioned.

The majority of the English army were housed in and around the Home Counties, with only a few regiments located within the South West, Midlands, and the north of the country in Berwick-upon-Tweed and Hull.

59 *London Gazette*, No. 2413, Monday, 24 December to Thursday, 27 December 1688, p.2.

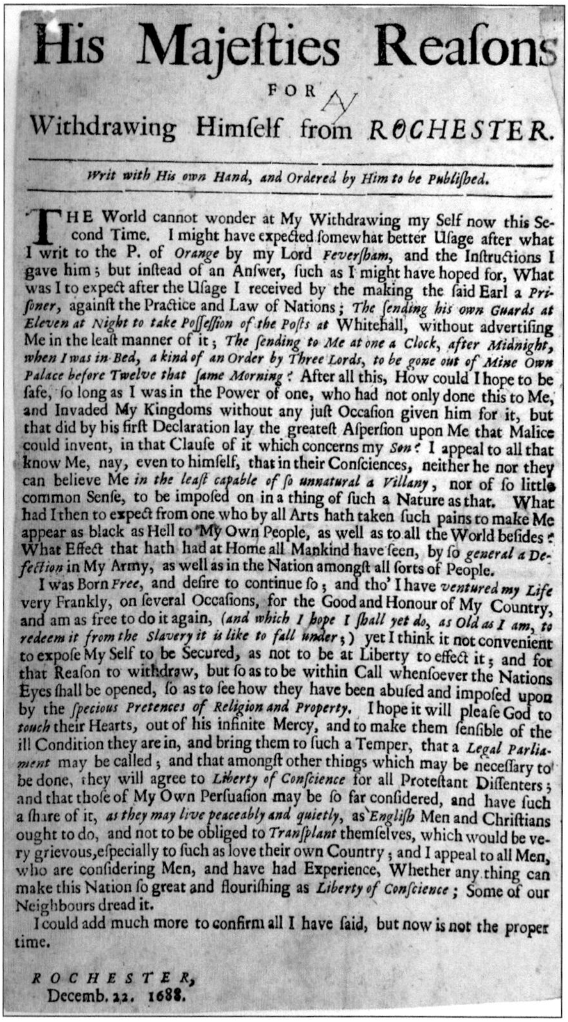

His Majeſties Reaſons FOR Withdrawing Himſelf from ROCHESTER.

Writ with His own Hand, and Ordered by Him to be Publiſhed.

THE World cannot wonder at My Withdrawing my Self now this Second Time. I might have expected ſomewhat better Uſage after what I writ to the P. of *Orange* by my Lord *Feverſham*, and the Inſtructions I gave him; but inſtead of an Anſwer, ſuch as I might have hoped for, What was I to expect after the Uſage I received by the making the ſaid Earl a *Priſoner*, againſt the Practice and Law of Nations; *The ſending his own Guards at Eleven at Night to take Poſſeſſion of the Poſts at* Whitehall, without advertiſing Me in the leaſt manner of it; *The ſending to Me at one a Clock, after Midnight, when I was in Bed, a kind of an Order by Three Lords, to be gone out of Mine Own Palace before Twelve that ſame Morning*: After all this, How could I hope to be ſafe, ſo long as I was in the Power of one, who had not only done this to Me, and Invaded My Kingdoms without any juſt Occaſion given him for it, but that did by his firſt Declaration lay the greateſt Aſperſion upon Me that Malice could invent, in that Clauſe of it which concerns my *Son*: I appeal to all that know Me, nay, even to himſelf, that in their Conſciences, neither he nor they can believe Me *in the leaſt capable of ſo unnatural a Villany*, nor of ſo little common Senſe, to be impoſed on in a thing of ſuch a Nature as that. What had I then to expect from one who by all Arts hath taken ſuch pains to make Me appear as black as Hell to My Own People, as well as to all the World beſides: What Effect that hath had at Home all Mankind have ſeen, by ſo *general a Defection* in My Army, as well as in the Nation amongſt all ſorts of People.

I was Born *Free*, and deſire to continue ſo; and tho' I have *ventured my Life* very Frankly, on ſeveral Occaſions, for the Good and Honour of My Country, and am as free to do it again, (*and which I hope I ſhall yet do, as Old as I am, to redeem it from the Slavery it is like to fall under*;) yet I think it not convenient to expoſe My Self to be Secured, as not to be at Liberty to effect it; and for that Reaſon to withdraw, but ſo as to be within Call whenſoever the Nations Eyes ſhall be opened, ſo as to ſee how they have been abuſed and impoſed upon by the *ſpecious Pretences of Religion and Property*. I hope it will pleaſe God to *touch* their Hearts, out of his infinite Mercy, and to make them ſenſible of the ill Condition they are in, and bring them to ſuch a Temper, that a *Legal Parliament* may be called; and that amongſt other things which may be neceſſary to be done, they will agree to *Liberty of Conſcience* for all Proteſtant Diſſenters; and that thoſe of My Own Perſuaſion may be ſo far conſidered, and have ſuch a ſhare of it, *as they may live peaceably and quietly*, as *Engliſh* Men and Chriſtians ought to do, and not to be obliged to *Tranſplant* themſelves, which would be very grievous, eſpecially to ſuch as love their own Country; and I appeal to all Men, who are conſidering Men, and have had Experience, Whether any thing can make this Nation ſo great and flouriſhing as *Liberty of Conſcience*; Some of our Neighbours dread it.

I could add much more to confirm all I have ſaid, but now is not the proper time.

ROCHESTER,
Decemb. 22. 1688.

His Majesties Reasons for Withdrawing Himself from Rochester, Rochester, 1688. (Author's Collection)

22 December 1688

Having received confirmation that the queen and his son, the Prince of Wales, had safely arrived in Louis XIV's court, James II finally decided to leave England and join his queen in France. His decision had been made easier by William's decision to reduce the number of soldiers guarding the king. James ordered the publication of a handbill stating *His Majesties Reasons for Withdrawing Himself from Rochester*, which outlines his reasons for leaving the country. His reasons include the arrest of Lord Feversham, William taking possession of his palace in the middle of the night, that he was 'born free', and that he had risked his life for the country on 'several occasions'.[60] There is no doubt that James II realised that William could not fulfil his ambitions while he lived and was in England.

23 December 1688

William ordered the Dutch foot guard under the command of Colonel Wiick to relax their guard on the king and his escorts and even issued the Duke of Berwick with blank passports for himself and his father.[61] James II, along with the duke, left their temporary quarters in Rochester and made their way to the coast in order to arrange passage from England and into the protection of Louis XIV of France. William allowed James to leave as this resolved a number of issues, including the potential risk of loyalists flocking to James's side and reigniting the conflict, possibly resulting in a protracted civil war.

24 December 1688

The Prince of Orange, while still waiting for the formal declaration of his power, started to govern the country and instructed Samuel Pepys to arrange the transport of a regiment of foot to the islands of Guernsey and Jersey and to arrange for the return of the seven companies of the Princess Anne of Denmark's Regiment of Foot currently stationed on the islands back to

60 King James II, *His Majesties Reasons for Withdrawing Himself from Rochester* (Rochester: NP, 1688).

61 Beddard, *A Kingdom Without a King*, p.64.

England.[62] James II departed England for France. This departure, along with him throwing the Great Seal into the River Thames when he first departed London, would be used by the lords to confirm that he had abdicated the throne of England. William of Orange was finally in control of the country without any major military conflict and with James II supposedly leaving the country by his own choice.

25 December 1688

The Lords Spiritual and Temporal requested that William take up the administration of the country, both civil and military, including the disposal (use) of all public finances for the protection of religion (Protestant) and for the peace of the nation. The request stipulated that this would be until a Convention was called for on 22 January 1689, although the lords' message was clear that the Convention was being held to ratify the agreement and to ensure that there was no subsequent legal basis to challenge William's succession.[63] The request stipulated a convention, and not for Parliament to be convened, because only the king could call for a new Parliament and England no longer had a king within the realm. The request was for William to take control of the country, and not for William and Mary to rule as joint monarchs or in joint control. At this time there was not any clear decision

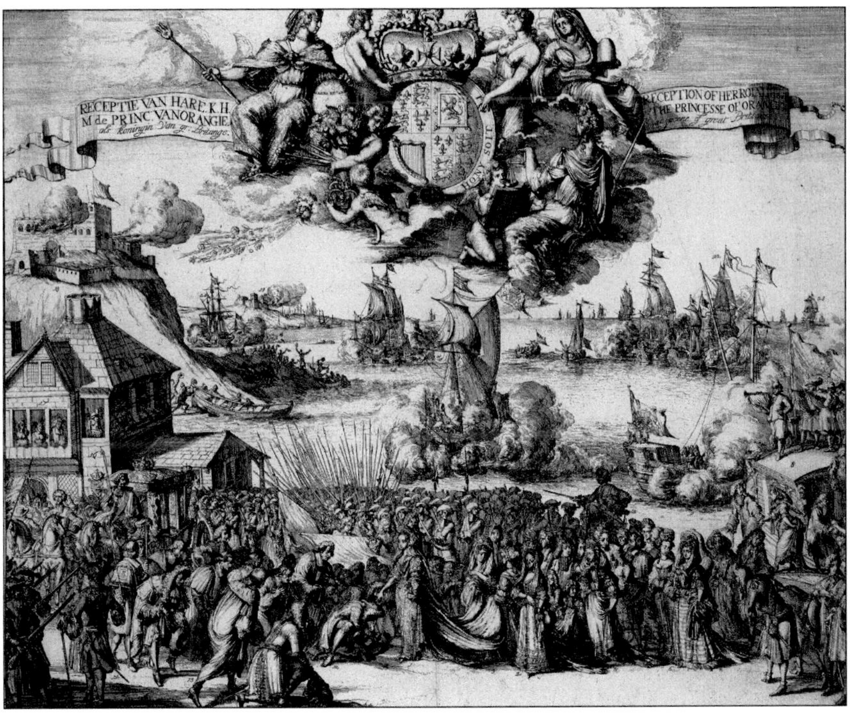

The reception of the Princess of Orange as Queen of England, a print by Romeyn de Hooghe, northern Netherlands, 1689. (Rijksmuseum: RP-P-OB-79.451, Public Domain)

62 NA: WO4/1, f.121.
63 Beddard, *A Kingdom Without a King*, p.166.

as to who would be 'invited' to rule England, William or Mary as a single monarch, or both as a dual monarchy.

28 December 1688

William of Orange officially accepted the responsibility for governing the country after previously issuing letters to each constituency for electing a Convention, although he had in all aspects been in charge of the country since mid-December. Even at this stage, the authority was solely with William – Mary had no formal role within the administration.

5

Aftermath

With William in charge of the country and in control of the army, the interregnum government refunded the States General for the full cost of raising and funding the invasion of England with the sum of 6 million Dutch guilders.[1] English troops were banned from being within 20 miles of London until the spring of 1690, with the capital effectively being under Dutch military occupation.[2] The Garde te Voet continued to guard St James's Palace, Whitehall, and Somerset House, while the regiments from the Anglo-Dutch and Scots-Dutch brigades were encamped within the Tower of London and in Lambeth.[3] William ordered the disbandment of numerous English regiments raised in the last months of James II's reign, including Lord Brandon's Regiment of Horse, while in March 1689 William ordered the raising of new regiments in London and several parts of the country.[4] In 1689 William ordered 8,000 English troops to the Netherlands in order to 'act against the French' in accordance with the Treaty of Nijmegen (1678), which shows that he had faith in the abilities and prowess of English troops.[5] During the convention of 22 January 1689, both houses of Parliament eventually agreed that both William and Mary should be offered the crown as joint monarchs. This was after the convention had declared that James II had abdicated the throne of England. This decision was reached after taking into account that the king had abandoned his authority by throwing the Great Seal into the Thames, and his people and throne by voluntarily leaving England for France. The offer of joint monarchy was based on William and Mary accepting of the Bill of Rights (1689), limiting the power of the monarchy, and securing the future role of Parliament and the Lords.

The Irish regiments had in effect found themselves to be foreign troops in a hostile country, but they generally conducted themselves with honour and according to military discipline. A number of the officers from the Irish

1 Glozier, *The Huguenot Soldiers of William of Orange*, p.107

2 A. van Poot, *Engelands gods-dienst en vryheid hersteld, door sijn Hoogheid den heere Prince van Oranjen* (Amsterdam: Marcus Doornik, 1689), pp.164–67.

3 Luttrell, *A Brief Historical Relation of State Affairs*, pp.488–89.

4 Luttrell, *A Brief Historical Relation of State Affairs*, pp.495, 511.

5 Israel, 'The Dutch Role', p.134; Luttrell, *A Brief Historical Relation of State Affairs*, p.507.

regiments had already given up their commissions, including Lord Forbes and six Protestant officers of the Irish foot guards.[6] While some troops did try to make their way home following the disbanding of the English army, including a large detachment of troops who unsuccessfully tried to take control of a Levant trading ship on the Thames, the majority still believed themselves to be in the service of the state. Troops from all the regiments remained together under their officers and even petitioned the Privy Council for protection. Officers from Lord Forbes's Regiment of Foot sent the following petition:[7]

> The humble petition of Lieutenant-Colonel Tuite and the disbanded officers and Soldiers of the Lord Forbes's Regiment… The said Officers and soldiers desire your Lordship's protection; and that you would propose some means for their security and subsistence in case you will have them continue here; or to give them a speedy licence to depart, either to their own country, or to the service of any Prince, that may be consistent with the interest of this Kingdom.

This was followed by a request from senior officers of the English army, who sent a petition to the Prince of Orange stating that:[8]

> We thought fit to report to your Highness the condition of the Irish forces now here in England. They being very ready to submit and lay down their armes. Our humble request in their behalf is that they may be assured of safety to retire separately or otherwise, at your highness shall think fit for their safety.

The Irish troops who were under the orders of the interregnum government were ordered to march to Portsmouth, where they were to be transported to the Isle of Wight, being held in internment while a solution was found for their service.[9] By the start of January 1689, it was suggested that about 1,500 'Irish' soldiers were quartered in Portsmouth awaiting transport.[10] Troops arrived in Portsmouth in good order and with good morale, with 250 troopers from Colonel Butler's Regiment of Dragoons arriving mounted.[11] The original plan was to house them within Carisbrook Castle and the surrounding town of Newport. William ordered the Board of Ordnance to provide sufficient bedding for the soldiers and for them to be guarded by four companies, each of 80 men.[12] The Board of Ordnance confirmed on 10 January 1689 that there were enough ammunition beds (seventeenth-century slang for camp beds) available at the Tower of London and in Portsmouth to accommodate the Irish troops. On 15 January the board advised that they

6 Luttrell, *A Brief Historical Relation of State Affairs*, pp.483, 496.
7 Beddard, *A Kingdom Without a King*, pp.106–07.
8 NA: SP8/2, f.75.
9 H. Murtagh and D. Murtagh, *The Irish Jacobite Army* (Dublin: Four Courts Press, 2024), pp.31–35.
10 BL: C161, f.2 75, English Newspapers, *The Universal Intelligence* No. 8, Tues., Jan. 1 to Thur., Jan. 3 1689 and *Orange Gazette* No. 5, Thur., 10 Jan. to Thur., 17 Jan. 1688/9.
11 Childs, *William III*, p.10.
12 NA: WO4/1, f.118.

had been mistaken and they could not provide any beds for the soldiers.[13] The Governor of the Isle of Wight, Sir Robert Holmes, was ordered to allow the Irish officers to keep their swords and to store all other weapons 'in such a manner' that they would be in a good condition when they (the weapons) were restored to the soldiers prior to their departure.[14] Troops were billeted in tents on Camp Hill and seemingly had the ability to travel to all the towns within the island and interact with the inhabitants, with some marrying local women. Sir Robert Holmes stated in a letter that, 'Those 'Irish' [that] are married since their arrival on the Island and do not care wither for [the continent] and we [find] them lurking and slacking about the island.'[15] In April 1689, William had secured an agreement with Emperor Leopold I of the Habsburg Empire to transfer 1,800 'Irish troops' to the Habsburg army for use on the eastern front against the Ottoman Empire.[16] The first group of troops left the Isle of Wight on 24 April 1689, bound for Hamburg, with approximately 1,000 soldiers departing later due to a lack of ships and illness (smallpox) within the camp.[17] Seven Imperial regiments were instructed that they were to receive foreign 'Irish' recruits; these were the Souches, Neuburg, Bufues, Carafte, Reusshofsantsley, Wallis, and Toblent regiments.[18] The 'Irish' soldiers were subsequently incorporated into one regiment due to integration issues within the seven original regiments. While tracking the service history of these men has so far been impossible, there were still at least 930 'Irish' soldiers serving in the Imperial army at the end of 1689.[19]

While the end of the invasion of 1688, or the 'Glorious Revolution' is generally considered to be James II's flight to France and the interim government's offer to William to succeed him, the last military campaign of William's invasion was actually in March 1689. On 12 March 1689 Scottish troops that had been incorporated into the English establishment mutinied, consisting of the majority of the Duke of Schomberg's Regiment of Foot, formerly under the command of Lord Dumbarton. This action resulted in Parliament ordering Dutch troops to intercept the mutinying troops and to bring them back under control by any means necessary, including by force of arms. The mutiny was reported in Parliament on Friday 15 March, when Mr Harbord stated incorrectly that the soldiers had declared for King James.[20] Parliament reported that 1,500 soldiers had deserted with their officers, pay chest, and with four pieces of light artillery (presumably the four battalion guns that were issued to the regiment). There was a general fear amongst the

13 NA: WO4/1, ff.119–20.

14 NA: WO4/1, ff.120–21.

15 IOW: Gw10/39, Letters of Sir Robert Holmes, f.9.

16 OSK: AFA 1690, Krieg Gegan Frankreich Turkenjring, Kt196, ff.158, 192–201; OSK, Bde 378, ff.606–07.

17 Luttrell, *A Brief Historical Relation of State Affairs*, p.525; *The Manuscripts of S.H. Le Fleming Esq of Rydal Hall* (London: HMSO, 1890), p.232; NA: ADM106/387, f.159; IOW: Gw10/39, f.13.

18 OSK, Bde 379, Registrat Protocoll, 1689, f.146.

19 D. Murphy, *The Irish Brigades, 1685-2006: A Gazetteer of Irish Military Service, Past and Present* (Dublin: Four Courts Press, 2007), pp.7–8.

20 William Harbord (1635–92), Member of Parliament for Launceston, Cornwall and Thetford, Norfolk. He accompanied William during his invasion and was made a Privy Counsellor in 1689. *Dictionary of National Biography* (1st supplement) (London: Smith Elder & Co, 1901).

new government that if this mutiny was not suppressed quickly, the actions of the mutineers would attract more dissenters and disillusioned soldiers and they would become an army if not stopped.[21] The reasons behind this mutiny are definitely not as simple as declaring for King James, as stated by Colonel Birch in his speech to Parliament. The majority of these soldiers had enlisted with a peacetime army and were now being asked to fight on the Continent in a foreign war for a foreign nation, namely Holland. In addition, they were being asked to fight alongside Dutch soldiers, who were paid more than the 8d English soldiers received a day.[22] The loyalties of soldiers are a complex issue and cannot be distilled down into a simple generalisation. Soldiers could be loyal to their regiment, their colonel (in this case Dumbarton and not Schomberg), or their country (Scotland, England, or both) as well as to Parliament or the king. As the stated aim of the mutineers was to return to their home country, Scotland, their nationality or perceived nationality certainly would have played a part in their decision. The Scottish army had been temporarily transferred onto the English establishment, but these regiments obviously considered themselves Scottish and not English. Their request to return to Scotland does suggest an element of national identity; however, practical issues might have been a more pressing reason.[23] Following the disbandment of the army on 11 December 1688, the precarity of army life and pay would have been brought to the forefront. The Scottish regiments would have wanted to return to a location friendly to them, and back to their families where they were sure they could survive the end of winter and the upcoming spring. With the army in flux and without pay or links to the community, the officers and soldiers would have found it hard to secure winter quarters among the civilian population of England.

These mass desertions brought the loyalty of all English troops into the forefront of the debate within Parliament, and also within William's close circle of advisers. William never fully trusted English or Scottish officers who had not served within the Anglo-Dutch brigades and did not fully trust those officers who had delayed in changed their loyalty from James to William.[24] During the Parliamentary debate of 15 March 1689, the Member of Parliament for Cirencester urged Parliament and the King to only send Dutch troops after the deserting troops bound for Scotland, stating, 'I know not which else to trust.'[25] While this statement obviously demonstrates the feelings of some of the members of Parliament, it was countered by a declaration of loyalty to their Majesties (King William and Queen Mary) by the officers and men of Lord Mordant's Regiment of Foot. The colonel of the

21 Speech by Colonel Birch, 15 March 1690, *Grey's Debates of the House of Commons: Volume 9* (London: T. Becket and P.A. De Hondy, 1769).

22 NA: WO24/12, ff.1–6; BL: Add MS 15897, f.88. Private soldiers of the foot guards and the Coldstream Guards received 10d a day, while troopers in regiments of horse received 2s 6d a day. The disparity in pay is due to troopers having to pay for to look after their horse. All pay was subject to stoppages and was always paid in arrears.

23 NA: SP8-2, ff.77–78.

24 Manning, *An Apprenticeship in Arms*, p.346.

25 John Grubham How (1657–1722), MP for Cirencester, Gloucestershire, between January 1689 and February 1690 and was appointed as Vice-Chamberlain to Queen Mary in 1689.

regiment 'assured him [the King] of standing in such manner and place as he shall command', offering to send his regiment to intercept the mutineers.[26] Even before these instances had been resolved, they sparked fierce debate within Parliament and instigated the call for a Mutiny Act to replace the outdated legislation. The debate called for the mutineers to be charged with 'levying war on the King and Queen' while the deserters were accused of 'deserting [too] and corresponding with the King's Enemies', both of which were treasonable acts.[27]

Concurrent debates within Parliament focused on the 'growing insolence of Papists' and reports of 'Papists' burning houses and refusing to give up arms and although there was no correlation between these acts and the acts of the regiments destined for Holland, it added to the atmosphere of fear within Parliament and the country. William and Parliament ordered one of his Dutch commanders, Lieutenant-General Godart van Reede van Ginkel, heer van Amerongen, to pursue the mutineers with a sufficient force of horse and dragoons to 'oblige them to submit to the King's mercy'.[28] The warrant specified that the mutineers were not to be punished but to be transported to Holland with the rest of the army, as their original order had stated.

Ginkel's pursuit force consisted of the three companies of his own regiment of horse that were in England and all ten companies of the Dutch Gardes Dragonders, along with two newly raised regiments of English horse. The English regiments had been raised by William's supporters during or immediately after the invasion and, therefore, their loyalty to William was not in any doubt. Although the two English regiments were green, they would ensure that if any military action was needed, it would not just be Dutch troops fighting Scottish and English troops. The troops were despatched on 19 March 1689 and intercepted the mutineers outside Sleaford in Lincolnshire. Despite their appearance, the Scottish troops did not have any coherent plan or unified objective, and numerous small bodies of men had already left the column of march and dissipated throughout the countryside. Lieutenant Barnesley, along with nine other soldiers, was apprehended by the authorities in Cambridge while a further seven soldiers were caught near Gravesend in Kent with horses.[29] By the time Ginkel intercepted the

26 NA: WO55/401, f.6; Luttrell, *A Brief Historical Relation of State Affairs*, p.512; Taylor, *The Entring Book of Roger Morrice, IV*, p.400. Henry Lord Viscount Mordant returned from Holland with William of Orange and was commissioned to raise a regiment of foot in late December 1688 by William of Orange (BL: C161 f.2 75, English Newspapers, *The English Currant*, Wed., Jan. 2 to Friday, Jan. 4 1688/9, f.1). This regiment was not sent with the force raised to intercept the mutineers; it was instead sent down to the Isle of Wight: Newport, Isle of Wight, NP: D1 1986–2728, pp.12–13; NP: Newport Corporation MSS Convocation Book, Vol. II (1669–1760), p.225.

27 Speech by Mr. Hampden, 15 and 16 March 1689, British History Online, <https://www.british-history.ac.uk/greys-debates/vol9/pp148-172#fnn1>.

28 Lieutenant-General Godart van Reede van Ginkel, heer van Amerongen (1644–1702) commanded a Dutch regiment of horse which accompanied the Prince of Orange's invasion force in 1688. He later accepted the Jacobite surrender at the second siege of Limerick in 1691 which ended the War of the Two Kings in Ireland (1689–91) and became the Earl of Athlone in 1691. M. McNally, *St Ruth's Fatal Gamble: The Battle of Aughrim 1691 and the Fall of Jacobite Ireland* (Warwick: Helion & Co, 2018), pp.47–48.

29 NA: SP44/97, ff.45-46, 49.

mutineers, their ranks had been reduced from the reported 1,500 soldiers to approximately 20 officers and 500 men. After a brief peaceful standoff with the government forces and being informed that the royal warrant stated that there would be no additional punishment if they returned to the army, the remaining mutineers were convinced that their only option was to return with Ginkel's force and head to the coast for onward transport for Flanders. However, after the mutineers had complied with William's and Parliament's orders, they were made prisoners and all their arms were seized, including the four battalion guns that they had brought with them.[30] While the latter part of the order regarding no additional punishment was true for the majority of those involved, a number of soldiers were singled out for arrest and tried for treason. This included all the officers, who were deemed to be ringleaders, and, in an act reminiscent of the ancient Roman punishment of decimation, a percentage of the enlisted soldiers were selected for punitive punishment.[31] Nineteen officers and the selected soldiers were transported to London to stand trial, arriving in London on 26 March 1689. The rest of the soldiers were taken to ports under guard and transported to Holland to join up with the main English army.[32] The Duke of Schomberg's (Dumbarton's) Regiment of Foot tried to make up the shortfall following the desertions by instigating a levy and emptying jails and tolbooths of military-aged men, but by July 1689 it was still some 500 men below full strength.[33]

While a number of the new regiments raised by James II were dissolved, some were incorporated into William's new English army. On 15 December 1688, the soldiers of Colonel Solomon Richard's Regiment of Foot unanimously laid down their arms and then immediately took them up for William. The regiment has the distinction of being one of the last regiments to be commissioned by James (27 September 1688) and was subsequently one of the first to be re-commissioned by William, on 21 December 1688.[34] William re-armed the regiment and sent it to Ireland as one of the first regiments to relieve the Siege of Londonderry, which confirms that William was willing to show loyalty to those officers who declared their loyalty to him and to Mary. These actions of re-commissioning regiments originally raised by James caused a rift between William and the lords, which resulted in the Lords Spiritual and Temporal appointing a commission 'inquiring into the hinderance to the expedition to Ireland and why Richard's regiment, being

30 Luttrell, *A Brief Historical Relation of State Affairs*, p.514.

31 The term decimation refers to the Roman practice of selection every tenth man to be put to death as a punitive sanction in cases of desertion, mutiny, or other crimes (*Oxford English Dictionary*).

32 HMC, *The Manuscripts of S.H. Le Fleming, Esq of Rydal Hall* (London: HMSO, 1890), p.232; M. Knight (ed.), *The Entring Book of Roger Morrice*. Vol. V, *The Reign of William III 1689-91* (Woodbridge: The Boydell Press, 2007), p.74; Luttrell, *A Brief Historical Relation of State Affairs*, pp.514-15.

33 H. Paton (ed.), *The Register of the Privy Council of Scotland*: Third Series, Vol. XIII, *A.D. 1686-1689* (Edinburgh: HMSO, 1932), pp.180 81, 548, 580; H. Paton (ed.), *The Register of the Privy Council of Scotland*: Third Series, Vol. XIV, *A.D. 1686-1689* (Edinburgh: HMSO, 1933), pp.234, 268, 619.

34 WO55/336, f.75; *CSPD: James II, 1687–89*, pp.284-85; Dalton, *English Army Lists*, vol. II, p.252.

the last raised by King James is the first to be sent against him'.[35] While William was allowed to send his chosen regiment to Ireland, the lords used this as a reason to tighten the wording of the Test Act and the Act of Supremacy with more direct 'anti-papist' language.

The Mutiny Act of 1688/89 was a direct response to the mass mutinies and desertions by elements of the English army and would remain one of the main legacies of the events of November 1688. The act would put the army on a clear legal basis and would separate civil and military crimes and jurisdictions and would form the basis for all future military legislation and army regulations.[36] The initial act was originally in effect from 12 April 1689 until 10 November 1689, but was subsequently extended. The first section stated that in accordance with the Declaration of Rights, the Monarchy could not raise or keep a standing army without the consent of Parliament and that: 'During this time of Danger several of the Forces which are now on foot should be continued and others raised for the Safety of the Kingdome for the Common Defence of the Protestant Religion and for the reducing of Ireland.' The act's original nine sections dictated how any court martial should be raised, how many members it should have and of what rank, depending on the rank of the offender. A tenth section was added stating that in the event of a sentence of death, at least nine of the thirteen members of the court must agree on the verdict.

An allegory of the coronation of William and Mary as King and Queen of Great Britain, 1688, a print by Romeyn de Hooghe, northern Netherlands, 1689. (Rijksmuseum: RP-P-OB-79.335, Public Domain)

35 HL/PO/JO/10/1/409, f.124; HMC, *Fleming*, p.244.

36 Wm. & Mar. I, c 5, 'An Act for Punishing Officers or Soldiers who shall Mutiny or Desert Their Majestyes Service.' (Mutiny Act 1688.)

6

Conclusion

> In all revolutions the vanquished are the ones who are guilty of treason, even by the historians, for history is written by the victors and framed according to the prejudices and bias existing on their side.[1]

The events of November and December 1688 have been ingrained into the collective memory of the British population as the Glorious Revolution, as made clear by Margaret Thatcher's speech in Parliament on the tricentenary of the events. However, there have always been a number of questions that need answering: how to define the events, why the English army failed to stop the Dutch, and what were the main reasons for William's involvement – religious saviour or political and military opportunist? There has been a longstanding debate amongst historians and academics regarding how to define the events of 1688: was it a revolution, a coup, or an invasion? When looking at most accounts covering the event, they call it a revolution. However, we need to differentiate between causation and correlation when we are looking at the outcome of William's and James's actions. The events covered within this book have been known by numerous names over the last 300 years; some, such as 'the English Revolution', were designed to evoke differences and a sense of 'being more civilised', separating the events of 1688 and the anarchy of the American Revolution (1775–83) or the French Revolution (1789–99).[2] The terms 'Bloodless Revolution' and 'Peaceful Revolution' were again designed to differentiate the events from the later bloody revolution on the Continent and in the Americas. However, as shown within this book, while there were no pitched battles, the events were definitely not bloodless. Soldiers were killed on both sides, at Cirencester, Wincanton, and at Reading, while the Dutch also lost men of the invasion fleet. Whig historians have been eager

---

1 G.G. Vest, *Kansas City Gazette*, 21 August 1891. Vest was a Missouri senator and had been a congressman at the Confederate Congress.

2 See R. Price, 'A celebration of the Revolution of 1688-1689, November 4, 1789', and E. Burke, 'The Significance of the revolution of 1688-1689, 1790', in S. Pincus (ed.), *England's Glorious Revolution 1688-1689: A Brief History with Documents* (Boston: Yale University Press, 2006), pp.50–55.

to separate the events in Scotland in 1689 and the long campaign in Ireland (1689–91) from the events of 1688, even though the overthrowing of James II was the direct cause of these events and the subsequent Jacobite rebellions of 1715, 1719, and 1745. Even looking past the minor skirmishes of 1688, the events cannot be described as peaceful, with riots within numerous cities and towns throughout the country, Catholic chapels and homes being destroyed and mass hysteria following the reports of the 'Irish Fright'. Troops and militia had to be stationed on the streets of London and other towns to protect life and property and while William had instigated some of the anti-Catholic feeling with his propaganda, it reached levels where even he needed to act to quell the unrest.

While James II was not 'technically' forcibly evicted from the throne of England at bayonet point, either in his first attempted flight from London or in his later escape to France, James did not leave of his own free will: he was, in effect, banished from his country. With foreign troops in control of London and the Home Counties, and Williamite supporters in control of large swathes of the country, England was in effect in a state of occupation by Williamite forces. James's actions, including throwing away the state seal, helped ensure the Whig victory, allowing them to conclude that James II had abdicated the throne, thus leaving it open to William and Mary. However, the vote confirming the abdication of James II and the transfer of the crown was neither straightforward nor unanimous as there were numerous objectors, including Bishops of the Church of England, with the vote only passing by 64 votes to 46.[3] William had played his part well: the fifth column in the guise of the Treason Club and the Immortal Seven had ensured that the army and navy were crippled from within. William and Whig propaganda, along with the collective memory of the Civil War, had ensured that the civilian population either stayed out of the events or bought into the false narrative of 'Papist' uprisings, rape, and pillage, including the 'Irish Fright'.

As for the term 'Glorious Revolution', there is no doubt that the events of 1688 caused a major shift in the political structure of England. England, and later Britain, had been transformed from a monarchy based on divine right to a constitutional monarchy with Parliament separating itself from the whims and constraints of the monarch. The Bill of Rights (1689) was formed as a direct result of what Parliament deemed to be the monarch's (James II's) absolutism and excesses and was designed to limit William's and any future monarchs' powers. The later Act of Settlement (1701) would inhibit Catholics in general and James II's children in particular from the succession, resulting in the line of succession falling to George Ludwig of Hanover, who became George I of Great Britain following the death of Queen Anne on 1 August 1714, leading to our current monarch, King Charles III. The Act of Settlement had stipulated that George's mother, Sophia, Electress of Hanover, was next in line to the throne until her death on 8 June 1714. While William's involvement did eventually lead to these changes, they were completely unforeseen at the time. William's intent was to ensure that

---

3 Israel, 'The Dutch Role', p.131.

James II did not support Louis XIV in his war against Holland and to take the English crown for himself and for his wife. William's preparations for the invasion of England started in 1687, a year before the engineered letter from the 'Immortal Seven' inviting him to save the country from 'Popery and Slavery'. The Dutch diplomacy during 1687 ensured the support of Protestant nations, securing German and Swedish forces to free up Dutch troops for the invasion, as well as support from Catholic states including Emperor Leopold I of the Habsburg Empire and Pope Innocent XI.

There has been an argument that the events of 1688 constituted a coup d'état, with some of the evidence at first glance seeming to support this interpretation. There were a small group of English lords, both spiritual and temporal, alongside army and naval officers who colluded to illegally remove James II from the throne of the country. These actions, at first glance, could constitute the textbook definition of a coup; however, this does not tell the full story, which is that they were reliant on a foreign power to be able to accomplish this. Members of this group had been in contact with William and his supporters in the year prior to the 'letter of invitation' being sent to William, so these events fall outside of the scope of a coup d'état. While the events did cause a revolution in how Parliament and the monarchy interacted, this was not the intent at the time. So if not a revolution or a coup, then it just leaves invasion as a definition.

The actions, or rather inaction, of the English army to stop the invasion and then to fail to bring the Williamite force to a pitched battle has often been explained as proof that the English forces were of poor quality, in equipment, in training, and in morale. If the English forces were of such poor quality, the question needs to be asked: why was William so concerned about the possibility of their involvement in the Continental war on the side of Louis XIV of France and why was he so angry when the army was dissolved on 11 December 1688? The answer is simply that the English army, although it had little experiences in the large-scale battles of the Franco-Dutch War (1672–78), was not an insignificant force. The process of modernisation of the army had started almost as soon as James II succeeded to the throne, and following his experience in the failed Monmouth Rebellion. James had instigated yearly training camps, the implementation of new, modern equipment and tactics, and the standardisation of formations. There were newly formed regiments that had received little or no training and some of the regiments raised in the last days and weeks before the invasion did suffer from a lack of men and equipment. However, these issues were only localised problems which did not impact the whole army, so if the failure of the army was not down to training or equipment, it could only be put down to morale and the loyalties of their officers. The members of the Treason Club had done their job well: officers of all ranks defected to William, while others including Churchill continued to feign loyalty to James until their situation became untenable. These fifth column officers spread fear, uncertainty, and doubt within the ranks of their regiments, resulting in a reduction in the units' morale. While records for this period are far from complete, very few of the rank and file defected with their officers, confirming that the general loyalty within the army remained fairly secure. James II did, however, have a failure in his morale and confidence in his army commanders, and in the army as a whole. His uncertainty, increased poor health, and lack of confidence can be tracked based on the numbers and seniority of those abandoning him during November and December 1688. While the army was within close range of the enemy on numerous occasions, it was always ordered to retire and not to face the Dutch in a pitched battle. In short, the failure of the English army was down to the fifth column operating within its command structure and not to issues with the training or equipment of the army. James II's order to Lord Feversham regarding the disbanding of the forces under his command was poorly worded and did at least as much damage to the English as the actions of the Treason Club and the Dutch army. Feversham's order was also open to interpretation, with some officers disbanding their entire regiments, while others just dismissed all Catholic and Irish soldiers from within their ranks. With the king departing London, many soldiers used this opportunity and period of ongoing chaos and uncertainty to withdraw from army life and return to their civilian occupations and homes.

The size and disposition of England's military forces during November and December 1688 has always been in question and needs further clarification to fully understand the ease with which the Williamite forces took control of the country. While the fifth columnist activities of the Williamite Whigs and members of the Treason Club had a large impact on the result of the invasion, the actual size of England's forces needs to be taken into account. While this is a history of the land campaign, the Royal Navy's involvement or lack thereof needs to be taken into account in order to be able to understand the larger military and political picture within England and the resulting impact on the Dutch fleet's free and unrestricted movement within English waters. The movements of the English fleet have been previously reported on, but the size of the English navy needs some clarification. On 18 December, the interregnum government received an update on the location and current size and readiness of the English fleet. The report confirmed that the Channel fleet consisted of 52 ships between third and sixth-raters, along with four yachts and 20 fireships. The vast majority of the fleet was located on 18 December at Spithead (53 ships of all classes) and all but 12 ships were within home waters.[4] There have always been issues with understanding the true size of the English army during November and December 1688 and historians have tended to overestimate the size of the standing army. One reason for this is a breakdown of the English army presented to the ruling lords on or about 18 December 1688. The document, titled 'A List of King James's Army Clothed and Armed', states that the English army had 53,716 men under arms, which has been used to prove the size of the English army.[5] This states that the army consisted of:

Eight regiments of horse (each of nine troops with 53 men)	3,816 men
Eight regiments of dragoons (each of 10 troops of 60 men)	4,800 men
48 regiments of foot (each of 13 companies of 60 men)	37,440 men

4 NA: SP8/2, ff.93–95. See Appendix IV for the full location of the fleet.
5 NA: SP8/2, f.99.

French foot	5,000 men
Foot guards (22 companies of 100 men)	2,200 men
Two troops of horse guards (each of 200 men)	400 men
One troop of horse (described as amateurs)	60 men

In addition to the number of complete regiments, the report also stated that there were an additional four regiments to be fitted out. However, there are a number of serious errors and inaccuracies within this account; most importantly, the inclusion of 5,000 'French foot' clearly shows that this is nothing but Williamite or Whig propaganda. James II never brought over any 'French troops' and never accepted any offer from Louis XIV of any troops until 1689, when French troops landed in Ireland. Even by late December there were three troops of horse guards, the fourth troop having already been disbanded as it was supposedly all 'Catholic', any Protestant troops being absorbed into the three other troops. In addition to the missing troop, the entry for the horse guards fails to include the troop of 60 horse grenadiers attached to each troop. The entry only shows one and not two regiments of foot guards and, lastly, each regiment is quoted at its full paper strength and does not take into account the collapse of the army following William's invasion and the disbanding of the army on 11 December 1688. The numbers of regiments involved within this document are far closer to the English army under William in May–July 1689, when the army was ready for service in England, Ireland, and in Flanders.[6] Even with the new recruits, the regiments being sent to Flanders in May and June 1689 were understrength, with the muster rolls for five regiments of foot recording a shortage of 758 soldiers.[7]

Lastly, when looking at William's (and Mary's) motives behind the intervention in English politics, the issue of propaganda versus intent needs to be investigated. There's no doubt that William's published reasons prior to arriving within England stated that his intention was to save the country's Protestant population from enslavement under a 'Popish' and absolute monarchy. These declarations were repeated upon his arrival in Torbay and repeated throughout the country; however, William was not anti-Catholic. The Dutch army, like Holland, was not solely Protestant – the only issues were the loyalty of troops to the Stadholder and States General, and as previously stated, William's force contained more Catholics than the English army. William's anti-Catholic rhetoric was designed to destabilise the country by pitting English Protestants against Catholics within the army, navy, and the civilian population. William became concerned following the departure of James II that the anti-Catholic propaganda had gone too far, resulting in numerous riots and disorder, causing William to change the narrative and calm the situation in London and the surrounding counties. On taking command of the English army, William's first act was to order the army to swear loyalty to him and his wife. The order included all troops, regardless of

6 NA: WO24/9, ff.3–9; WO24/10, ff.3–16; WO24/12.

7 NA: SP8/5, f.104. A further five regiments of foot failed to provide detailed muster figures. Muster figures from September 1689 show a sickness rate of 25 percent and an absence rate of 3 percent (NA: SP8/5, f.323).

their religion, and had no mention of the anti-Catholic declarations within the Test Acts. It was Parliament, not William, that forced all soldiers to swear their loyalty again while using the wording of the Test Act, and instigated further amendments to the acts to ensure that wording of the Test Act became more anti-Catholic and more extreme. Parliament objected to regiments raised under James serving under William; such objections included Colonel Solomon Richard's Regiment of Foot, which was one of the first regiments to be ordered to defend Londonderry. William continued to defy the will of Parliament by recruiting Catholics into his army, within both his English and Dutch regiments. During the later stages of the war in Ireland (1689–91), William commissioned Catholic officers to govern captured towns in order to ensure a smooth transition of power. This constant use of Catholics within his forces is in direct contradiction to the continued use of William's image as the Protestant saviour, portrayed on a rearing white horse, which is nothing more than a continuation of his successful propaganda of 1688. Images filled with religious and chivalric symbology were published following the events of 1688, linking William's actions to St George and his fight against the evil dragon. This imagery, along with references to soldiers carrying flaming swords, referenced Biblical texts and was designed to project William's image as a saviour of the Protestant faith. William's agreement with Pope Innocent XI, confirming his intention of securing Mary's succession to the English throne and that his intention was not to subjugate the English Catholic population, can be seen as a direct contradiction of this Biblical image. William's aim was to secure the English throne, preferably without the use of force, but he was ready and willing to use whatever force was needed. He arrived in Torbay with a naval force greater than the Spanish Armada of 1588, and with one of the largest armies to ever land on English soil. His army included some of the best foot and mounted soldiers of the Dutch states, a large train of artillery, and a pontoon bridge, as well as enough supplies for a long-term campaign. The inclusion of bullion and equipment to mint coinage suggests that this was never intended as a short-term action to redirect James II back onto a Protestant path and engage with Parliament and call for free elections. William's intention was to control England's resources, including the army and navy, for his ongoing war against Louis XIV, and to deny France their use or abstention from the conflict. William and Mary's intentions were never to instigate a parliamentary democracy or a constitutional monarchy; they agreed to the Bill of Rights as a matter of pragmatism rather than as a prerequisite for their intervention. William had a number of confrontations with Parliament and the Lords. The support for his succession was not unanimous, with numerous lords, both spiritual and temporal, refusing to take the oath of loyalty to William and Mary. Despite the lords' concerns regarding James II's religion and policies, a number still believed that the king was appointed by the divine right of God, and therefore they could not intervene with God's will.

The 'Immortal Seven' never intended for the events of late 1688 to revolutionise England, either in the interactions between the monarchy and the people, or between the monarchy and Parliament – they just wanted England to be ruled by a Protestant king. The letter they sent on 30 June

1688 was not an impromptu invitation for urgent assistance from William, but a pre-arranged signal designed to confirm the legitimacy of William's preplanned actions. When looking at William's motives, you can believe either the reason he gave to Pope Innocent XI, that his only concern was to secure his wife's succession to the English throne, or those within his later statements and actions regarding securing England's allegiance and armed forces for his ongoing war with France. Whichever of his reasons is believed, neither required a revolution within England. William had no reason to diminish either his or Mary's power within England, as although his position within Holland as Stadholder was not hereditary and dependant on the authority of the Dutch states, he was aware that the crown of England was not. His belief in the right of kings can be seen in his interactions with Parliament during the entirety of his reign. Therefore, these events can only be realistically seen as a successful foreign invasion, and not a revolution or a coup. The invasion and subsequent propaganda have been so successful, in fact, that the actual act of invasion has been forgotten and the events of November and December 1688 have been immortalised as the Glorious Revolution.

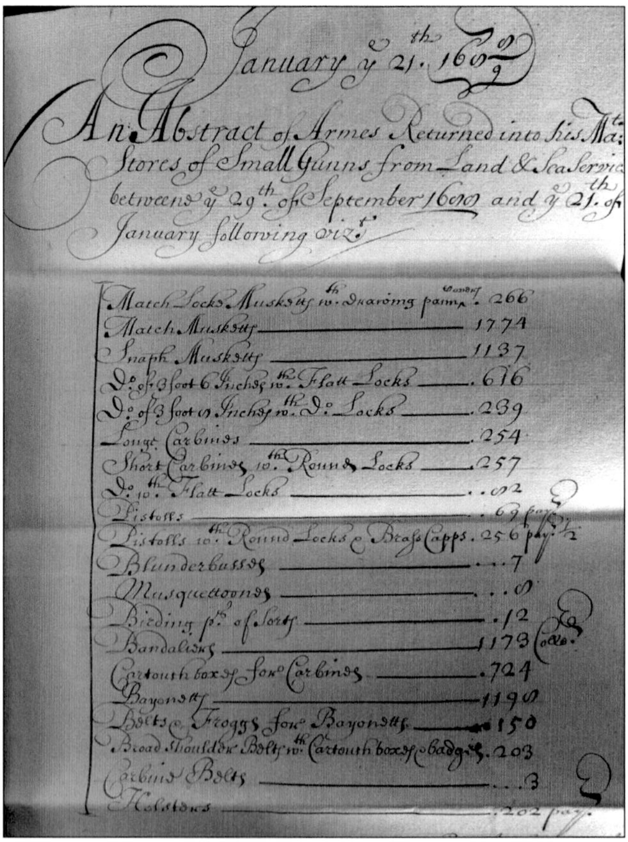

January ye 21th. 1688/9

An Abstract of Armes Returned into his Mats: Stores of Small Gunns from Land & Sea Service betweene ye 29th. of September 1688 and ye 21th. of January following viz.t

Match Locks Musketts wth. drawing pairs	266
Match Musketts	1774
Snaph Musketts	1137
Do. of 3 foot 6 Inches wth. Flatt Locks	616
Do. of 3 foot 0 Inches wth. Do. Locks	239
Longe Carbines	254
Short Carbines wth. Round Locks	257
Do. wth. Flatt Locks	02
Pistolls	69 pairs
Pistolls wth. Round Locks & Brass Capps	256 pay. ½
Blunderbusses	7
Musquettoons	0
Birding pcs. of Sorts	12
Bandaliers	1173 Colls.
Cartouch boxes for Carbines	724
Bayonetts	1190
Belts & Froggs for Bayonetts	150
Broad Shoulder Belts wth. Cartouch boxes & badges	203
Carbine Belts	3
Holsters	202 pay.

'An Abstract of Armes Returned into His Majesties Stores,' 1689. (Author's Collection)

Colour Plate Commentaries

Plate A. Regiment Ginkel, Colonel Godard van Reede, Heer van Ginkel

Raised 1665, this regiment of horse was commanded by one of Williams main commanders, who would later be responsible for tracking down the Scottish 'deserters' in early 1689. Three squadrons landed at Torbay in November 1688 (123 men). The regiment was involved in the main actions of the war in Ireland including the Battle of the Boyne, and the Battle of Aughrim and Sieges of Cork, Kinsale. Dutch cavalry was armed with a flintlock carbine, a pair of holster pistols and a sword. The trooper is dressed in a typical Dutch white coat without a collar, lined in white which shows on the turnbacks and on the cuffs, with brass buttons, and he is wearing white breeches.

Plate B. Regiment s'Gravemoer, Colonel Adam van der Duyn, Heer van s'Gravemoer

One squadron of 52 men landing in Torbay in November 1688, after which they remained in English service until 1697. The two remaining squadrons were active in the conflict against Louis XIV on the Continent. The trooper is shown wearing the regiment's white coat, with green lining, showing at the cuffs and where the top button is turned back, with tin buttons. The trooper has green breeches under his cavalry boots. Dutch cavalry did not wear the cuirass at the time, this was only reintroduced in 1707.

Plate C. *Gardes Dragonders* (Eppinger), Colonel Commandant Abraham Van Eppinger.

The *Gardes Dragonders* had an establishment strength of 800 men in 10 companies and while the colonel of the regiment was Willem III, Prince of Orange, the actual commander of the regiment was Abraham van Eppinger, who held the post between May 1679 and October 1700. He was granted the rank of Major-General in 1699. The regiment landed in England with its full strength in November 1688 and remained in English service until 1697, when the States General resumed paying for the regiment. The trooper is shown wearing the regiment's distinctive blackish-grey coat, with black lining, silver lace at each buttonhole including on cuffs and pocket flaps. The hat is a low, black fur, dragoon hat with brown bag handing behind. Dragoons were typically armed with a flintlock musket and sword; in addition, they carried a pistol and a hatchet on their saddle.

Plate D. Regiment Grobën, Colonel Christoffel Erhard van Grobën

As with most regiments of this period the regimental name changed with the colonel; with this regiment, Ernst Christoffel van Marwitz was awarded the colonelcy of the regiment in February 1688, however Williamite documentation during the campaign of 1688 refers to the regimental colonel still being van Grobën. The regiment landed at Torbay with eight companies, reportedly understrength at only 440 men. The regiment was returned to Holland in 1689 where it took part in the Battle of Walcourt on 25 August 1689. The establishment strength of Dutch line dragoon regiments should have been eight companies with 640 troopers. This trooper is shown wearing a red coat lined white with silver buttons, and a black hat with white edging, and white breeches.

Plate E. *Gardes te Voet*, Colonel Godard van Reede, Heer van Ginkel

The *Gardes te Voet*, the 'Dutch Blue Guards', was the senior regiment of the Dutch Army and had a strength of 27 companies in three battalions. Twenty-five companies landed with William in November 1688; one battalion remained in England and two battalions travelled to Ireland in 1689. It was the *Gardes te Voet* that secured St James Palace and King James II. Each battalion had a grenadier company, and the regiment, unusually, also had a cadet company. The figure is shown in the regiment's distinctive uniform of mid-blue coat lined yellow, with brass buttons, and red neck cloth, and yellow breeches and stockings. The image shows the distinctive extra buttons above the pocket flaps; two sets of two buttons set vertically. The figure is holding the Dutch pattern flintlock musket with a plug bayonet with a 12-inch blade fitted.

Plate F. Regiment Holstein-Norburg, Colonel Rodolf Frederik, Duke of Holstein-Norburg

The regiment landed at Torbay in November 1688 with 10 companies. Dutch infantry regiments generally had a peacetime strength of 10 companies (550 men) which was expanded to 12 companies (660 men) in wartime. Each company consisted of a captain, lieutenant, ensign, two sergeants, two drummers, forty-four privates, and four ancillary personal (servants and clerks). One soldier in five of each infantry regiment would normally be armed with a 4.5-metre long pike. The figure is dressed in the regiment's red coat, lined red, cuffs and pockets are edged with white lace with four buttons on the pocket flaps, red breeches and stockings, and a white neck cloth. Buff waist belt holding a sword, plug bayonet and cartridge pouch.

Plate G. Colonel Henry Sidney's Regiment of Foot. Better Known Under the Name of its Colonel Commandant, John Cutts

This regiment was one of the regiments belonging to the Anglo-Dutch brigade which had been in the pay of the States General since the late sixteenth century with the soldiers being recruited from England. William of Orange had refused James II requested the Anglo-Scots Brigade to be returned to England prior to November 1688, however, some officers and enlisted men returned to serve James II against William. The figure is shown wearing the regiments red coat lined in pale yellow, all troops within the regiment unusually had lace buttonholes with silver or tin buttons pale yellow breeches with off white stockings.

Plate H. Colonel Hugh Mackay's Regiment of Foot

The senior regiment in the Scots-Dutch Brigade. While the Anglo-Dutch brigade was disbanded in 1697, the Scots-Dutch Brigade was only disbanded in 1795. The regiment arrived in Torbay with all 12 companies and would later serve in the campaign in Scotland including serving at the Battle of Killiekrankie on 26 June 1689 along with the two other regiments of the brigade (Balfour's and Ramsay's). Drummers of the regiment followed tradition, and their coat colours were reversed, so had a blue coat with red lining. The figure is shown wearing a coat described as red-brown in colour, with a blue-grey lining, four brass buttons on the flap and three brass buttons on the cuff, yellow edging to the hat and a white neck cloth. The breeches are described as either red or light grey. The general 'rule' was that if a regiment used tin or white-metal buttons then the hat trim would be in white, and if the regiment used brass or gold buttons then it would be yellow.

Appendix I

Dutch Invasion Army

Cavalry Regiments

1. Gardes te Paard (Blue Guards), Colonel Hans Willem Bentinck, six companies, 480 men.[1]
2. Gardes du Corps, Captain Hendrik van Nassau-Ouwerkerk, one company, 197 men.[2]
3. Regiment Oyen, Colonel Matthias Hoeufft van Oyen, two companies, 82 men.[3]
4. Regiment Ginkel, Godard van Reede, Heer van Ginkel, three companies, 123 mcn.[4]
5. Regiment Waldeck, Colonel George Frederik, Graaf van Waldeck-Pyrmont en Culemborg, four companies, 208 men.[5]
6. Regiment Nassau-Zuylenstein, Colonel Willem Frederik van Nassau-Zuylenstein, two companies, 104 men.[6]
7. Regiment Obdam, Colonel Jacob van Wassenaer, Heer van Obdam, three companies, 156 men.[7]
8. Regiment Nassau-Saarbrücken, Colonel Prins Walrad, Graaf van Nassau-Saarbrücken, three companies, 156 men.[8]
9. Regiment Hayden, Colonel Frederik Willem, Baron van Hayden, three companies, 156 men.[9]
10. Regiment Montpouillan, Colonel Armand Nompar Caumont de la Force, Marquis de Montpouillan, three companies, 156 men.[10]

---

1 Hall, *Flags and Uniforms of the Dutch Army* Vol 1, pp.97–100.
2 Hall, *Flags and Uniforms of the Dutch Army* Vol. 1, pp.100–02.
3 Hall, *Flags and Uniforms of the Dutch Army* Vol. 1, pp.51–52.
4 Hall, *Flags and Uniforms of the Dutch Army* Vol. 1, pp.52–54.
5 Hall, *Flags and Uniforms of the Dutch Army* Vol. 1, pp.57–58.
6 Hall, *Flags and Uniforms of the Dutch Army* Vol. 1, pp.69–71.
7 Hall, *Flags and Uniforms of the Dutch Army* Vol. 1, pp.63–65.
8 Hall, *Flags and Uniforms of the Dutch Army* Vol. 1, pp.71–73.
9 Hall, *Flags and Uniforms of the Dutch Army* Vol. 1, pp.74–75.
10 Hall, *Flags and Uniforms of the Dutch Army* Vol. 1, pp.79–81.

11. Regiment Flodroff, Colonel Adriaan Gustaaf van Flodroff, three companies, 156 men.[11]
12. Regiment Lippe, Colonel Otto, Graaf von de Lippe, three companies, 156 men.[12]
13. Regiment Riedesel, Colonel George, Baron van Riedesel, three companies, 156 men.[13]
14. Regiment Quadt-Soppenbroek, Colonel Willem Roeleman, Heer van Quadt-Soppenbroek, two companies, 104 men.
15. Regiment Schack, Colonel Bogislaf Sigismund Schack, three companies, 156 men.[14]
16. Regiment s'Gravemoer, Colonel Adam van der Duyn, Heer van s'Gravemoer, one company, 52 men.[15]

Dragoons

1. Gardes Dragonders (Eppinger), Colonel Commandant Abraham van Eppinger, 10 companies, 860 men.[16]
2. Regiment Marwitz, Colonel Ernst Christoffel van Marwitz, eight companies, 440 men.[17]

The mounted element consisted of elements of 16 cavalry regiments, comprising 45 companies with a paper strength of 2,598 men, with two dragoon regiments of 18 companies and 1,300 men at full strength.

Infantry

1. Gardes te Voet, Colonel Godard van Reede, Heer van Ginkel (in English pay until 1699), two battalions, 25 companies, 2,522 men.[18]
2. Regiment Wynbergen, Ditmar van, Heer Va Horssen & de Poll, 12 companies, 660 men.[19]
3. Regiment Birkenfeld, Johan Karek, Prins en Paltsgaft von, 10 companies, 550 men.[20]
4. Regiment Holstein-Norburg, Rodolf Frederik, Duke, 10 companies, 660 men.[21]
5. Regiment Fagel, Francois Nicolaas, 10 companies, 550 men.[22]

---

11 Hall, *Flags and Uniforms of the Dutch Army* Vol. 1, pp.83–85.
12 Hall, *Flags and Uniforms of the Dutch Army* Vol. 1, pp.88–90.
13 Hall, *Flags and Uniforms of the Dutch Army* Vol. 1, pp.90–92.
14 Hall, *Flags and Uniforms of the Dutch Army* Vol. 1, pp.104–05.
15 Hall, *Flags and Uniforms of the Dutch Army* Vol. 1, pp.105–07.
16 Hall, *Flags and Uniforms of the Dutch Army* Vol. 1, pp.128–30.
17 Hall, *Flags and Uniforms of the Dutch Army* Vol. 1, pp.131–32.
18 Hall, *Flags and Uniforms of the Dutch Army* Vol. 2, pp.100–01.
19 Hall, *Flags and Uniforms of the Dutch Army* Vol. 2, pp.127–29.
20 Hall, *Flags and Uniforms of the Dutch Army* Vol. 2, pp.110–11.
21 Hall, *Flags and Uniforms of the Dutch Army* Vol. 2, pp.121–22. The Duke of Holstein Norburg died in December 1688 and was succeeded by Ernst Willem van Salisch on 30 December 1688.
22 Hall, *Flags and Uniforms of the Dutch Army* Vol. 2, pp.124–26.

6. Regiment Brandenburg, Colonel Prinz Albrecht Friedrich, Prince of Brandenburg-Ansbach (in English pay until 1697), 10 companies, 550 men.[23]
7. Regiment Nassau-Saarbrücken, Van der Beke (Ottweiler) (in English pay until 1697), 12 companies, 660 men.[24]
8. Regiment Hagedoorn, Marquette Pallandt, 10 companies, 550 men.[25]
9. Regiment Gröben, Hans Wolf van (in English pay until 1697), 12 companies, 660 men. (Often listed as Regiment Bornig.)[26]

Anglo-Dutch Brigade – English regiments in Dutch Pay (All were transferred onto the English establishment in 1689)

10. Colonel Thomas Tollemache's Regiment of Foot, 12 companies, 660 men.[27]
11. Colonel Babington's Regiment of Foot, 12 companies, 660 men.[28]
12. Colonel Henry Sydney's Regiment of Foot (better known under the name of its Colonel Commandant, John Cutts), 12 companies, 660 men.[29]

Scots-Dutch Brigade – Scottish regiments in Dutch pay (All were transferred onto the English establishment in 1689)

13. Colonel Hugh Mackay's Regiment of Foot, 12 companies, 660 men.[30]
14. Colonel Barthold Balfour's Regiment of Foot, 12 companies, 660 men.[31]
15. Colonel George Ramsay of Carriden's Regiment of Foot, 12 companies, 660 men.[32]

William's infantry consisted of fifteen regiments of foot, comprising 16 battalions with a paper strength of 11,322 men.

Artillery

William's artillery train consisting of 21 field guns, which were each to be drawn by 16 horses.[33] The artillery was crewed by 16 artillery officers and 66 cannoneers.

23 Hall, *Flags and Uniforms of the Dutch Army* Vol. 2, pp.115–17.
24 Hall, *Flags and Uniforms of the Dutch Army* Vol. 2, pp.62–64.
25 Hall, *Flags and Uniforms of the Dutch Army* Vol. 2, pp.71–73.
26 Hall, *Flags and Uniforms of the Dutch Army* Vol. 2, pp.104–05.
27 Hall, *Flags and Uniforms of the Dutch Army* Vol. 2, p.166.
28 The regiment was quoted in the Dutch army list *Het Staatsche Leger* under its old colonel as Regiment Bellasis, when Sir Henry Bellasis (alternative spelling Belasyse) had been replaced as colonel of the regiment on 7 April 1688 by Philip Babington.
29 Hall, *Flags and Uniforms of the Dutch Army* Vol. 2, p.165.
30 Hall, *Flags and Uniforms of the Dutch Army* Vol. 2, pp.159–62.
31 Hall, *Flags and Uniforms of the Dutch Army* Vol. 2, pp.162–64.
32 Hall, *Flags and Uniforms of the Dutch Army* Vol. 2, pp.167–69. The Dutch army list *Het Staatsche Leger* referred to the regiment under its old colonel's name, John Wauchope's. However, Wauchope was one of the officers who returned to England following the recall of the English and Scots regiments in Dutch service by James II in March 1688.
33 Van Nimwegen, *De Subsistentie Van Het Leger.*

Appendix II

Williamite Order of March[1]

These lists are taken from the daily order of march documents in the William Blathwayt Collection at Dyrham Park, Chippenham; the information has been translated from the French original. They list either the daily order of march or the end points and can refer to senior officers' locations or to the location of complete or part regiments. All locations have been changed to their modern names. The list uses the European calendar but has been changed to the old system for ease of use. The lists have been transcribed in full. It must be noted that they do contain errors (for example, constant use of four battalions of the Garde te Voet rather than the three that accompanied William) and inconsistencies in the names used, as well as the use of the term 'gardes' without differentiating between foot guards and the mounted regiments of guards. Where units are not mentioned on a specific day, the assumption is that they stayed in their previous location.

6 November 1688

Unit/Officer Name	Location
Two battalions of Guards	Newton Abbot
Tollemache, Macquay [Mackay], Wynbergen, Bierkinfeld, Nassau, and Fagel	West Ogwell
Two battalions of Guards, Sydney, Balford	East Ogwell
Holstein, Hagedoorn, Carlesson, Brandenburg, and Ramsey	Abbotskerswell
Babington	Coffinswell
The cavalry	Paignton

1 Marquess of Cambridge, 'The March of William of Orange from Torbay to London – 1688', *Journal of the Society for Army Historical Research,* 44.179 (1966), pp.152–74.

8 November 1688

Two battalions of Guards, Sydney, and Balford	Chudleigh
Two battalions of Guards	Kenn
Tollemache	Kennford
Holstein, Haguedorp, Carleson, Brandenbourg, and Ramsey	Kenton
Bierkinfeld, Mackay, Wynbergen, Nassau, and Fegel	Kingteignton
Garde a Cheval, Gardes du Corp, and dragoons	Newton Abbot
Ginkel, Oye, Nassau, Schack, Zuylenstein, Soppenbroek, Riedesel, Obdam, and Flodroff.	Kingskerswell
S'Gravemoer and Lippe	Haccombe
Benting, Heiden, and Montpouillan	Coffinswell

9 November 1688

Two battalions of Guards, Tollemache, Babington, and Garde du Corps	Exeter

The rest of the Infantry and cavalry either stayed where they were or marched to Pinshave, Bishops Clyst, Farringdon, Sowton, Clyst St George, Aylesbear, and Salterton.

10 November 1688

Ginkel, S'Gravemoer, Oye, and Riedesel	Alfington
Nassau and Soppenbroek	Exminster
Montpouillan, Heyde, Schack	Woodbury
Heyde	Kenton
Waldeck, Obdam, and Benting	Ede*
Flodroff, and the artillery horses	Whipton
Zuylenstein	Pinn

The rest of the infantry and horse were located at Exeter, Kent, and Abston.

14 November 1688

Waldeck and Lipp	Clyst Honiton and Whipton
Schack	Buckerel
Zuylenstein	Owlescombe
S'Gravemoer	Whimple
Nassau	Wiggaton

Ginkel and Oye	Cullumpton
Soppenbroek	Beare
Riedesel	Clyst St Lawrence
Obdam	Clyst Bydon
Flodroff, Benting, and Heyde	Silverton
Gardes te Paard	Broad Clyst

16 November 1688

Flodroff	Tallaton
Heyde and Bentin	Broadhembury
Montpouillan	Pehembury
Two battalions of Guards	Clyst Honiton and Bishops Clyst
Sydney	Heavitree
Nassau	Sowton
Wynbergen	Harington*
Carlisson	St George's*

20 November 1688

Babington	Achard*
Four battalions	Ottery St Mary

22 November 1688

Two battalions of Guards	Honiton
Two battalions of Guards	Gittisham
Two others at Colyton.	
Fagel, Haguedorp, and Mackay	Wiggaton
Holstein, Birkenfeld, and Brandenburg	Ottery St Mary

23 November 1688 – Cavalry

Waldeck and Lippe	Chard
Schack and Zuylenstein	Chardstock
S'Gravemoer and Nassau	Dalwood
Ginkel and Oye	Shute
Soppenbroek and Riedesel	Cotleigh
Obdam	Monkton
Flodroff	Offwell
Benting and Eyde	Kilmington
Montpouillan	Widworthy
Garde a Cheval	Membury
Royal Dragoons	Yarcombe and Upottery
Dragoons de Marwitz	Stockland and Monkton

23 November 1688

Two battalions of Guards	Axminster
Two battalions of Guards, Babington, Tollemache, Wynbergen, and Carkesson	Chard
Sydney, Nassau, and Ramsey	Lyme
Artillery and Balford	Ottery St Mary
125 dragoons	Chard
One battalion of Guards	Masbury*
One battalion of Guards	Kilmington
Gardes du Corps	Charmouth

24 November 1688

Sydney, Nassau, and Ramsey	Beaminster
Four battalions	Bettiscombe
Gardes de Axminster?	Pilsdon
Tollemache, Carlesson, and the English volunteers	Ilminster
Wynbergen Babington	Chellington
Birkenfeld, Mackay, Hagedoorn, and Brandenburg	Chard
Artillery and Fagel	Honiton
Balford	Memsbury
Count Nassau, Gardes Dragoons, and Marwitz Dragoons	Speckington
Schack	Seavington St Michael
Zuylenstein and Oye	Seavington St Mary
Nassau	Merriot
S'Gravemoer	Hinton St George
Soppenbroek	Dunnington
Benting	Kingstone
Heyden	Dowlish Wake
Flodroff	Cheddington
Montpouillan	Cudworth
Cornbury Dragoons**	Chardstock
Langston Horse**	Wambrook
Waldeck	Stockland
Lippe	Dalwood
Ginkel	Lambrook

** This refers to the portion of the Royal Regiment of Dragoons that defected under Cornbury and the remnants of Langston's Regiment of Horse that defected to William.

25 November 1688

Neighbourhood of the cavalry and dragoons	Crewkerne and Sherborne
Location of the Guards less the officers	Over Compton
Waldeck, Nassau, Montpouillan, and Heyden	Nether Compton
S'Gravemoer, Lippe, Soppenbroek, and Riedesel	Mudford
Oye, Benting, Ginkel, Flodroff, Schak, and Zuylenstein	Marston*
Prince's Dragoons	Trent, Lamford, and Kinston

27 November 1688

Four Guards battalions	Sherborne
Garde du Corps	Preston Plucknett
Artillery and wagons	Ashington
Unspecified unit	Beaminster
English volunteers	Ilchester
Dragoons	Queen Camel
Waldeck, Nassau, Montpouillan, and Heyden	West Camel
S'Gravemoer, Lippe, Soppenbroek, and Riedesel	East Camel*
Oye, Benting, and Ginkel	Yeovil
Flodroff, Schack, Zuylenstein, and Obdam	Nortucell*
Cornbury's Dragoons	Chinnock
Langston's Horse	Middle Chinnock and Odcombe
Dragoons and artillery	Barwick and Sloford
Refugee officers (Huguenot)	Thorne and Montacute
English officers come over from James II	Goathill and Purse Caundle

30 November 1688

Headquarters and a battalion of Guards	Wincanton
Three battalions of Guards	Temple Combe, Horsington Marsh, Horsington, and Cheriton
Wynbergen Brigade and English volunteers	Mere
Hagedoorn	Upton Henstridge

Ramsey	Stalbridge
Sydney, Nassau, Tollemache, and Fegel	Milbornewick
Balford	Milborne Port
General Nassau, Waldeck, Lippe, and Benting	Bruton
Marwitz and Prince's Dragoons	Stourton, Brewham, and Burcomlinge*
Heyden	Wyke
Soppenbroek	Hashpin* and Pitcombe
Nassau, S'Gravemoer, Ginkel, Flodroff, and Obdam	Shepton Mallet
Zuylenstein	West Compton
Schack	Pilton
Montpouillan	Pykke
Gardes du Corps	South Cadbury
Gardes te Paard	North Cadbury
Cornbury's Dragoons	Compton Pauncefoot
Langston's Horse	Galhampton
Dragoons and artillery	Evercreech
My Lord Maxfield	Gillingham
Tollemache	Corton Denham and Sandford Orcas
Carlesson	Long Sutton? and Weston*

1 December 1688

Headquarters and battalion of Guards	Hindon
Wynbergen Brigade	Fonthill Bishop
Three regiments and Scottish lords	Fonthill Gifford
Prince Birkenfeld's Brigade	Fovant and Teffont
Sydney's Brigade	Wincanton
Gardes du Corps	Kilmington and Porton
Gardes te Paard	Maiden Bradley and Iarenwill
Cornbury's Dragoons	Stour Provost
Langston's Horse	East Knoyle and West Knoyle
Artillery	Sedgehill
English foot	East Hatch
Lord Makefield	Kingston Deverill
English lords and volunteers	Longbridge Deverill
Refugee officers	Hill Deverill

Royal Dragoons	Baverstock, Ugford, Barford St Martin, and Wishford
Marwitz Dragoons	Wylie and Teffont
Waldeck	Boyton
Lippe	Sherrington
Benting	Cortington, Tytherington, and Sutton Veny
General Nassau and his regiment and Soppenbroek	Chelmarsh?
Ginkel, Oye, and Riedesel	Cucklington
Flodroff and Obdam	Kington Magna
Zuylenstein	Stour
Schack	West Stour
Montpouillan	Chilton*

3 December 1688

One battalion of Guards	South Newton and Chilhampton
Three battalions of Guards	Kingston Deverill and Deverill Longbridge
Birkenfeld's Brigade	Hill Deverill, East Knoyle, West Knoyle, and Semley.
Sydney's Brigade	Mere
Wynbergen's Brigade	Rests where it is
Garde du Corps	Remains where it is
Garde a Cheval	Chicklade, Pertwood, and Chilmark
Cornbury's Dragoons	Wylie, Teffont, and Bapton
Langston's Horse	Stockton and Sherrington
English foot	Boyton
Lord Makefield	Winterbourne Stoke
Dragoons and artillery	Corton
Refugee officers	Boscombe
Waldeck and Lippe	Shrewton
Benting	Holston
Heyden	Milston and Figheldean
Soppenbroek and S'Gravemoer	Bulford
Nassau and his regiment.	Upavon
Ginkel	Combe Bisset
Oye	Compton Chamberlayne

Riedesel	Quere*
Flodroff and Obdam	Sutton Mandevil
Zuylenstein	Swallowcliffe
Schack and Montpouillan	Flamston
Marwitz Dragoons	North Tidworth and South Tidworth
Royal Dragoons	Remain where it is

4 December 1688

One battalion of Guards	Amesbury
Birkenfeld	Hindon
Wynbergen Brigade	Netheravon, Enford, and Compton
Garde du Corps	Durrington
Garde a Cheval	Orcheston St George and Maddington
Lords of the Council and English volunteers	Woodford and Orcheston St Mary
Cornbury's Dragoons	Shrewton
Langston's Horse	Tilshead
English foot, dragoons, and artillery	Wishford and Lacke*
Ginkel	Idmiston
Oyc and Riedesel	Porton
Flodroff	Winterslow
Obdam	Winterbourne Gunner
Zeilstein	Winterbourne Earls
Schack and Montpouillan	Winterbourne Dauntsey
Waldeck and Lippe	Hangston*

5 December 1688

Headquarters, Two battalions of Guards and the Garde du Corps	Salisbury
One battalion of Guards	Durrington
Wynbergen's Brigade	Amesbury
Birkenfeld's Brigade	Winterslow, Porton, Winterbourne Gunner, Winterbourne Dautsey, and Winterbourne Earls
Sydney's Brigade	Wiston*, Fisherton, and Emilston*
Gardes te Paard	Orcheston St George and Maddington

Lord Makefield	Winterbourne Stoke
English lords	Orcheston St Mary
Scottish lords	Amesbury
Cornbury's Dragoons	Shrewton
Langston's Horse (recorded as dragoons)	Tilshead
English foot	Wilsford
S'Gravemoer regiment	Figheldean
Soppenbroek regiment	Bulford
Nassau regiment	Upavon
Ginkel's regiment	Charlton
Oye regiment	Compton
Riedesel and Flodroff regiments	Russeck*
Obdam regiment	Enford
Zuylenstein regiment	Fittelton
Schack regiment.	Netheravon
Marwitz Dragoons	North Tidworth and South Tidworth
Royal Dragoons	Allington, Newton Tony, and Shellerton*

6 December 1688

Headquarters	Collingbourne Kingston
Marshal's quarters	Collingborn St Andre*
One battalion of Guards	East and West Everley
Three battalions of Guards	North Tidworth, South Tidworth
Prince Birkenfeld	Chute
Birkenfeld's Brigade	Appleshaw, Saddesdon*, Kimpton, and Thruxton
Sydney's Brigade	Amesbury?
English lords and volunteers	Ludgershall
Scottish lords	Amport
Royal Dragoons	Tidcombe, Wexcombe, and Marten
Marwitz Dragoons	Shalbourne, Ham, and Buttermere, and Harding*
General Nassau and a regiment from Wynbergen's Brigade	Great Bedwyn
Waldeck and Lippe	Stoke
One regiment from Wynbergen's Brigade	Little Bedwyn

Two regiments from Wynbergen's Brigade	Burbage
Benting	West Grafton
Heyden and Soppenbroek	East Grafton
S'Gravemoer	Milton Lilbourne
Nassau	Easton Royal
Ginkel	Draycot Fitz Payne
Oye and Riedesel	Pewsey
Flodroff and Obdam	Manningford Abbots
Zuylenstein and Schack	Wilcot
Montpouillan	Manningford Bruce
Cornbury's Dragoons and Lanston's Horse	Marlborough
Dragoons and artillery	Preshute Within
English foot	Wootton Rivers
Gardes te Paard	Beeching Stoke and Wilsford
Lord Makefield	Overton
Officer refugees	Boxcombe*

7 December 1688

Headquarters	Hingerford
Prince Birkenfeld and one battalion Guards	Chilton Foliat
Three battalions of Guards	Tidcombe, Wexcombe, and Marten
Birkenfeld's Brigade	Shalbourne, Bedwyn, and Burbage
Sydney's Brigade	East and West Everley
Wynbergen's Brigade	Hamsted*
Artillery	Shouborne*
English infantry, cavalry, and dragoons	Lambourne
All Dutch dragoons, Waldeck, Lippe, General Nassau, and Hayden	Newbury
Soppenbroek and S'Gravemoer	Wickham
Nassau	Newton*
Ginkel, Oye, and Riedesel	Avington
Flodroff and Obdam	Enborne
Zuylenstein, Schack, and Montpouillan	East or West Woodhay
Gardes du Corps and Gardes te Paard	Kimbury
English lords	Shefford

8 December 1688

Headquarters and four battalions of Guards	Newbury
Birkenfeld's Brigade	Kimbury and Amsted*
Sydney's Brigade	Hungerford
Wynbergen's Brigade	Kingsclere
English cavalry and dragoons	Wallingford
English foot	East and West Everley
Garde du Corps	Demistocast*
Garde a Cheval	Chapel Row and Winterbourne
Royal Dragoons	Burfeld* and Silham*
Marwitz Dragoons	Tilehurst and Purley
Lippe and Waldeck	Basildon
Benting and Heyde	Streatley
Soppenbroek	Moulsford
S'Gravemoer	Ashampstead
Nassau	Stanford*
Ginkel	Mulbury*
Riedesel and Oye	Chilton
Zuylenstein	Sulham
Flodroff and Obdam	Theale
Northern cavalry**	East Garston and Letcombe Basset
Lord Makefield	Wickham
English lords	Sydmonton
Scottish lords.	Pudworth*
Refugee officers and artillery.	Compton*

** Northern cavalry possibly refers to volunteer cavalry that arrived in William's camp from the Midlands and the North of England.

11 December 1688

Prince of Orange	Abingdon
Headquarters and three battalions of Guards	Wallingford
One battalion of Guards	Brightwell
Sydney's Brigade	Brightwell
Birkenfeld's Brigade	Thatcham and Chapel Row
Wynbergen's Brigade	Brewham and Stanford Dingley

All the dragoons, Waldeck. Lippe, and Heyde	Reading
Benting	Streatley
Soppenbroek regiment	Moulsford
S'Gravemoer regiment	Ashampstead
Nassau regiment	Stanford Dingley
Ginkel regiment	Blewbury
Oye and Riedesel regiments	Chilton
Schack and Montpouillan regiments	Aldworth
Zuylenstein regiment	Salham
Flodroff regiment	Theale
Obdam regiment	Burghfield
Cornbury's Dragoons	South and North Morton
Langston's Horse	Appleford, Long Wittenham, and Little Wittenham
English foot	Cholsey
Cavalry from the north	East Garston and Letcombe Basset
Mackay's regiment	Peasemore and Beedon
English lords	Penenton*
Artillery	East and West Ilsley
Refugee officers	Compton

13 December 1688

Headquarters	Henley
Birkenfeld's Brigade	Reading
Sydney's Brigade	Tilehurst, Purley, Theale, and Sulham
One battalion of Guards	Remenham
Three battalions of Guards	Twyford and Wargrave
Mackay's regiment	Nettlebed and Checkendon
Wynbergen's regiment	Wokingham
Conte de Nassau, Marwitz Dragoons, Lippe, Flodroff, and Obdam regiments	Maidenhead
Waldeck and Heyde regiments	Bray
Benting's regiment	Ruscombe
Nassau's regiment	Warborough
Royal Dragoons	Beaconsfield
Soppenbroek's regiment	Hambledon
S'Gravemoer's regiment	Fingest

Ginkel and Oye regiments	Bix
Schack's regiment	Bixgeben*
Riedesel's regiment	Assenton
Montpouillan's regiment	Grey's Court
Zuylenstein regiment	Rotherfield Peppard
Detachment of the Garde du Corps	Hurley
English lords	Brightwell and Ewelme
Langston's Horse	Binsington*
Lord Makefield	Shiplake
Cornbury's Dragoons and artillery	West Wycombe
Garde a Cheval	Wallingford
Refugee officers	Turfelde*
English foot	Radnage

14 December 1688

Headquarters	Windsor
Four battalions of Guards	Windsor, Colnbrook, and Datchet
Mackay	Wraysbury
Wynbergen's Brigade	Wraysbury and Watham St Lawrence
Birkenfeld's Brigade	Windlesham, Bagshot, and Bromwell*
Artillery	Reading
Conte De Nassau, Marwitz Dragoons, Lippe, and Flodroff regiments	Maidenhead
Obdam regiment	Remains where it is
Benting's regiment	Ruscombe
Nassau regiment	Medmenham
Soppenbroek's regiment	Hedsor
S'Gravemoer Regiment	Woodburn
Ginkel, Oye, and Riedesel regiments	Great Marlow
Schack regiment	Little Marlow
Montpouillan regiment	Coleshill
Garde du Corps	Staines
Garde a Cheval	Wimbledon
Langston's Horse, Cornbury's Dragoons and the artillery	West Wycombe
Refugee officers	Farnham

English foot and 400 men of Douglas regiment	Hughenden
Scottish lords	Wesham
English lords	Fulmer

16 December 1688

Guard regiments	Brentford
Royal Dragoons	Kingston
Gardes du Corps	Hounslow
Marwitz Dragoons	Colnbrook
Lippe and Flodroff regiments	Horton
Obdam and Waldeck regiments	Wraysbury
Heyde, Benting, and Nassau regiments	Egham
Soppenbroek regiment	Dorney
S'Gravemoer regiment	Burnham
Ginkel and Oye regiments	Stoke Poges
Riedesel regiment	Upton
Schack, Zuylenstein, and Montpouillan regiments	Datchet
Gardes te Paard	Uxbridge
Refugee officers	West Drayton
Mackay's Brigade	Enfield?
Sydney's Brigade.	Maidenhead
Birkenfeld's Brigade	Toplay*, Hotson*, and Wooburn

17 December 1688

Headquarters	Sion and Brentford
Gardes du Corps	Knightsbridge
Gardes te Paard	Ealing, Chiswick, and Fulham
Royal Dragoons	At rest in Kingston
Marwitz Dragoons	Perivale, Kingston, and Staines
Lippe, Obdam, and Flodroff regiments	Hounslow
Waldeck, Benting, and Heyde regiments	Petersham
Conte de Nassau and his regiment, and Soppenbroek regiment	Richmond
S'Gravemoer regiment	These*
Ginkel and Oye regiments	Teddington
Riedesel and Schack regiments	Twickenham

Zuylenstein and Montpouillan regiments	Hampton
Refugee officers	West Drayton
Balford regiment	Neasden
Babington and Carlsson regiments	Acton
Mackay's regiment	Turnham Green
Wynbergen's regiment	Ealing
Sydney's regiment (possible brigade)	Colnbrook
Birkenfeld's regiment (possible brigade)	Wexham, Farnham, and Stoke Poges
Three battalions of Guards	Walham Green and Kensington

18 December 1688

Headquarters, four battalions of Guards, Gardes du Corps, and Gardes te Paard	London
Sydney, Tollemache, and Babington regiments	The Tower [of London]
Mackay's regiment	Lambeth
Balfor and Ramsey regiments	Highgate
Birkenfeld regiment (possible brigade)	Hammersmith, Fulham, Parsons Green, Kensington, Gravel Pits, and Walham Green
Carlesson regiment	Chelsea and Knightsbridge
Brandenburg regiment	Marylebone, Paddington, St Pancras, and Kentish Town
Hayden regiment	Highgate and Hampstead
Fagel	Deptford?
Wynbergen regiment	Dartford, Greenhill, Sutton, Barkeley, and Erith
Four companies of Holstein regiment	Woolwich and Greenwich
Waldeck regiment	Kingston and Petersham
Lippe regiment	Epping and Eppingstret*
Conte de Nassau regiment	Putney
Benting regiment	Wandsworth and Wimbledon
Soppenbroek regiment	Clapham. Tooting, Pretham*, and Battersea
Heyde regiment	Croydon, Carshalton, and Mitcham
S'Gravemoer regiment	St Mary Cray, Farningham, Chelsfield, and Oprington

Marwitz Dragoons	Lewisham, Bromley, Scadbury Park, Eltham, and Beckenham
Refugee officers	Edgware
Montpouillan's regiment	Shepperton, Charlton, Kenton, and Sunbury
Schack's regiment	Kingston, Ditton, and Hampton Wick
Zuylenstein's regiment	Hounslow and Thistleworth
Obdam's regiment	Brentford, Ealing, and Chiswick
Flodroff's regiment	Edmonds Street* and Thornham Street*
Ginkel's regiment	Waltham Cross and Waltham Abbey
Oye's regiment	Cheston*, Thebase*, and Wormley
Riedesel's regiment	Hoddesdon and Oswell*
Royal Dragoons	Ingestone, Romford, Ilford, and Hornchurch

Appendix III

English Army, November 1688

Unless otherwise stipulated, all figures are for the establishment strength of the regiment and not the actual strength. As shown within the text, regiments were never normally at full strength, and some regiments, especially the Irish regiments were far from full strength.

English Forces[1]

Horse

Four troops of horse guards	Four troops of 200 men
each with a troop of horse grenadiers	Four troops of 60 men
Royal Regiment of Horse (Duke of Berwick)	Nine troops of 60 men
Queen's Regiment of Horse	Nine troops of 50 men
Sir John Fenwick's Regiment of Horse	Nine troops of 50 men[2]
Major-General Werdon's Regiment of Horse	Nine troops of 50 men
Earl of Arran's Regiment of Horse	Nine troops of 50 men
Colonel Hamilton's Regiment of Horse	Nine troops of 50 men
Princess Anne's Regiment of Horse	Nine troops of 50 men
The Queen Dowager's Regiment of Horse	Nine troops of 50 men
Marquis de Miremont's Regiment of Horse	Six troops of 50 men[3]
Lord Brandon's Regiment of Horse	Six troops of 50 men[4]

1 NA: WO24/8, Part 5, ff.44–49.

2 Sir John was paid the sum of £3223 10s 08d by William for outstanding debts of the crown on 18 January 1689 (NA: WO24/3138, f.1).

3 The marquis was paid the sum of £5,246 11s 08d by William for outstanding debts of the crown on 17 January 1689 (NA: WO25/3138, f.1).

4 Lord Brandon was paid the sum of £4,932 02s 10d by William for outstanding debts of the crown on 17 January 1689 (NA: WO25/3138, f.1).

Earl of Salisbury's Regiment of Horse	Six troops of 50 men
Colonel Slingsby's Regiment of Horse	Six troops of 50 men
Captain John Anderson's Independent Troop of Horse	50 men[5]
Independent Troop of Horse	50 men[6]
Dragoons	
Royal Regiment of Dragoons	Eight troops of 60 men
The Queen's Regiment of Dragoons	Six troops of 60 men
Princess Anne of Denmark's Regiment of Dragoons	Six troops of 60 men
Foot	
First Regiment of Foot Guards	24 companies of 80 men**
Coldstream Regiment of Foot Guards	24 companies of 80 men**
Royal Regiment of Foot	18 companies of 60 men**
Queen Dowager's Regiment of Foot	13 companies of 60 men*
Prince George of Denmark's Regiment of Foot	13 companies of 60 men*
The Holland Regiment of Foot	13 companies of 60 men*
The Queen's Regiment of Foot	13 companies of 60 men*
Colonel John Hales's Regiment of Foot	13 companies of 60 men*
Royal Regiment of Fusiliers	13 companies of 60 men*
Princes of Denmark's Regiment of Foot	13 companies of 60 men*
Colonel Henry Cornwall's Regiment of Foot	13 companies of 60 men*
The Earl of Bath's Regiment of Foot	13 companies of 60 men*
The Lord Montgomery's Regiment of Foot	13 companies of 60 men*
The Earl of Lichfield's Regiment of Foot	13 companies of 60 men*
The Earl of Huntington's Regiment of Foot	13 companies of 60 men*
Colonel Edward Hales's Regiment of Foot	13 companies of 60 men*
Sir James Lesley's Regiment of Foot	13 companies of 60 men*
Colonel Skelton's Regiment of Foot	13 companies of 60 men*
Colonel Henry Gage's Regiment of Foot	13 companies of 60 men*
Colonel Sackville Tufton's Regiment of Foot	13 companies of 60 men*
Colonel Caines Regiment of Foot	13 companies of 60 men*[7]
Earl of Salisbury's Regiment of Foot	13 companies of 60 men*
Earl of Stafford's Regiment of Foot	13 companies of 60 men*

5 NA: SP44/165, f.134.

6 NA: WO55/335, f.90r.

7 The colonel was paid the sum of £1,278 11s 02d by William for outstanding debts by the crown on 17 January 1689 (NA: WO25/3138, f.1).

Colonel Solomon Richard's Regiment of Foot	13 companies of 60 men*
Duke of Newcastle's Regiment of Foot	13 companies of 60 men*
Three Independent Companies of Chelsea Pensioners[8]	3 companies of 60 men
Irish Forces on the English Establishment[9]	
Irish Battalion of Foot Guards	Eight companies of 80 men*
Lord Forbes Regiment of Foot	13 companies of 50 men*
Colonel Hamilton's Regiment of Foot	13 companies of 50 men*
Colonel MacElligott's Regiment of Foot	13 companies of 50 men*
Colonel Butler's Regiment of Dragoons	10 troops of 50 men
Scottish Forces on the English Establishment[10]	
Troop of Scots Horse Guards	One troop of 118 men
The Royal Regiment of Horse	Six troops of 49 men
Scottish Regiment of Foot Guards	14 companies of 79 men*
Colonel Buchan's Regiment of Foot	14 companies of 50 men*
Colonel Wauchope's Regiment of Foot	13 companies of 70 men*
Regiment of Scots Dragoons	Six troops of 49 men

* Denotes regiments that had one company of grenadiers.

** Denotes regiments that had two companies of grenadiers.

8 NA: WO55/335, f.94.

9 NA: WO24/8, Part 5, ff.50–52. WO24/6, Part 2 states that that battalion of Irish Guards consisted of seven companies of 80 men and not eight companies.

10 NA: WO24/8, Part 5, ff.53–55.

William III attends a session of Parliament as king, in 'Allegory of Events of 1688 and 1689,' a print by Jan Luyken, Amsterdam, 1689. (Rijksmuseum: RP-P-1896-A-19368-701, Public Domain)

Appendix IV

Members of The Privy Council

Privy Council from 1685 to 1688

Prince George of Denmark
The Duke of Queensbury
The Earl of Perth
The Earl of Mulgrave
The Earl of Berkeley
Sir Edward Herbert
The Viscount Preston
The Earl of Plymouth

Privy Councillors appointed in 1688

The Lord Crew
The Earl of Powis
The Lord Arundell of Wardour
The Lord Belasyse
The Lord Dover
The Earl of Tyrconnell
The Earl of Castlemaine
Sir Nicholas Butler
Edward Petre
Silius Titus

Appendix V

Location of the English Fleet, 18 December 1688[1]

Location	Rate					
	3	4	5	6	Yacht	Fireship
Spithead	9	21		3	4	16
Sheerness	1	2		1		2
Chatham		1				
Plymouth		1				
Poole						1
Bristol				1		1
On station – coming home		4	2	6		
Ships to be laid up at Portsmouth		2				
Ships being fitted out		5	1			4

1 NA: SP8/2, ff.93–95.

Appendix VI

The Numbers of the Militia in the Several Counties in England and Wales[1]

County	Horse			Foot			Total
	Regiments	Troops	Men	Regiments	Companies	Men	
Berkshire	—	3	170	1	—	900	1,070
Buckinghamshire	—	3	180	1	—	800	980
Bedfordshire	—	2	100	1	—	450	550
Bristol	—	—	—	1	(12)	960	960
Cambridgeshire	—	2	140	—	5	700	840
Cheshire	—	2	100	1	—	970	1,220
Chester	—	—	—	—	1	150	
Cinque Ports	—	—	—	—	20	2,000	2,000
Cornwall	—	2	120	4	—	3,200	3,320
Derbyshire	—	2	120	—	4	400	520
Dorset	—	2	120	2	—	2,154	
Lyme	—	—	—	—	1	)	
Poole	—	—	—	—	1	) 300	2,574
Weymouth	—	—	—	—	1	)	
Devonshire	1	—	240	6	—	4,800	5,040
Gloucestershire	1	—	240	4	—	4,000	4,240

1 NA: SP8/8, f.81.

Hampshire	—	2	120	6	—	2,450	4,520
Isle of Wight	—	—	—	2	(8)	1,600	
Southampton	—	—	—	—	1	200	
Winchester	—	—	—	—	1	150	
Hertfordshire	—	3	160	1	—	1,100	1,260
Herefordshire	—	2	120	1	—	900	1,020
Kent	1	(5)	320	?	?	3,400	3,720
Lancashire	—	3	150	3	—	1,800	1,950
Leicestershire	—	3	180	—	6	600	780
London – Militia	1	(8)	400	?	?	8,600	9,000
London – Auxiliaries	—	—	—	?	?	6,000	6,000
Lincolnshire	1	(6)	266	2	—	1,630	2,026
Lincoln city	—	—	—	—	1	130	
Middlesex	—	1	60	1	—	705	765
Monmouthshire	—	1	50	1	—	700	750
Norfolk	1	(6)	370	4	—	3,087	4,841
Lynn	—	—	—	—	2	258	
Norwich	—	—	—	1	—	700	
Yarmouth	—	—	—	—	4	426	
Northamptonshire	—	3	150	1	—	800	950
Nottinghamshire	—	2	120	1	—	420	540
Northumberland	—	2	100	—	3	330	430
Oxfordshire	—	1	180	1	—	800	980
Purbeck Isle	—	—	—	—	4	300	300
Rutland	—	1	60	—	1	120	180
Shropshire	—	2	120	1	—	920	1,140
Shrewsbury		—	—	—	1	100	
Suffolk	1	—	230	4	—	2,209	2,599
Ipswich	—	—	—	—	2	160	
Staffordshire	—	2	140	—	5	500	640
Surrey	—	2	120	1	—	1,000	2,620
Southwark	—	—	—	1	—	1,500	
Sussex	—	4	200	2	—	1,500	1,700
Tower Hamlets	—	—	—	2	—	1,920	1,920

Warwickshire Coventry	— —	3 —	170 7	1 —	— 1	600 40	817
Wiltshire	1	(4)	232	4	—	2,266	2,498
Worcestershire	—	2	120	1	—	813	933
Wales, North Wales, South	? ?	? ?	505	? ?	? ?	6,100	6,605
North Riding	—	3	180	3	—	950	1,130
West Riding	—	3	200	4	—	2,300	2,500
Durham	—	2	120	—	8	800	920
Somersetshire	—	3	120	4	—	3,200	3,320
Total	8	68*	6,800	74	29*	85,686	92,486

* Indicates the numbers of independent companies and troops and does not include the numbers of companies or troops that are part of a militia regiment which are notated in brackets ( ).

Appendix VII

New Units Raised by James II in Late 1688

The following appendix records new units raised by James II between September 1688 and December 1688. Companies and troops were either raised as independent commands or as part of an existing regiments; all companies and troops are independent commands unless otherwise stipulated. Unless noted, the main source for the information is the *CSPD: James II, 1687–89*.

Troops of Horse

* Raised as a new troop for an existing regiment.

Date Raised	Captain	Catholic or Dissenter	Notes
27/11/1688	Stephen Tempest		Never raised
21/11/1688	Sir Louis Palmer		Raised
26/11/1688	John Grosvenor*		Raised
27/11/1688	James, Earl of Salisbury*		Raised; given his own regiment of horse on 5/11/1688
29/09/1688	Francis Radcliffe		Raised
30/09/1688	Edward Widdrington	Catholic	Raised
03/10/1688	John Anderson		Raised
10/10/1688	Charles Lord Baltimore		Raised
11/10/1688	Sir John Yate		Raised
12/10/1688	Sir John Gifford		Raised

Companies of Foot

* Raised as a new company for an existing regiment.
** Raised from soldiers in the Royal Hospital, Chelsea.
*** Companies amalgamated into the Duke of Newcastle's new regiment of foot

Date Raised	Captain	Catholic or Dissenter	Notes
21/09/1688	Adam Cuningham*		Raised and served under William III
23/09/1688	Alex Pearson*		Raised and served under William III
02/10/1688	Anthony Power		Raised
24/09/1688	Anthony Vane*	Catholic	Raised and served under William III
02/10/1688	Benjamin Laney		Raised
29/09/1688	Charles Collier***		Raised[1]
02/10/1688	Charles Palmer		Raised
25/09/1688	Charles Potts*		Raised
24/09/1688	David McAdam*		Raised and served under William III
28/09/1688	Edward Braughel		Raised
06/10/1688	Edward Picking**		Raised and served under William III
28/09/1688	Edward Rupert		Raised
01/10/1688	Edward Wolf		Raised
28/09/1688	Francis Edwards*		Raised and served under William III
30/09/1688	Francis Watson		Raised
26/09/1688	Fraser Napier*		Raised and served under William III
27/09/1688	Fraser Shadwell*		Raised and served under William III
28/09/1688	George Cony**		Raised and served under William III
25/09/1688	George Roberts*		Raised

1 Previously captain of a company that was raised for the Monmouth Rebellion and transferred to the Irish establishment in October 1685 (BL: Add MS 15897, f.71).

27/09/1688	George Wingfield*		Raised and served under William III
02/10/1688	Henry Bruning		Raised
30/09/1688	Henry Crofton	Catholic	Raised
29/09/1688	Henry Davies***		Raised
27/09/1688	Henry Fielding*		Raised and served under William III
01/10/1688	Henry Pounds		Raised
01/10/1688	James Bowles		Raised
30/09/1688	James Courtney		Raised
22/09/1688	James McCraken*		Raised and served under William III
25/09/1688	John Barber		Never raised
29/09/1688	John Cornwall*		Raised and served under William III
29/09/1688	John Drake*		Raised and served under William III
01/10/1688	John Leeds		Raised
30/09/1688	John Mair		Raised
28/09/1688	John Prideaux*		Raised and served under William III
02/10/1688	John Sibley		Never raised
01/10/1688	John Widdrington		Raised
25/09/1688	Lancelot Ord*	Catholic	Raised
08/10/1688	Matthew Smyth		Raised
30/09/1688	Maurice Flynn		Raised
28/09/1688	Richard Anthony		Raised
27/09/1688	Richard Leigh*		Raised
28/09/1688	Richard Smith**		Raised and served under William III
29/09/1688	Robert London***		Raised
24/09/1688	Robert Lucas*	Catholic?	Raised served under William III[2]
29/09/1688	Samuel Arnold*		Raised
30/09/1688	Sandy Williams		Raised
25/09/1688	Thomas King*		Raised

2 Served as captain in the Tower Hamlets militia. *CSPD: William and Mary 1689–90*, p.20.

02/10/1688	Thomas Motley		Incorporated into Bevil Skelton's Regiment of Foot
03/10/1688	Thomas Motley*	Catholic	Raised
02/10/1688	Thomas Neale		Raised
27/09/1688	Thomas Raleigh*		Raised
29/09/1688	Thomas Styles		Raised and served under William III
02/10/1688	Thomas Witham		Raised[3]
30/09/1688	Ulick Bourk	Catholic	Raised
30/09/1688	William Gibbons		Raised
24/09/1688	William Herbert*		Raised and served under William III
30/09/1688	William Low		Raised
30/09/1688	William Sandy*		Raised

New regiments raised by James II

Date Raised	Colonel	Catholic or Dissenter	Foot or Horse	Notes
09/10/1688	Archibald Douglas		Foot	Colonel removed but regiment served under William[4]
09/10/1688	Bevil Skelton		Foot	At least five companies were raised, armed, and later served under William III, although Bevil Skelton surrendered his commission of 10/12/1688.
01/10/1688	Charles Lord Brandon[5]	Catholic	Foot	Raised and armed, later disbanded[6]

3 Not armed as of 23 November 1688, when the company was incorporated into Colonel Bevil Skelton's Regiment of Foot. A. Browning, *Memoirs of Sir John Reresby* (London: RHS, 1991), p.531.

4 Dalton, *English Army Lists*, vol. II, p.188.

5 *CSPD: James II, 1687–89*, p.282. Lord Brandon was offered the commission of either a regiment of horse or of foot by James II on 25 September 1688.

6 NA: WO24/6, Part 2, f.71.

05/11/1688	Earl of Salisbury		Horse	Part raised and armed; later disbanded[7]
10/10/1688	George Holman	Catholic	Horse	Raised; possibly not armed
04/10/1688	Henry Duke of Newcastle		Foot	Continued to serve William III[8]
29/09/1688	Henry Duke of Newcastle		Horse	Received arms 13/10/1688 [9]
27/09/1688	Henry Gage	Catholic	Foot	Eight or nine companies armed on 03/10/1688[10]
03/10/1688	Henry Slingsby		Horse	Disbanded 05/01/1689[11]
08/11/1688	Henry Stafford		Foot	Only seven companies raised[12]
13/10/1688	John Carne		Foot	Part raised and armed[13]
03/10/1688	Lord Dunbar[14]		Foot	
22/10/1688	Marquis de Miremont		Horse	Raised and armed; disbanded 24/05/1689[15]

7 NA: WO24/6, Part 2, f.71.
8 NA: WO55/400, f.226; NA: WO55/335, f.101.
9 NA: SP44/56, f.448. The regiment raised from new recruits and from militia cavalry.
10 D. Hosford, *Nottingham, Nobles and the North: Aspects of the Revolution of* 1688 (Springfield, Archon Books, 1976), p.104; NA: WO55/400, f.224.
11 Dalton, *English Army Lists*, vol. II, p.185.
12 NA: SP44/166, f.5. As of 8 November 1688.
13 Ordered to stop recruiting on 27 November 1688. Dalton, *English Army Lists*, vol. II, pp.151–58.
14 NA: SP44/165, f.96.
15 *CSPD: William and Mary, 1689-90*, p.117.

Bibliography

Manuscripts

Austrian State Archives: Kriegsarchiv – OSK
AFA 1690, Bde 378, Bde 379

British Library – BL
Add MS 15897, Add MS 41837, Add MS 28938, Add MS 38695, Add MS 41805,
Add MS 41821, Add MS 75392, C161/f2/75, MS Egerton 2717

Exeter Archives – EA
312M/8/F/2

Parliamentary Archives
HL/PO/JO/10/1/405, HL/PO/JO/10/1/409

Isle of Wight Archives – IOW
Gw10/39

National Archives – NA
ADM 77/3, ADM 106/387, PC 2/72, SP 8/1 King William's Chest, SP 8/2, SP 8/5
SP 8/8, SP 31/4, SP 44/56, SP 44/69, SP 44/70, SP 44/71, SP 44/97, SP 44/139
SP 44/163, SP 44/164, SP 44/165, SP 44/166, SP 44/167, SP 44/336, SP 44/338
SP 44/339, SP 63/340, WO 4/1, WO 5/3, WO 24/8, WO 24/9, WO 24/10
WO 24/12, WO 25/3138, WO 55/335, WO 55/397, WO 55/339, WO 55/400
WO 55/401

Newport Records Office – Isle of Wight: NP
D1 1986-2728, Newport Corporation MSS Convocation Book

Nottingham University – NU
PwA 2188/8: Planned list of landing sites, PwA 2197/2: Plan of the order of sailing of the Dutch Fleet

PwA 2206, PwA 2231, PwA 2235, PwA 2251: Requisition order for oxen and wagons

Staffordshire Archives – SA
D(W) 1778/V/71 PART 1, D(W) 1778/V/1377, D(W)1778/V/1380

Primary Sources

The *Orange Gazette*: various issues available at www.thegazette.co.uk.

Anon., *An Account of Last Sundays Engagement BETWEEN His Majesty's, and the Prince of Orange's Forces, in the Road between Reading and Maidenhead, amongst which, its said, a Blue-Garter fell. With a True Account of some Occurrences at Portsmouth* (London: WD, 1688).

Anon., *An Exact diary of the Late Expedition of His Illustrious Highness the Prince of Orange (now King of Great Britain) from His palace at the Hague, to His Landing at Torbay and from thence to His Arrival at White-Hall* (London: Richard Baldwin, 1689).

Anon., *A Letter from a Gentleman in Exeter to his Friend in London* (London: NP, 1688).

Anon., *A Letter of Advice to all Protestant Soldiers, and Sea-men Showing how Inconsistent it is with their Duty to God, and the Law of England, to Fight for a Popish Interest* (London: NP, 1688).

Anon., *A True and Exact Relation of the Prince of Orange: His Publick Entrance into Exeter* (Exeter: NP, 1688).

Anon., *A View of the Court of St Germain: Since the Year 1690 with an Account of the Entertainment Protestants meet with there* (Dublin: Andrew Cook, 1696).

Anon., *Prince of Orange Letter to the English-Fleet and the Form of Prayer used in the Dutch Fleet* (NL: NP, 1688).

Anon., *Rules and Articles for the better Government of His Majesties Land-Forces in Pay during this present Rebellion: Published at His Majesties Command* (London: John Bill Deceased, Henry Hill and Thomas Newcomb, 1685).

Fagel, Gaspar, *A letter Writ by Mijn Heer Fagel, Pensioner to the Great and Mighty Lords, the States of Holland and Westfriesland* (Holland and Westfriesland: J. Schelsus, 1687).

King James II, *His Majesties Reasons for Withdrawing Himself from Rochester* (Rochester: NP, 1688).

Prince of Orange, *By the Prince of Orange, A Declaration* (Savoy, London: Ede and Jones, 1688).

W. Prince of Orange, *The Reasons Inducing Him to Appear in Arms in the Kingdom of England, for Preserving of the Protestant Religion, and for Restoring the Laws and Liberties of England, Scotland, and Ireland* (Hague: NP, 1688).

W. Orange, *The Declaration of William, Prince of Orange, of the Reasons Inducing Him to Appear in Arms in England* (Hague: Arnout Leers, 1688).

Secondary Sources

Ashley, M., *The Glorious Revolution of 1688* (London: Hodder and Stoughton, 1966).
Beddard, R., *A Kingdom without a King: The Journal of the Provisional Government in the Revolution of 1688* (Oxford: Phaidon, 1988).
Beddard, R. (ed.), *The Revolution of 1688: The Andrew Browning Lectures 1988* (Oxford: OUP, 1991).
Berkovich, I., *Motivation in War: The Experience of Common Soldiers in Old-Regime Europe* (Cambridge: CUP, 2017).
Best, B., *William of Orange and the Fight for the Crown of England: The Glorious Revolution* (Barnsley: Pen and Sword, 2021).
Bevan, B., *King William III: Prince of Orange, The First European* (London: Rubicon Press, 1997).
Black, J., *Beyond the Military Revolution: War in The Seventeenth-Century World* (Basingstoke: Macmillan Press, 2011).
Black, J., *How the Army Made Britain a Global Power 1688-1815* (Oxford: Casemate Publishers, 2021).
Blackmore, D., *Destructive & Formidable: British Infantry Firepower 1642-1765* (London: Frontline Books, 2014).
Brandon, P., *War, Capital and the Dutch State (1588-1795)* (Chicago, IL: Haymarket Books, 2016).
Callow, J., *James II: King in Exile* (Stroud: History Press, 2017).
Carswell, J., *The Descent on England: A Study of the English Revolution & its European Background* (London: Cresset Press, 1969).
Carter, A., *Neutrality or Commitment: The Evolution of Dutch Foreign Policy, 1667-1795* (London: Edward Arnold, 1975).
Chandler, D., *The Art of Warfare in the Age of Marlborough* (London: B.T. Batsford, 1976).
Childs, J., *The Army, James II, and the Glorious Revolution* (Manchester: Manchester University Press, 1980).
Childs, J., *Armies and Warfare in Europe 1648-1789* (Manchester: Manchester University Press, 1982).
Childs, J., *The British Army of William III, 1689-1702* (Manchester: Manchester University Press, 1987).
Childs, J., *The Nine Years' War and the British Army 1688-97: The Operations in the Low Countries* (Manchester: Manchester University Press, 1991).
Childs, J., *Warfare in the Seventeenth Century* (London: Cassell, 2001).
Childs, J., *The Williamite Wars in Ireland 1688-1691* (London: Hambledon Continuum, 2007).
Childs, J., *General Percy Kirke and the Later Stuart Army* (London: Bloomsbury, 2014.)
Cibber, C., *An Apology for the Life of Mr. Colley Cibber, Comedian, and Late Patentee of the Theatre-Royal* (2nd ed, London: John Watts, 1740).
Claydon, T., 'William III's Declaration of Reason and the Glorious Revolution', *The Historical Journal*, 39 (1996), pp.87–108.
Claydon, T., *Europe and the Making of England 1660-1760* (Cambridge: CUP, 2007).

Cruickshanks, E. (ed.), *By Force or By Default? The Revolution of 1688-1689* (Edinburgh: John Donald Publishing, 2001).

Coward, B., *The Stuart Age: England 1603-1714* (3rd ed, Harlow: Pearson Education, 2003).

Cox, B., *King William's European Joint Venture* (Assen: Van Gorcum & Co., 1995).

Ede-Borrett, S., *The Army of James II 1685-1688: The Birth of the British Army* (Solihull: Helion & Co., 2017).

Gibson, W., *James II and the Trial of the Seven Bishops* (Basingstoke: Palgrave Macmillan, 2009).

Glozier, M., *The Huguenot Soldiers of William of Orange and The Glorious Revolution of 1688: The Lions of Judah* (Brighton: Sussex Academic Press, 2008).

Glozier, M., and Onnekink, D. (eds), *War, Religion and Service: Huguenot Soldiering, 1685-1713* (London: Routledge, 2007).

Grew, M., *William Bentinck and William III: (Prince of Orange) The Life of Bentinck Earl of Portland from the Welbeck Correspondence* (London: John Murray, 1924).

Guy, A., and Spencer-Smith, J. (eds), *1688 Glorious Revolution? The Fall and Rise of the British Army 1660-1704* (London: National Army Museum, 1988).

Hall, R., Stanford, I., and Roumegoux, Y., *Flags and Uniforms of the Dutch Army 1685-1715*, 2 Vols (Romford: Pike and Shot Society, 2014).

Hoak, D., and Feingold, M. (eds), *The World of William and Mary: Anglo-Dutch Perspectives of the Revolution of 1688-89* (Stamford: Stamford University Press, 1996).

Hilton-Jones, G., *Convergent Forces: immediate Causes of the Revolution of 1688 in England* (Ames, IA: Iowa State University Press, 1990).

Hutton, R., *The Glory of 1688* (NL: Royal Stuart Society, 1995).

Israel, J. (ed.), *The Anglo-Dutch Moment: Essays on the Glorious Revolution and its World Impact* (Cambridge: CUP, 2003).

Jackson, M., *Soldier* (London: Transworld Publishing, 2007).

Jones, D., *War and Economics in the Age of William III and Marlborough* (Oxford: Basil Blackwell, 1988).

Jones, D.L., *A Parliamentary History of the Glorious Revolution* (London: HMSO, 1988).

Jones, J.R., *The Revolution of 1688 in England* (London: Weidenfeld and Nicolson, 1972).

Kampmann, C., 'Communication: The English Crisis, Emperor Leopold, and the Origins of the Dutch Intervention in 1688', *The Historical Journal*, 55 (2012), pp.521–32.

Keay, A., *The Last Royal Rebel: The Life and Death of James, Duke of Monmouth* (London: Bloomsbury, 2018).

King, H., *Brandenburg and the English Revolution of 1688* (Oberlin: AUS, 1914).

Lynn, J., *The Wars of Louis XIV 1667-1714* (London: Longman, 1999).

Manning, R., *An Apprenticeship in Arms: The Origins of the British Army 1585-1702* (Oxford: OUP, 2006).

Martines, L., *Furies: War in Europe 1450-1700* (London: Bloomsbury Press, 2013).

Meerwijk, M., 'Negotiating the Grand Alliance: the role of the King-Stadholder's Corps Diplomatique in Establishing a New Alliance Between 'Austria', the Dutch Republic and England, 1688-1690', Unpublished Bachelors' thesis, Utrecht University, 2001.

Mijers, E. and Onnekink, D. (eds), *Redefining William III: The Impact of the King-Stadholder in International Context* (Aldershot: Ashgate, 2007).

Miller, J., *Popery & Politics in England 1660-1688* (Cambridge: CUP, 1973).

Miller, J., *James II* (London: Yale University Press, 2000).

Murtagh, H. and Murtagh, D., *The Irish Jacobite Army* (Dublin: Four Courts Press, 2024).

Ogg, D., *England in the Reign of James II and William III* (Oxford: Clarendon Press, 1957).

Oakley, S., *William III and the Northern Crowns During the Nine Years War 1689-1697* (London: Garland Publishing, 1987).

Onnekink, D., *The Anglo-Dutch Favourite: The Career of Hans Willem Bentinck, 1st Earl of Portland (1649-1709)* (Aldershot: Ashgate, 2007).

Pincus, S., *1688: The First Modern Revolution* (London: Yale University Press, 2009).

Pincus, S., *England's Glorious Revolution 1688-1689: A Brief History with Documents* (Boston, MA: Bedford/St Martin's, 2006).

Pinkham, L., *William III and the Respectable Revolution: The Part Played by William of Orange in the Revolution of 1688* (Cambridge: Harvard University Press, 1954).

Powley, E., *The English Navy in the Revolution of 1688* (Cambridge: CUP, 1998).

Pull, W., *William III: From Prince of Orange to King of England, A History 1650-1689* (London: Unicorn Publishing, 2021).

Quinn, S., 'The Glorious Revolution's Effect on English Private Finance: A Microhistory. 1680-1705', *The Journal of Economic History* [Online] 61.3 (2001), pp.593–615.

Raven, G., and Rodger, N. (eds), *Navies and Armies: The Anglo-Dutch Relationship in War & Peace 1688-1988* (Edinburgh: John Donald Publishers, 1990).

Rule, J. (ed.), *Louis XIV and the Craft of Kingship* (Ohio: Ohio State University Press, 1969).

Schwoerer, L., *"No Standing Armies!": The Antiarmy Ideology in Seventeenth-Century England* (Baltimore, MD: Johns Hopkins University Press, 1974).

Schwoerer, L. (ed.), *The Revolution of 1688-1689: Changing Perspectives* (Cambridge: CUP, 1992).

Shearwood, M., *The Perfection of Military Discipline: The Plug Bayonet and the English Army 1660-1705* (Warwick: Helion & Co., 2020).

Shearwood, M., 'A Summer on Hounslow Heath: Combined Army Operations in late Seventeenth-Century England', *War in History* (29.3) July 2022.

Smith, H., *Armies & Political Change in Britain 1660-1750* (Oxford: OUP, 2021).

Speck, W.A., *Reluctant Revolutionaries: Englishmen and the Revolution of 1688* (Oxford: OUP, 1988).

Stapleton, J., 'Forging a Coalition Army: William III, The Grand Alliance, and the Confederate Army in the Spanish Netherlands, 1688-1697', Ph.D. Thesis, Ohio State University, 2003.

Trevelyan, G.M., *The English Revolution, 1688-1689* (Oxford: OUP, 1938).

Troost, W., *Stadhoulder-Koning Willem III, Een Politieke Biografie* (Hilversum: Verloren b.v., 2001).

Turner, F.C., *James II* (London: Eyre & Spottiswoode, 1948).

Vallance, E., *The Glorious Revolution: 1688 – Britain's Fight for Liberty* (London: Abacus, 2006).

Van Der Kiste, J., *James II and the First Modern Revolution: The End of Absolute Monarchy* (Barnsley: Pen and Sword, 2021).

Van Nimwegen, O., *The Dutch Army and the Military Revolutions 1588-1688* (Woodbridge: Boydell Press, 2010).

About the author

Mark Shearwood is an independent early-modern historian specialising in late seventeenth- and early eighteenth-century military history, with a main focus on the reign of James II and William III. He was awarded a MA in War and Strategy and PhD from the University of Leeds. He has written two other books for Helion on the history of the plug bayonet (The Perfection of Military Discipline) and Wargaming the Great Northern War (Waking the Bear).

About the artist

Marco Capparoni is an artist and illustrator for wargames, fiction & nonfiction publishers, and private commissions. Specialising in history and military history, Marco's works also include natural history, portraiture, and book illustrations.

Century of the Soldier 1618-1721

'This is the Century of the Soldier', Fulvio Testi, Poet, 1641

The 'Century of the Soldier' series covers the period of military history c. 1618–1721, the 'golden era' of Pike and Shot warfare. This time frame has been seen by many historians as a period of not only great social change, but of fundamental developments within military matters. This is the period of the 'military revolution', the development of standing armies, the widespread introduction of black powder weapons and a greater professionalism within the culture of military personnel. The series examines the period in a greater degree of detail than has hitherto been attempted, and has a very wide brief, with the intention of covering all aspects of the period from the battles, campaigns, logistics and tactics to the personalities, armies and their material culture.

Submissions

The publishers would be pleased to receive submissions for this series. Please email info@helion.co.uk, or write to Helion & Company Limited, Unit 8 Amherst Business Centre, Budbrooke Road, Warwick, CV34 5WE

You may also be interested in:

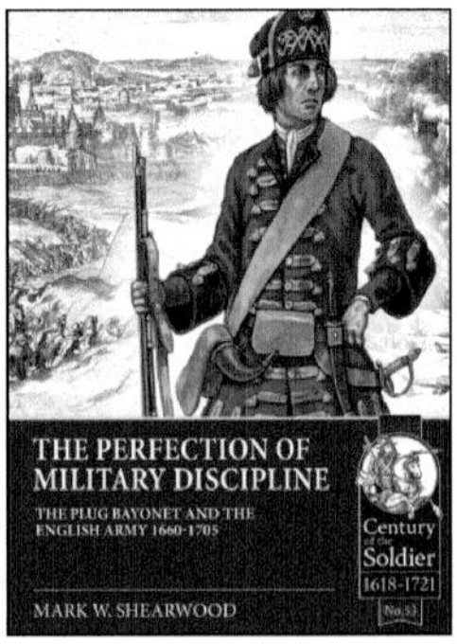

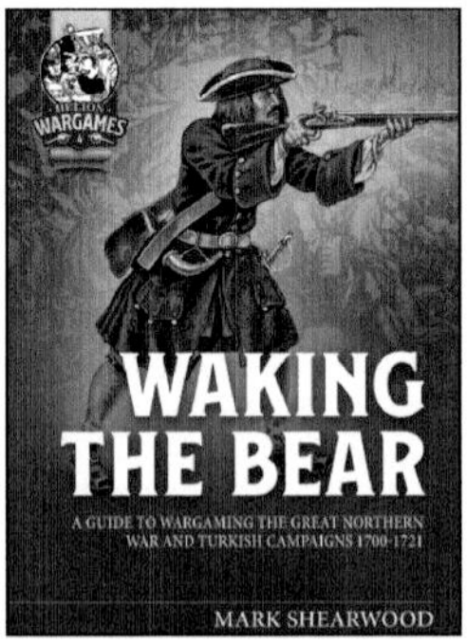